A CUP OF COMFORT®

Devotional

Daily reminders
of God's love
and grace

Edited by James S. Bell
& Stephen R. Clark

adamsmedia

Avon, Massachusetts

Published by
Adams Media, an F+W Publications Company
57 Littlefield Street, Avon, MA 02322. U.S.A.
www.adamsmedia.com and *www.cupofcomfort.com*

ISBN 10: 1-59869-657-2
ISBN 13: 978-1-59869-657-8

Printed in the United States of America.

J I H G F E D C B A

Library of Congress Cataloging-in-Publication Data
A cup of comfort devotional / edited by James S. Bell
and Stephen R. Clark.
p. cm.
1. Devotional literature. I. Bell, James S. II. Clark, Stephen R.
BV4801.C87 2004
242--dc22
2004009158

This publication is designed to provide accurate and authoritative
information with regard to the subject matter covered. It is sold with the
understanding that the publisher is not engaged in rendering legal,
accounting, or other professional advice. If legal advice or other expert
assistance is required, the services of a competent professional person should
be sought.

—From a *Declaration of Principles* jointly adopted by a Committee of the
American Bar Association and a Committee of Publishers and Associations

Many of the designations used by manufacturers and sellers to distinguish
their products are claimed as trademarks. Where those designations
appear in this book and Adams Media was aware of a trademark claim, the
designations have been printed with initial capital letters.

Unless otherwise noted, the Bible used as a source is *Holy Bible: New Living
Translation*, Tyndale House Publishers (March 1997).

Photographs © Brand X Pictures

*This book is available at quantity discounts for bulk purchases.
For information, call 1-800-289-0963.*

CONTENTS

ACKNOWLEDGMENTS

We would like to thank all of the gracious contributors, as well as those who submitted stories and devotionals that did not make it into this book. Thank you for being willing to share some of the intimate moments you have had with the Lord.

I (Jim) would also like to thank my family whose personal stories of God's dealings are precious to me. This includes my wife Margaret and my children Rosheen, Brendan, Brigit, and Caitlin.

I (Stephen) want to extend my gratitude to my parents, now with the Lord, who each lived lives of devotion and grace. And special gratitude to my amazing son, Michael, who has added multiplied joys to my life.

INTRODUCTION

The Bible is often depicted as a set of rules for living as well as a teaching manual for beliefs about God. It is both of those things, but we must remember that it takes place in time and space, weaving through history, and though it is also seen as a sweeping epic drama, it involves the stories of people with limitations and faults just like you and me.

So what makes up our historic Judeo-Christian faith comes from the fears and foibles and the hopes and triumphs of kings and prostitutes, farmers and tax collectors. Some of the stories involve momentous events, like Moses at the burning bush. But others deal with what seem to be minor details like a group of beggars who wander into the riches in the camp of a fleeing army. It's an exotic tapestry—just like life itself.

Like the Bible, our faith is largely based on stories, and its nurture is often compared to a journey. And though the pages of the Bible have closed, when Jesus left this earth he promised that through his spirit the work of God would go on in and through those who believed in Him. A *Cup of Comfort Devotional* contains stories of everyday folks whose lives are touched by an awesome God. Sometimes these stories depict seeming miracles, sometimes only a realization that a loving God is in our midst, but they all have simple but profound lessons to teach concerning how we might, even in small ways, get closer to God ourselves.

Some of the stories can help us to see God in the precious small things we might otherwise miss. A sparrow picks up a sunflower seed and feeds it to another sparrow. What a lesson from God's creation! Some of the stories help us deal with senseless tragedy. A girl's brother is shot to death in a veteran's hospital by a deranged older veteran who reacts to the United States' invasion of Afghanistan. Contributors like this sister tell us also how they deal with adversity through the grace of God.

We all live busy lives and find it difficult to retain a lot of information first gleaned in the morning. Ideally, these devotionals aim at delivering a quick spiritual jump start to begin your day, a key concept that you can take with you found in the narrative material and reinforced with a Scripture verse and concluding principle.

These selections are meant to be inspirational rather than providing in-depth teaching on biblical truth. They are indeed meant to provide some comfort and peace in knowing that God is in control of your life, even in the mundane circumstances, and loves you deeply. You will hear from people just like yourself who have been touched by God's love and power, rather than theologians who may be one step removed. May you see God today in your own spiritual journey—in others, in the vast expanse of stars, and in the tiniest snowflake.

—JAMES S. BELL AND STEPHEN R. CLARK

JANUARY

FAITHFUL UNDER FIRE
—RACHEL WALLACE-OBERLE

"And God, in his mighty power, will protect you until
you receive this salvation, because you are trusting him."
1 PETER 1:5

S EVERAL YEARS AGO A NOTORIOUS NEWSPAPER publisher hired me as a freelance writer and reporter. Numerous people described him as a malicious, vindictive man and claimed he deliberately went out of his way to antagonize and offend. They refused to have anything to do with him or his newspaper. I considered the prospect of writing for a local paper an interesting challenge and paid little attention to the warnings. I figured that as a freelancer I would seldom be in the office anyway.

I *was* seldom in the office, but whenever I went in, I realized that the publisher's unpleasantness permeated the workplace—even when he wasn't there. Coworkers were slandered; most of the town's council members and mayor were openly attacked and ridiculed; and community figures, particularly pastors, were constantly criticized. All this hostility spilled onto the pages of the newspaper, often outraging the residents in the community.

On top of all this, it didn't take me long to discover that Barbara, the assistant editor, disliked me. Still, I felt that my being placed in this environment was not an accident. God could perform a work of eternal significance through my life if I let Him.

I determined to show the love of Christ and do my work with excellence, but still struggled with the spitefulness at the office and Barbara's coldness and criticism. I decided on a new approach. I began bringing coffee for Barbara when I visited the office. She was unsure how to handle this new development and would sometimes snap, "I'm too busy to stop for a coffee right now." I simply left the coffee on her desk and said I would catch her another time.

Over time, from various other staffers, I learned Barbara's story. Her parents had crushed her dreams to attend university in the country where they lived. Disregarding their daughter's hopes and keen mind, they had sent her to Canada and arranged a marriage for her. Now she was trapped in a low-paying job with two children and a husband involved in flagrant affairs, and she lashed out at everyone.

Seeing that Barbara wore the same nondescript wardrobe week after week, I began bringing her clothes I was unable to use. Barbara seemed to appreciate the gesture. One afternoon I brought in a spring coat. Barbara tried it on and it fit beautifully. She tightened the belt around her waist and put up the collar. "I don't often get clothes this nice," she admitted, fingering the fine fabric. I think it was then she began to thaw.

Her face would light up with one of her rare smiles when she saw me. Our visits began to take place in the break room and at times stretched to forty-five minutes, which was unheard of in that hectic environment. When I bought her a Christmas present, she threw her arms around me and exclaimed, "You just made my day, my whole week, my month!"

One afternoon as I sat with Barbara in the break room, I realized the moment to share Christ with her had come. I felt overwhelmed. Barbara and most of the staff had never shown anything but contempt for Christian matters. We talked about all sorts of things for almost fifteen minutes as I silently beseeched Him for words of wisdom. I usually share the Gospel with joy and confidence, but this time was different.

Finally, my heart racing, I reached across the table, took her hand, and said, "I know, Barbara, that God has sent me here to write for this newspaper for a reason. I believe that reason is to tell you how much He loves you, how precious you are to Him, and that He sent His Son to die on the cross for you."

As I spoke I sensed the power of God in the room. Barbara stared at me in wonder. When I asked her if she wanted to pray the sinner's prayer with me, she nodded and said slowly and clearly, almost as if she couldn't believe what she was saying, "Yes. Yes, I think I would." Heads bowed, holding each other's hands, we prayed together. When we finished, Barbara looked up, awed. And then she smiled. Her face was radiant. She just sat there speechless, eyes shining.

Over the next few days I gave Barbara a Bible and a devotional book. A new peace seemed to fill her and the harshness that had always clung to her was gone. When I asked how the decision to accept Christ had affected her, she thought for a moment and then said with surprise, "I feel different. I don't lose my temper as often."

A short time later I felt the Lord leading me on to write for other sources. When I gave my notice, a look of shock swept over Barbara's face and her eyes filled with tears. She grabbed me and hugged me. "Oh, Rachel," she said, her voice breaking. "Those stories, your wonderful stories. Who will write those beautiful stories now?"

Several months later, to the amazement of the entire community, the publisher who had held his position for twenty-four tumultuous years left, and his place was filled by a young Christian woman. On the masthead in every edition, a Bible verse now appears: "Whatsoever things are true, whatsoever things are honest, whatsoever things are just . . . think on these things" (Philippians 4:8, KJV).

New Year's Resolutions

"Open my eyes to see the wonderful truths in your law."
Psalm 119:18

"Mom, what New Year's resolutions are you making this year?" my daughter asked at the first of the year.

"I don't make New Year's resolutions," I said. "I only break them."

"You have to make at least one," Ann said. "Listen to my list." She rambled through about a dozen. Not to be outdone by an eighteen-year-old, I promised to make at least one resolution.

First thing the next morning, as usual, I grabbed the newspaper and read about fatal accidents, drive-by shootings, child abuse, and domestic violence. That's when I came up with my resolution.

I resolved to change the way I begin each day. Every morning I've decided that the first imprint on my mind will be words that have stood the test of time—the encouraging, eternal words of God's Word.

Reading God's Word renews your mind and heart,
lifting you out of what is, to what God has planned for you.

—JEWELL JOHNSON

Get New Furniture

"You must display a new nature because you are a new person, created in God's likeness righteous, holy, and true."
Ephesians 4:24

"Wherever you go, there you are." Kind of a dumb but very true saying.

I once lived in a tiny, but cozy, attic apartment. From time to time, for a change of perspective and in an attempt to open up more space, I'd rearrange the furniture.

Moving the couch to the other side of the room did offer a fresh perspective, but, as far as space was concerned, only incremental improvement could be achieved. Why? No matter how much I rearranged the furniture, it was still the same furniture.

If the stuff of your life is holding you back from living a holy life, then it's time to get new stuff. Incessant rearranging of your inner furniture won't bring peace or healing.

In Christ everything is new (2 Corinthians 5:17), not just rearranged. To be truly changed, get rid of old thought patterns and habits and furnish your life with new behaviors and attitudes.

You can't live the same way and expect new results.

—SRC

My Job His Job

"Keep on asking, and you will be given what you
ask for. Keep on looking, and you will find.
Keep on knocking, and the door will be opened."
Matthew 7:7

Have you ever prayed for a friend to know the Lord? I've been praying for a friend of mine for many years. Sometimes this effort seems to be fruitless.

Prior to a recent meeting with my friend, I prayed, "Lord, I'll wait for you. You direct the conversation." We discussed everything. We even danced around salvation by talking about church.

I was puzzled. Why didn't God take this opportunity? I was ready to assist. Just before I pulled out of the parking lot, my friend knocked on the car window.

"I have a favor to ask. Last year my focus was decorating. This year's emphasis is my spiritual life. Will you pray for me?" Totally dumbfounded, I responded, "Yes."

I need to be still and know that He is God. Heart surgery takes precision and timing. I have enough trouble doing my job. God's got His down just fine. Prayer is fruitful.

Persistence, prayer, and patience are a part of God's plan.

—LORI WILDENBERG

Blessed Blindness

"The LORD opens the eyes of the blind.
The LORD lifts the burdens of those bent beneath
their loads. The LORD loves the righteous."
Psalm 146:8

Whenever I ride an elevator and look at the dots embossed on the operating panel, I am reminded to thank God for Louis Braille, one of my favorite characters in history.

Braille was born on January 4, 1809, in France. At three years old, he was blinded permanently in an accident. At age fifteen he invented the Braille system of six raised dots that have allowed blind people all over the world for nearly two centuries to read with their fingertips. Braille was also a dedicated teacher and a talented organist.

What would Braille have done with his life had he not been blind? And what would he have accomplished if he had been bitter about his affliction?

How can you take your personal challenges and do something positive with them for God, who knows what is best for you?

You were once spiritually blind,
but with your new ability you can please God.

—JAN SEALE

Peanuts!

"For others will treat you as you treat them.
Whatever measure you use in judging others,
it will be used to measure how you are judged."
Matthew 7:2

Consider how brave you would need to be if you were the first person to eat a peanut! A strangely shaped, bumpy little pod found in the dirt under a plant one day while you were out digging around. Brushing off the dirt, you open the pod, see two little brown nuts inside, open your mouth and pop them in!

Judging by their outward appearance, who would think that peanuts could be so many things? George Washington Carver discovered over a hundred different ways to use peanuts, and it all started with a bumpy little seedpod that someone took a chance on.

Sometimes people and situations are like that. You have to go beyond outward appearances and take a look inside. Given the opportunity, peanuts can be so much more than a bumpy pod. You can't judge a peanut's value by its appearance, now can you?

You shouldn't judge by outward appearances.

—Anna Seden

Daily Exercise

"Then he said to the crowd, 'If any of you wants to be
my follower, you must put aside your selfish ambition,
shoulder your cross daily, and follow me.'"
Luke 9:23

We know the importance of daily exercise and how essential
it is to good health. The Bible puts emphasis on daily exercise—but of a spiritual nature. Luke records about the apostles, "And every day, in the Temple and in their homes, they
continued to teach and preach . . ." (Acts 5:42). Often
people only stress spiritual thinking for certain events and
activities such as weddings, funerals, or holidays. But the
Bible underscores daily spiritual exercise.

David prayed to the Lord "morning, noon, and night"
(Psalm 55:17). Paul "went to the synagogue to debate with
the Jews and the God-fearing Gentiles, and he spoke daily in
the public square to all who happened to be there" (Acts
17:17). Jesus ". . . taught daily in the Temple" (Luke 19:47).

Take time daily for God's Word and prayer.

*Daily spiritual exercise is required
for ongoing spiritual health.*

—STEPHEN D. BOYD

New Beginnings

"If you believe, you will receive
whatever you ask for in prayer."
Matthew 21:22

Most of us can rattle off a list of New Year's resolutions that we didn't keep. How many of us actually lost ten pounds, balanced our checkbooks, organized our closets, or took a class in auto mechanics? Most likely, these goals fell by the wayside as everyday life happened to us.

The problem is, no one really expects us to keep our resolutions. But God does.

When we believe and ask Jesus into our hearts, we feel His presence every day of every year. We start with the promise that God will walk with us, listen to us, and guide us. Then, when life intervenes and "stuff happens," we discover His strength to cope. With His help, a few of those smaller goals may be realized along the way.

Each day, as well as each new year,
can be a new beginning in Christ.

—ROBIN BAYNE

Bread from Heaven

"You parents—if your children ask for a loaf of bread, do you give them a stone instead? Or if they ask for a fish, do you give them a snake? Of course not! If you sinful people know how to give good gifts to your children, how much more will your heavenly Father give good gifts to those who ask him."

Matthew 7:9–11

Last year, our furnace broke on a cold winter morning. Watching the workmen finish the installation, we reviewed our already stretched finances.

"Can you budget on $60 a week?" my husband asked.

With $30 allocated for diapers and gas, this left $30 for groceries. I swallowed, and headed to the pantry to take stock of what we had.

A long-forgotten sack of flour sat on a back shelf. I hauled the neglected bread machine out of the cupboard and measured ingredients. Soon the smell of fresh-baked bread filled our tiny house.

We ate bread that month. Wonderful, gourmet breads baked from leftover ingredients—unwanted jars of baby fruit and a stale granola bar became delicious apple granola bread, and cinnamon and oatmeal made cinnamon nut bread. God provided our daily bread—in a way that I never expected.

God will always provide what you need.

—MICHELLE PETERS

Kingdom Music

"When you go through deep waters and great trouble, I will be with you. When you go through rivers of difficulty, you will not drown! When you walk through the fire of oppression, you will not be burned up; the flames will not consume you."

Isaiah 43:2

I loved to watch Grandpa make violins. He began with a smooth piece of wood. Slowly, he would carve out the back and front to the desired thickness. Achieving this, he would begin to bend and press the wood. I was afraid it would break. He assured me he knew just the right amount of pressure to make it a beautiful instrument. When done, Grandpa often inscribed his initials into the back of the completed instrument.

The Lord knows just how much we can take in times when we are pressed, bent, and feel as if we can't endure. He is careful not to allow us to be broken beyond repair. Christ allows trials to become part of our lives and he has placed His name on us as His prized children. He sees the final outcome and through these trials, "Kingdom music" is made.

You are shaped by God and his initials are on your heart.

—BEVERLY HILL MCKINNEY

Adopted into God's Heart

"Long ago, even before he made the world, God loved us and chose us in Christ to be holy and without fault in his eyes. His unchanging plan has always been to adopt us into his own family by bringing us to himself through Jesus Christ. And this gave him great pleasure."

Ephesians 1:4–5

Some days it's hard for me to get my arms around the truth that God, the Creator of the universe, actually chose to adopt me into His own family. And if that weren't enough, this verse then tells me that this brings God great pleasure.

When I'm able to tuck that truth in my heart, it changes everything. When the world tells me I don't measure up, this verse tells me I'm the daughter of the King. When I feel hurt, alone, or unloved, God tells me He's loved me before He even made the world. And not only that, God likes me! He tells me I make Him smile.

When I live in the light of God's smile and His love, I can't help but be a better wife, mother, sister, and friend. I can't help but want to be a daughter who relishes pleasing her Heavenly Father.

God takes great pleasure in making
you part of His eternal plan in Christ.

—SUE RHODES

A Firm Foundation

"Anyone who listens to my teaching and obeys me is wise, like a person who builds a house on solid rock. Though the rain comes in torrents and the floodwaters rise and the winds beat against that house, it won't collapse, because it is built on rock."

Matthew 7:24–25

"I've lived in this house for thirty-seven years," the distraught woman declared on the evening news. The story went on to reveal that a team of engineers had originally assessed her home to be in no danger. But they missed an uncharted mine shaft under the home. Even though the home appeared to be on a solid foundation, it wasn't. Just two days prior to the news report, the walls had been straight and the floors had been level. Now the home was askew and sinking into the shaft.

This story reminded me of the lesson Jesus taught about building our spiritual lives on a solid foundation. We can be fooled into thinking other foundations are suitable, especially the foundation of good works. Although activities may earn us praise, we are told in Scripture to build our lives on Jesus, the solid rock, lest we sink when the storms of life hurl themselves at us.

To stand strong, be sure your foundation is solid on the Rock.

—ELAINE INGALLS HOGG

A Lighthouse for God

"My health may fail, and my spirit may
grow weak, but God remains the strength
of my heart; he is mine forever."
Psalm 73:26

Last year I lost a treasured friend to pancreatic cancer. The worst part was, it came out of nowhere. He went in for routine hernia surgery, and came out with a terminal diagnosis. They gave him six to nine months. They were wrong. He had only three.

I try so hard not to ask, "Why?" But this time I couldn't help but ask, "Why now?" Sergio was at a peak point in his life serving God in ministry. He not only served at home, he served in a Mexican prison sharing the love of our Lord with troubled youths. He was making such a difference. It just didn't seem fair.

I looked for encouragement and strength, and found it in Sergio himself. He lived and shared his faith every day. Friends and family witnessed Jesus' light through him. His story, and his courage, continues to touch lives today.

*God can use your life as a legacy
to inspire others to serve Christ.*

—SUE RHODES

Angels All Around

"When Lot still hesitated, the angels seized his hand and the hands of his wife and two daughters and rushed them to safety outside the city, for the LORD was merciful."
Genesis 19:16

One winter day, my children and I decided to build a snowman. The powdery snow kept falling apart in our gloved fingertips. Nevertheless, my son and I persevered, patting and pressing the icy flakes into balls. My daughter, less patient with the uncooperative material, made snow angels instead.

The completed project looked laughable. Embedded in the snow, and forming a barrier of sorts, laid the shapes of several pixie-sized angels. Our crumbly snowman stood in the midst of them, leaning like an exhausted soldier threatening to collapse on the battlefield. His pink milk-cap eyes hung crookedly, oblivious to the glistening angels all around.

It made me reflect how God protects us in life. Our eyes, tired from daily stress and distractions, don't see that angels encamp around us. Like Lot, doubt and fear may immobilize us. Thankfully, we can count on God to act on our behalf.

God upholds and protects you because
He is merciful and loves you.

—LORI Z. SCOTT

Blobs and Lumps

"Thank you for making me so wonderfully complex! Your
workmanship is marvelous—and how well I know it."
Psalm 139:14

Gaze in the mirror. Do you see a spiritual blob, not yet finished by God? I hope so. God likes to work with blobs!

Imagine yourself as a lump of clay on the potter's wheel.
God, the Master Potter, will lovingly mold your character.
Intense shaping, carving, and forming will produce a beau-
tiful sculpture. You don't feel like a beautiful work of art?
Perhaps you see yourself as an ashtray.

Does a frustrated potter throw his hands in the air and
scream, "This clay will never amount to anything, I'll just
make an ashtray and be done with it!" No, he believes in his
abilities and he will not give up. Similarly, God will never
give up on His unique design for your life, and He will continue to mold and fine-tune your character until you draw
your last breath.

God's design is second to none and He personally signs
each distinct creation—just look for His fingerprints.

God is a perfectionist who creates and expects the very best.

—CHARLENE FRIESEN

Everything You Need

"Why be like the pagans who are so deeply concerned about these things? Your heavenly Father already knows all your needs, and he will give you all you need from day to day if you live for him and make the Kingdom of God your primary concern."

Matthew 6:32–33

I was thumbing through a magazine and came across a section listing various strange facts about animals. The first fact was that goldfish have a memory span of three seconds. I thought to myself how lucky that was for them. Otherwise, they would get very bored in their small living space. They had been given exactly what they needed to exist happily.

We have everything built into us that we need to cope with our circumstances. Goldfish may have boring lives, but they also have a tiny memory so it never seems boring to them. My life may sometimes seem stressful and almost too much, but I always seem to find just enough strength to cope. It seems that everything we really need has already been given to us.

Everything you need has already been given to you in Him.

—SHELLEY WAKE

Expectations

"Now there was a man named Simeon who lived in Jerusalem. He was a righteous man and very devout. He was filled with the Holy Spirit, and he eagerly expected the Messiah to come and rescue Israel."

Luke 2:25

How many people were in the temple when Jesus was presented? Fifty? One hundred? How many recognized Him? Only two, Simeon and Anna. Why were they aware of His identity while others blithely went about their daily tasks? Mary and Joseph were just another Jewish couple fulfilling the law of Moses concerning a firstborn son.

Simeon and Anna were ready for Him. They expected Him. Their hearts were open. They were waiting for the Messiah, anticipating His coming. Are we like them or do we immerse ourselves in busyness and the mundane? Just as Jesus was present in the temple then, so is He present with us today. Do we recognize Him? In others? In nature? In the humdrum of daily living?

Do we look for Him? Expect Him? Are our hearts open to Him? Do we ask Him to make us aware of His presence?

Jesus promised to be with you always. Expect His presence.

—NANCY BAKER

The Bread Machine

"Jesus replied, 'I am the bread of life. No one
who comes to me will ever be hungry again.
Those who believe in me will never thirst.'"
John 6:35

For Christmas, my mom received a wonderful bread
machine from my brother and his wife. I remember
watching as she tried it for the first time.

"Let's see, the instructions say to dump all of the ingredients in, close the lid, and in three hours we will have fresh homemade bread," she explained.

I went off to occupy my time. Later, a loud *BEEP, BEEP, BEEP* announced the bread was ready! I rushed to the kitchen just as my mom was pulling the bread out. It smelled so wonderful, and it tasted even better. I thought to myself, "I could live on eating this bread alone."

It's wonderful to know that Jesus was here as a spiritual "bread" for us. He tells us that if we partake of His wonderful bread, we will never hunger again.

Eat the bread of life and you will never be hungry again.

—STORMY NIEVES

Friendly Persuasion

"Taste and see that the LORD is good.
Oh, the joys of those who trust in him!"
Psalm 34:8

Is Maxwell House Coffee still "good to the last drop"? My cat thinks so, but Gracie prefers Barney's Gourmet Crème Brulee. She hovers to drink the last drops from my cup and she takes it black!

Growing up, every time I picked up an apple, Tam O'Shanter, our dachshund-mix, would rear back on his haunches like a sentinel, eyes fixed on the prize: my apple core. He assumed if I liked it, it must be good.

Today my adult daughter remembers my grandmother simmering turnip greens all day, delicately seasoned with salt pork, and eating them with such obvious relish, that she was converted at age four. Because she ate them, I eventually came around, too.

Amazing, isn't it? The power of a personal example. Delivered with love, the unpalatable becomes savory, the unlikely seems routine, and the ordinary can become divine.

Live your life in a way that invites others to "taste and see."

—MARCIA SWEARINGEN

Give God Your All, and Let the Adventure Begin!

"The eyes of the LORD search the whole
earth in order to strengthen those whose
hearts are fully committed to him."
2 Chronicles 16:9

"Girls, you know how you enjoy adventures?" my husband steered the conversation. "Well, we're going on a Big God Adventure to study and minister in Australia. How 'bout that?" Silence. Our three daughters were quite content in Suburban Sanctuary, USA, but the decision to leave every comfort and security we knew had been made.

Finally, our oldest daughter piped up, "Well . . . I don't want to be like Jonah. He disobeyed God and ended up in the belly of a fish!" After enjoying a good laugh, our discussion transitioned into the beauty of God trusting us to follow His commission. Since saying yes to His plan, our family has been blessed with amazing provision, faith, and encouragement to carry out His will.

*Don't limit God's power and He will
provide for your next big venture in faith.*

—BROOK CHALFANT

Learning to Wait

"Wait patiently for the LORD. Be brave and courageous.
Yes, wait patiently for the LORD."
Psalm 27:14

"I didn't say no, I said wait!" I reasoned as calmly as I could over the coup attempt in the backseat. We were running errands later than usual and I was withholding the lollipops from the bank drive-thru until my little boys ate lunch.

"Oh brother"—I rolled my eyes in thought—"I wish they could understand that I am making them wait for their own good."

"That's the way *you* act when I tell you to wait," I felt the Lord gently chide me. Touché! And ouch!

I can't stand to wait. Rationally I know the Lord says to wait because He is at work behind the scenes, but emotionally I feel like I'm on hold.

I realized that day I need the Lord to teach me how to wait, and I need Him to gently remind me that there are three answers given out of Love: yes, no, and wait.

Patience is a virtue God can help you learn.

—DenaRae Carlock

Hold Hands and Don't Get Lost

"How wonderful it is, how pleasant,
when brothers live together in harmony!"
Psalm 133:1

I walked up behind a set of two-year-old twins in a hospital corridor. At the same time the father turned and said to the boys, "Now hold hands so you don't get lost." He and his wife kept going.

The boys did as they were told and then looked up at me. One held up his hand and said, "Don't get lost." I took his hand and we strolled along behind their parents. The mother looked back and saw me walking along with the boys. She started laughing and soon we all joined in.

The family was black and I am white, but for that few minutes we were just people making our way holding hands and helping each other. Don't you think that is the way God intended life? If we could learn to join hands and help each other, imagine what the world would be like.

Seek to live in peace with those you meet.

—DON M. AYCOCK

Mind Transplant

"Don't copy the behavior and customs of this world, but let God transform you into a new person by changing the way you think. Then you will know what God wants you to do, and you will know how good and pleasing and perfect His will really is."

Romans 12:2

I met a lady several years ago who was going through a most difficult time. Even though she prayed and read her Bible, all she could think of was her problems. God revealed to me that she needed a mind transplant!

As believers we need to have the mind of Christ in every circumstance. Isn't it wonderful that we can know exactly what God is thinking about our situation? For me that is a great peace giver. When I apply the mind of Christ to my daily life, I find that I am less critical, less cynical, and less sinful.

Are you in need of a mind transplant today? Have today's worries taken the joy of Christ from you? Ask God to give you His mind. You can start to develop a new pattern for your life. A pattern that is Christ-minded and filled with joy!

Having the mind of Christ brings peace in all circumstances.

—JANE MORIN

Missing a Lot

"For God has not given us a spirit of fear and timidity,
but of power, love, and self-discipline."
2 Timothy 1:7

Some time after the funeral of his girlfriend of thirty years, a Tennessee man was asked why they'd never married. His response: "Well, I never brought up the subject, and neither did she." Then he added, "My friends tell me I missed a lot."

This applies to each of us in sharing the Gospel of Jesus Christ. When your friend is asked why he or she was not a Christian, will he or she give the same reply? "Well, I never brought up the subject, and neither did any of my friends. I've heard I missed a lot."

We must remember that Christ's command to go to "all the world" includes our own little world—our mechanic or hairdresser or convenience-store clerk or the young mother down the street. Pray silently, then be ready for the Spirit to guide you in what to say in bringing up spiritual matters. You'll be amazed at the positive responses you'll get!

Let others see and hear Christ in you.

—LANITA BRADLEY BOYD

Our Heavenly Mansion

"There are many rooms in my Father's home, and I am going to prepare a place for you. If this were not so, I would tell you plainly. When everything is ready, I will come and get you, so that you will always be with me where I am."

John 14:2–3

I listened to my girlfriends share a visit to another friend's home. Their excited and envious voices described a beautiful home with three stories, large windows, marble tubs, and spacious rooms. Every corner of the home left an impression.

As a result of what they'd seen, each expressed a desire to redecorate or buy a new home.

Jesus has promised us that He is preparing a mansion in heaven, His Father's home, for all of us. It is all right to long for a nicer house, as long as we keep in mind that our true home is in heaven. Our heavenly home will be decorated according to how we live now.

What does your spiritual décor look like?

Jesus calls you to stand at the ready for His return.

—STACY DECKER POOLE

Out of the Depths

"But we know these things because God has revealed
them to us by his Spirit, and his Spirit searches out
everything and shows us even God's deep secrets."
1 Corinthians 2:10

On a trip to Reykjavik, Iceland, I took a tour of the city. One of the most fascinating aspects of Reykjavik is that the entire city is heated with hot water that is piped straight out of the ground. Iceland sits atop a volcanic field that keeps the water below heated to extreme temperatures. Although the island is almost on the Arctic Circle, residents can take advantage of hot water in the depths of their nation to generate electricity and provide heat.

But let us suppose that the citizens of Iceland never bothered to tap into the natural resource below their feet. We would think they were anything but wise. Would they be any less wise than a Christian who will not tap into the riches of God's gifts? Today's reading speaks of "God's deep secrets." These are aspects of our walk with God that we will not experience until we dig deeper.

*God has great things to show you if
you will tap into the depths of His grace.*

—DON M. AYCOCK

Serving God Is Ageless

"Teach us to make the most of our time,
so that we may grow in wisdom."
Psalm 90:12

The day I turned forty, I felt life ended. Anger, depression, emptiness—they all took up residency in my soul. Despite the roses and the lighthearted, morbid humor, my family couldn't pull me out of the dumps.

Thankfully, someone aligned my thoughts with reality. The Lord reminded me of Caleb, who stated when he was eighty-five that he was "as strong as the day that Moses sent him." There was Moses, who at eighty rescued the Israelites. And don't forget Abraham. He was 100 before the Lord gave him Isaac and began to fulfill those wonderful promises.

Clearly age has nothing to do with God's purpose for our life. We need to make the most of our time and use the accumulated wisdom to glorify the Lord. Our seasoned years may bring that bountiful harvest.

Fret not over your age! Simply grow in grace and God's wisdom.

God's purpose for your life has nothing to do with your age.

—RHONDA LANE PHILLIPS

Spiritual Training

"Do not waste time arguing over godless
ideas and old wives' tales. Spend your time and
energy in training yourself for spiritual fitness."
1 Timothy 4:7

We would all love to find that quick fix, shortcut, or pill in a bottle that will speed us toward our goal of a leaner, trimmer body. Many of us have tried a miracle diet, only to be disappointed in the results. It is only through discipline and training that we are able to achieve the desired results.

When we try to approach our spiritual fitness in the same way, we are often disappointed when we don't grow as strong as we'd like. Paul tells us that we need to spend time and energy on developing our spiritual strength, just as we must do to develop physical strength. And both take discipline.

The more time we can spend with our Father, in word and prayer, the stronger we'll grow in our relationship with Him, and the more spiritually fit we'll become.

*Train to become stronger spiritually,
just as you train to become stronger physically.*

—SUE RHODES

Stepping Forward

"The priests will be carrying the Ark of the LORD, the Lord of all the earth. When their feet touch the water, the flow of water will be cut off upstream, and the river will pile up there in one heap."

Joshua 3:13

When our oldest daughter was about a year old, my husband and I tried and tried to get her to walk. We stood her against a wall away from other support and beckoned her toward us. After watching us for several seconds, Sarah would slide to the floor and crawl to us.

We wanted her to learn to move forward in a new way, trusting us to help her with the next step, but she was not ready.

Fortunately for Christians, our Heavenly Father knows when we are ready. At the right time, He stands us against a wall and urges us forward. He is ready to take our hand and lead us on to a better way of living the Christian walk. By trusting His leadership and taking that first tentative step, we can experience victory.

When you follow God, He helps you step out.

—SHERRY L. POFF

The Ultimate Wash

"'And now, why delay? Get up and be baptized, and have
your sins washed away, calling on the name of the LORD.'"
Acts 22:16

Maisie was new to the United States and to commercial
washers. The sign said "75 cents" but she deposited a
quarter and waited. She deposited another and waited some
more. Still nothing happened.

Another woman seeing the sign that now read "25 cents"
explained the process to Maisie. Maisie replied, "I don't need
a full tub of water; I don't have a full load of clothes." She
objected to small and large loads' costing the same.

Jesus' death provides an ample supply of mercy for
everyone, regardless of the size of the load: whether we bring
one small item of discontent, or one enormous bundle of
stresses; whether the life is covered with grime from the
past, or simply stained with consequences. Color is no
problem: White lies, green envy, red anger, black regrets all
disappear.

He made full payment for the wash. So plunge into His
water of Life and walk away cleansed by His power.

Jesus' death provides an ample supply of mercy for you.

—DORA ISAAC WEITHERS

Time to Redecorate!

"And the one sitting on the throne said, 'Look, I am making all things new!' And then he said to me, 'Write this down, for what I tell you is trustworthy and true.'"
Revelation 21:5

Once, as I was receiving communion, I asked God to enter fully into my life. At that moment I was transported back to the day I came home from school to find my room and furniture repainted.

I didn't have a headboard for my bed . . . until then. My mom had painted a floral trellis on the wall! My old brown chest and desk were now a pale pink accented with roses cascading down a flowing green vine! The effect was magical.

That night I lay awake too excited to sleep. Not only the beauty, but the love this represented made everything seem new.

How equally tender the love and creativity of a Heavenly Father who could prompt a prayer, re-create a memory, and remodel a life to give it an entirely new perspective!

Daily He converts liabilities into assets. He did it with a stable and a cross. Imagine what He can do with a life as precious as yours.

When you give God the key to your heart,
His renovations will delight and amaze you.

—MARCIA SWEARINGEN

In God, We Are Overcomers

"'Don't be afraid!' Elisha told him. 'For there are more on our side than on theirs!' Then Elisha prayed, 'O LORD, open his eyes and let him see!' The LORD opened his servant's eyes, and when he looked up, he saw that the hillside around Elisha was filled with horses and chariots of fire."

2 Kings 6:16–17

The king of Syria was not a happy man. What he was sharing with his own officers was being passed on to the king of Israel through the prophet Elisha as revealed by God. This prophesying was eventually discovered by the king. As a result, Elisha and his servant soon found themselves surrounded by a small army sent by the king of Syria, the end seemingly near.

But what Elisha knew to the depths of his soul was that a world exists beyond our own that possesses an army greater than anything the nations of earth can muster. They are servants of fire, God's very angels. And they do not know defeat. The prophet's faith was in the God he served, not in what his eyes could see.

In our daily living, life's trials can cause us to lose sight of the infinite power of the omnipotent God we serve. His limitless resources are there for us by faith, able to overcome any obstacle.

God's power trumps the forces arrayed against you.

—DAN EDELEN

FEBRUARY

DO YOU LOVE ME?
CHECK YES OR NO!
—MICHELLE LOUISE PIERRE

"Dear friends, let us continue to love one
another, for love comes from God. Anyone
who loves is born of God and knows God."

1 JOHN 4:7

*M*Y NIECE GENAVAE PIERRE DIXON IS A sweet gift from God. When she was around six, I had been playing with her between doing loads of laundry while also visiting with my sister, Rolanda, and brother-in-law, James. For eighteen years, I had been doing my laundry at their house, another gift from the Lord!

My niece was used to my being around and would follow me to the door to the basement where the washer and dryer were, and wait patiently for me to come back upstairs. I always closed the door so she wouldn't take a tumble.

One day when I went up, there was a little crumpled-up piece of paper sticking under the bottom edge of the door and not a sound coming from the other side, yet I knew Genavae was still there. I opened up the paper and in her childish scrawl was the question, "Do you love me?" Underneath the question was the simple instruction, "Please check yes or no."

It took me by surprise because I know, without a doubt, that Genavae knows, and has known all of her life, that her Auntie Shelly loves her with all of her heart. Even in moments when I had to chastise her for something, I always made sure she understood that, despite her behavior, I love her. Still, as we all do from time to time, she needed a little tangible affirmation.

I could almost hear her heartbeat as she waited on the other side of the door for my answer. She had also written, "Please put the note back under the door." I checked my answer, slipped the note back under the door, where it disappeared quickly.

When I finally opened the door, I was greeted with her bright eyes and a huge smile as she jumped up into my arms for a big hug and some quick kisses. Then she wiggled down and skipped off to her room to put the note in a secure place.

The love of a child is one of the most precious things that anyone can ever experience. On their faces is a look that says a thousand things, but most profoundly, "Do you love me?" Most often, in the silence that passes between us, our actions are their answers. Not all children are as precocious as my niece, so they will not all write these little notes. But, that does not mean that question is not always just below the surface of their smile or beautiful, twinkling eyes.

How many times over the course of our walk with the Lord have we slipped the Lord a little "note"? How many times have we wanted a response as tangible as a checkmark on a piece of paper, even though we know in our heart of hearts that He certainly does love us unconditionally?

When we express our love to and for Him, it blesses His heart and helps us adjust our behavior. Is there a note slipped under the door of your heart? Pick it up and answer the question, "Do you love Jesus?"— check yes!

The Heart of Trust

"Trust in the LORD with all your heart;
do not depend on your own understanding. Seek
his will in all you do, and he will direct your paths."
Proverbs 3:5–6

At a corporate retreat I had to take what's called a "trust fall." I stood on a platform seven feet high, crossed my arms over my heart, and trustingly fell backward into the arms of my coworkers.

From the ground, watching others do it, it looked easy. From the platform though, it felt impossible. I didn't fully trust that I would be caught!

We can trust the Lord with our whole heart, not just when we're in a position of safety. From the ground it's easy to say "God will provide." But He asks for our faith and trust when we are standing at the edge of the precipice, too. It takes courage, and yet God is eternally faithful in His promises. If we trust with our whole heart and let go, He will not let us fall.

The Lord is always faithful and worthy of your trust.

—ADRIAN WARD

Aliens

"But we are citizens of heaven, where the
LORD Jesus Christ lives. And we are eagerly
waiting for him to return as our Savior."
Philippians 3:20

We live in a world that is cautiously aware of differences in our society. If someone looks and acts differently than us, we assume that they are not citizens of our community, rather transplants that don't necessarily fit in among us.

One Sunday our pastor handed out green cards to everyone in the congregation. "Carry it with you at all times to remind you that you are not a citizen here. We are citizens of heaven and only temporarily here on Earth. When we look at each other through God's eyes, we realize that all of us belong to a greater community."

So, the next time that you sit down next to a stranger who looks different from you, remember that you don't belong here either. Smile and extend your hand to your neighbor, who just might be a part of your community in heaven.

As a child of God, your citizenship is in heaven.

—MICHELE STARKEY

Reason for Holiness

"For everything comes from him; everything
exists by his power and is intended for his glory."
Romans 11:36

Every appliance I have purchased has an instruction manual
with a section called "Important Safeguards." I am supposed
to read all instructions and follow them carefully. I should
never use my blender outdoors or with the cover off. I
should never use my hair dryer in the shower or tub and
should unplug it after each use. I should not use gasoline,
paint thinner, or insecticide on my portable stereo. A
catchall phrase at the end of many of these lists is, "Do not
use appliance for other than its intended purpose."

People misuse their lives every day and instead of getting the fulfillment the world promises, they get dissatisfaction and grief. We are given God's word, our instruction
manual, with important safeguards we ignore and then
wonder why our lives are a mess. Instead we should offer
ourselves to God and renew our minds with Bible study and
prayer every day.

God's Word is your owner's manual.

—MARY J. BAUER

Bowl of Cherries

"Lazy people want much but get little,
but those who work hard will prosper and be satisfied."
Proverbs 13:4

A coworker, Jack, stumbled over his own plastic waste-basket, scattering the contents all over the floor. Stems and dark pits from the cherries he had eaten earlier were strewn about, smudging the tile floor.

"Life's the pits," he told me, smiling at his own pun. "Work's the pits. Get it, pits?" He went back to his desk after a halfhearted attempt to clean his mess. In keeping with his everyday work ethic, he took the easy way out, complaining the entire time.

His assistant, Susan, saw the mess and scrubbed the red blotches until the floor shone again. Jack's boss noticed. Much to Jack's chagrin, Susan went home with the promise of a bonus in her next paycheck.

"God gives us our cherries when we need them," she confided to me later. Have faith that God takes care of our needs, and rewards hard work.

Hard work may feel like the pits,
but it yields cherry-sweet rewards!

—ROBIN BAYNE

Following the Crowd

"Then Saul finally admitted, 'Yes, I have sinned. I have
disobeyed your instructions and the LORD's command, for
I was afraid of the people and did what they demanded.'"
1 Samuel 15:24

When I was in first grade, my mother helped me make lacy
valentines for my classmates. But there was one boy who
wasn't liked. My friends thought he was different, so I did, too.
I told Mom not to make one for him. She told me I had to.

When she wasn't watching, I took a small discarded
paper heart and pasted a picture on it cut from a Sears cat-
alog. It was an ugly card. I wrote the boy's name on it and
took it to school.

On Valentine's Day when the teacher asked if everyone
had received valentines, the boy said sadly, "I only got one
and it's an ugly homemade one."

Years later I can still see his face and hear the heartache
in his voice. I did "what the people demanded" rather than
what was right and hurt that little boy.

When you disobey God, you hurt others, yourself, and God.

—LESLIE NIVENS

Strength in Weakness

"Oh, what a wonderful God we have! How great are his
riches and wisdom and knowledge! How impossible it is
for us to understand his decisions and his methods!"
Romans 11:33

With her two young children at her side, Linda had risked
everything to flee an abusive situation in South Africa.
Picking up the pieces of her life, she'd come to church that
Sunday seeking refuge. Answering an altar call for prayer, I
was the one assigned to counsel her.

The horrific abuse she'd fled left me speechless. Not
knowing what to say, I simply gave her a hug. As my arms
went around her shoulders, Linda held on to me as if she'd
found a long-lost treasure. Then she looked up at me and
said, "Thank you so much for the gift of your hug. You'll
never know how much it's meant. This is the first time
anyone has reached out to me since we fled South Africa."

Sometimes God's greatest gifts are His little ones—like
a hug.

A loving touch can turn a life around.

—LINDA KNIGHT

A Stranger's Mercy

"Are you called to help others? Do it with all the strength and energy that God supplies. Then God will be given glory in everything through Jesus Christ."
1 Peter 4:11b

I stood in the grocery store aisle and cried. I needed to finish shopping, but my six-week-old twins were screaming. I tried soothing each one in turn, but nothing worked, and I was so tired and overwhelmed I felt helpless and alone.

Then I saw a woman come to me with purpose in her step. She lifted my baby daughter out of her seat and held her and rocked her. I held my son, and after a few moments, both babies quieted and I was able to continue shopping.

I tried to thank the stranger, but she just smiled and said, "You looked like you needed some help. God bless you," and she walked away.

God had indeed blessed me with the tenderness and mercy of a woman whose name I'll never know, but whose loving kindness I will not forget.

Let God help you help strangers in need.

—ADRIAN WARD

Abounding Strength

"The Sovereign LORD is my strength!
He will make me as surefooted as a deer
and bring me safely over the mountains."
Habakkuk 3:19

Bounding over the mountains and crags of life not just with strength, but with grace, beauty, and abundance. Now there's a beautiful picture!

But would you believe that Habakkuk came to this powerful reality only after wrestling with the question, Where is God when bad things happen? The bad guys in Habakkuk's day were winning, everything was going wrong, and God seemed invisible as His people struggled for survival. In his frustration, Habakkuk wanted answers from God. God's reply? Wait. Consider who I am. Trust that I am completely wise and sovereign . . . period.

We still wrestle with injustice today, wondering at times if good guys really do finish last. And, still, God calls on us to persevere and trust His unchanging goodness.

*Your steadfast hope is your strength
as God takes you to new heights.*

—BROOK CHALFANT

Beautiful Feet

"How beautiful on the mountains are the feet
of those who bring good news of peace and salvation,
the news that the God of Israel reigns!"
Isaiah 52:7

Have you ever awaited the sound of familiar footsteps? You're so used to their footfall that you know who they are by the sound of their walk.

That's the way I feel about my husband. Rick suffered terrible injuries in an auto accident many years ago and still walks with what he calls a wobble. One of his feet strikes the ground harder than the other. The distinctive sound tells me he's on his way down the hall, shopping aisle, or sidewalk and enables me to sense his presence minutes before his actual appearance.

How beautiful are his footsteps to me! His feet and legs had to learn how to walk again, but he persevered in his physical therapy and is walking proof that God performs miracles!

We're never alone in our pain and frustration because God is always with us, ready to surround us with His comforting presence.

*Rest in the comfort that God's
plans are better than your own.*

—ANNA M. POPESCU

Bound by Chains

"Give us our food for today."
Matthew 6:11

When I was a teenager, a woman from church kindly offered to teach me how to crochet. After I learned the basics, she sent me home with a pattern for a simple, yet colorful afghan. After repeatedly reading the instructions, I became thoroughly disheartened. I returned to her home to seek assistance.

"But this isn't difficult," she said. "Sit next to me and I'll help you."

"Chain 250 stitches," she read from the pattern. Bit by bit, I chained the required stitches.

"Excellent! Now, single crochet across, and back and forth until your work measures two inches." An hour later, I showed her my work.

"What was so hard about that?" she lightheartedly inquired.

"But what about changing colors?" I lamented.

"Don't worry about that until you get there," she replied. "Don't look so far ahead!"

What awesome counsel—not just for crocheting, but also for every minute of every day.

It's hard to live for today when
you're worried about tomorrow.

—S. (SHAE) COOKE

49

Extraordinary Lives

"I don't understand myself at all,
for I really want to do what is right, but I don't do it.
Instead, I do the very thing I hate."
Romans 7:15

I remember the day I realized people in the Bible weren't on a superspiritual plane that I'd never attain. It happened as I cruised through chapter 7 in Romans, rushing through my daily reading. My gaze snagged on verse 15. I had to reread it. Paul struggled with sin? The man whose letters filled most of the New Testament? I was shocked. He was just like me.

That day was a turning point. I had a new view during my quiet time. Biblical characters weren't playing a role; they were real people with struggles, failures, and successes. James summed it up: "Elijah was as human as we are, and yet when he prayed earnestly that no rain would fall, none fell . . ." (James 5:17). The great heroes of the Bible were people just like me, but they allowed God to work through them and use them.

Though you struggle with sin you can still do great things.

—SARA ROSETT

Grace—Saving and Amazing

"The God of peace will soon crush Satan under your feet.
May the grace of our LORD Jesus Christ be with you."
Romans 16:20

I stood beside the grave of Barbara, who had died of cancer after a mere three months of illness. A Bible scholar, mother, and wife, she had shocked the entire community by slipping away.

I had a huge lump in my throat and my hands shook as I held my flute. In a safe moment over the phone with her husband, I had agreed to play "taps" for my friend. Now I wasn't sure I could do it. My personal grief was about to swamp me.

Then God said, "Take a deep breath and begin. I will send you help." All was quiet, all eyes and ears waiting. Suddenly, from a nearby tree a mockingbird called out loud and clear. It made me and everyone else smile. I relaxed and began to play "Amazing Grace." People joined in singing.

The amazing comfort of our Lord was provided.

The grace of Christ is with you daily.

—JAN SEALE

High Maintenance

"And this same God who takes care of me
will supply all your needs from his glorious riches,
which have been given to us in Christ Jesus."
Philippians 4:19

Do you know any high-maintenance people? They are men and women who pay top dollar to have their hair coiffed, their fingernails and toenails polished to perfection. They adorn themselves with the finest silk suits and dresses, and they drive the most expensive cars. Their children wear only designer clothes and own every computer game imaginable.

Perhaps God thinks that each of us is high mainte-nance as He listens to our requests each day. Like Santa Claus reviewing our Christmas list of requests: "Father, I want this and that. Can you please supply this request, ful-fill this need . . . ?" Our wish lists are endless, and yet, God grants our requests and fills our needs (but not all our wants). This is our promise from the Father who loves us enough to supply all our needs—high maintenance or not.

You are never too high maintenance in His eyes!

—MICHELE STARKEY

Guard Your Heart

"Above all else, guard your heart,
for it affects everything you do."
Proverbs 4:23

It is so easy to allow our hearts to be distracted. I may love a certain book, a hairdo, the sweater I saw in a magazine. My attachments aren't always toward material things though. I can be enamored with people, places, even styles of church and worship.

I am learning that it will be easier to love God with all my heart if I guard my emotions from running after everything that may hold an attraction for me.

Not guarding my heart from wildly chasing after everything that awakens my interest is a surefire way to find myself distracted from God's best. It's a test I face every day. How I come out in the test affects everything else I do.

A pure, uncluttered heart leads me closer to Him.

*Guarding your heart is one of
the wisest choices you will ever make.*

—CATHEE A. POULSEN

Listening Ears

"So if you break the smallest commandment and teach others to do the same, you will be the least in the Kingdom of Heaven. But anyone who obeys God's laws and teaches them will be great in the Kingdom of Heaven."

Matthew 5:19

"Grant, did you see the bad word on that sign?" one of my young sons whispered to his brother. We were on our way to town and the boys were in the backseat. I looked up at the billboard Russell had seen. In big, bold letters was the word S-E-X.

Grant read the sign and whispered back, "That isn't a bad word."

"Yes, it is," his brother argued.

"No, it isn't. The preacher said it Sunday in church and Pastor Joey wouldn't say a bad word."

Russell thought that over and then agreed, "You're right. Pastor Joey wouldn't say anything wrong."

The sermon on Sunday had been about the sin of adultery and the boys had appeared uninterested. Evidently they were listening more closely than I had thought they were.

Every word you speak is
teaching something to whoever hears.

—TERESA BELL KINDRED

Spit out the Pits

"But giving thanks is a sacrifice that truly
honors me. If you keep to my path, I will
reveal to you the salvation of God."
Psalm 50:23

Cherries are delicious. But their pits aren't.

I know a young woman who is bright, attractive, and who has been repeatedly blessed. Yet, despite the "cherries" she's been given in her life, she has chosen to chew on the "pits."

How does she view her life? It "stinks!" she says. Instead of being thankful for having received a car, an apartment, and scholarships that have paid the major part of her college education, she complains endlessly about her life, her "parental units," her jobs, her friends, and more.

Even the most blessed of lives has an occasional downside. Bad things happen along with the good. Our perspective is our choice. We can choose to spit out the pits and pick another cherry, or chew on the bitter negatives.

I'd rather spit and pick!

*Honor God through thankfulness
for the good things in your life.*

—SRC

Making the Menial Meaningful

> "I have given you an example to follow.
> Do as I have done to you."
> John 13:15

What glory is there in cleaning up after your incontinent parent? What joy is to be found in washing sheets and pajamas after your sick child whimpers, "I couldn't make it to the bathroom, Mama"?

It takes a lot of motivation to cook yet another pot of soup to take to a family in crisis. Great determination is also required to do another load of laundry, while mountains of it stare you in the face.

I used to daydream of doing great things for Him. The Lord showed me, by the example of washing His disciples' dusty feet, that acts of kindness and service don't have to be big. They do have to be done with love and humility.

To make menial acts meaningful, I must see a purpose in doing them beyond pleasing myself. Understanding this now makes all the difference in the world in the way I approach serving others.

You serve Christ by serving others.

—ELAINE YOUNG MCGUIRE

Lord, Keep Us Faithful

"You used the lovely things I gave you to make shrines
for idols, where you carried out your acts of prostitution.
Unbelievable! How could such a thing ever happen?"
Ezekiel 16:16

God compared His people to an unfaithful woman. He married her; provided her with food, fine clothes, and jewelry; and made her popular. Then she cheated on Him.

"How could such a thing ever happen?" God asked. We want to be loyal, but it is so easy to become unfaithful without realizing it. We spend more time with the jobs He gives us than with Him. We shift our worship from Him to the possessions He helps us to acquire. We flaunt our physical beauty instead of His beauty of character in us.

We are privileged to have a God who loves first, unconditionally and always! Our many acts of disloyalty should never happen. And only if we repent and return to His embrace can we find real happiness.

God loves always and forgives you when you repent.

—DORA ISAAC WEITHERS

Fresh Blooms

"Yes, I am the vine; you are the branches. Those
who remain in me, and I in them, will produce
much fruit. For apart from me you can do nothing."
John 15:5

Pam appeared one day at our church service, shabbily
dressed, strung out on drugs, and grumbling to herself.
Amidst our well-attired, properly behaved congregation,
Pam stuck out like a sore thumb.

At the end of the service, two young mothers went up
to Pam and took her under their wings. They welcomed her,
hugged her, and invited her to go out for lunch with them. It
was truly a miracle to see Pam's face change from a scowl to
a smile as she happily accepted.

All God needs is a willing heart to make a difference, to
heal a hurt, to graft a broken branch back onto the vine so it
can bloom again.

All it takes to work a miracle is your willing heart.

—LINDA KNIGHT

Puzzles and Plans

"Unless the LORD builds a house, the work of the builders is useless."

Psalm 127:1

My grandson has a monster puzzle that's bigger than he is. When he decides that a certain piece fits a specific spot, there's no changing his mind. He pounds on it, saying, "It WILL fit!"

Sometimes I act that way, stubbornly trying to force the pieces of life to fit my own plans without seeking God's guidance. When my plans go against His, they can't prosper.

My husband and I fell in love with a Victorian house and determined to buy it even though we couldn't afford the cost. We planned to work second jobs, take in renters, and sell one car. When the house sold to someone else before we made our offer, we were disappointed. Later, though, we realized that we would have been sorry if we had gotten what we so desperately wanted.

Thank God that he'd worked out *His* will instead of letting us have our way!

Seek His guidance instead of force-fitting your own plans.

—MARSHA JORDAN

Seek the Lord

"Run from anything that stimulates youthful lust. Follow anything that makes you want to do right. Pursue faith and love and peace, and enjoy the companionship of those who call on the LORD with pure hearts."

2 Timothy 2:22

Sometimes when we move we promise our neighbors and friends we will keep in touch. Years go by and we get busy in our lives. We stay in touch at first and gradually drift away. The odd Christmas card gets sent, but the closeness that was shared is lost.

Isaiah says to call on God while He is near. God is always near. It is us who move away from Him. We drift or, worse, erect a barrier between Him and ourselves.

Seek God now. He is, and always will be, near.

God is always near and waiting for your call.

—NANCY F. REVIE

The Belt of Truth

"Stand your ground, putting on the sturdy belt
of truth and the body armor of God's righteousness."
Ephesians 6:14

Remember the Western gunslinger putting both hands on his gun belt to make sure it was secure before facing the enemy? Think of the batter hitching up his pants before he bats. Visualize that symbol on your dashboard that reminds you to fasten your seat belt.

Belts are important. They keep things together. They keep you safe. They complete your outfit.

God gives us a belt to protect us against the dishonesty in the world. The belt He gives us is truth.

When you get dressed, don't forget to put it on to protect you against that master of deceit, the Devil.

*In a world of misprints, errors, half truths,
and lies, God's truth protects you.*

—MERRY E. VARGO

A Tissue of Comfort

"But his officers tried to reason with him and said, 'Sir, if the prophet had told you to do some great thing, wouldn't you have done it? So you should certainly obey him when he says simply to go and wash and be cured!'"

2 Kings 5:13

I always felt like I had to do great things for God until I understood the story of Elisha, Naaman, and the servant girl. It's a truth embodied in a friend of mine.

Sheila suffers from a bipolar mental illness and is open about her struggles. Despite medication and good medical care, she often has to be hospitalized. One day she shared her ministry, although I don't think she would have called it by that name.

During her hospitalizations, Sheila often encounters other depressed patients who cry uncontrollably. She comforts them, gives them tissues, hugs them, and stays with them until the doctor arrives.

What a lesson this was for me! I know the Lord must be saying of her, as he did the widow of Mark 12:42, "She . . . has given everything she has" (Mark 12:44).

It pleases God when you serve Him in small ways.

—ELAINE YOUNG McGUIRE

The Warmth of God's Love

"But my life is worth nothing unless I use it for doing the work assigned me by the LORD Jesus—the work of telling others the Good News about God's wonderful kindness and love."

Acts 20:24

"Finish your dinner! Think of the poor children who have to do without!" my mother used to admonish. She always thought of the less fortunate, even though we ourselves were poor.

In the wintertime, she told me that many children suffered because their parents couldn't afford warm clothes for them. One bitter-cold day, I had an epiphany. If everyone opened the doors and windows and let the heat escape from their homes, the outside would warm up and no one would freeze!

My childlike reasoning offered a simple solution to the plight of the poor, though not an effective one. Our heating bills would skyrocket! However, my idea had merit. What would happen if we opened the door of our hearts, and let the warmth of God's love escape? Would the poor in spirit feel the heat of God's unconditional love? God constantly replenishes our love supply, so giving generously won't drain our resources.

God's love—there's plenty of it to go around.

Warm another by sharing God's love.

—S. (SHAE) COOKE

63

Up, Up, and Away!

"The LORD continued,
'Stand here on this rock beside me.'"
Exodus 33:21

Recently, I took my niece, Shannon, rock climbing at an indoor facility for her tenth birthday. As I watched, Shannon skillfully climbed from one rock to the next. If she got stuck, she climbed down to look at the entire wall. Then, she would ask my advice on where to go next and carefully plan her route. She was determined to climb all the way up. And she did, several times! A boy nearby marveled at Shannon. He climbed only about twelve feet before he was completely paralyzed with fear, unable to move up or down.

When you get into a tough situation, does fear overwhelm you? Or are you like Shannon and step away from it to gain perspective? Do you seek the counsel of the Lord when you don't know which direction to go? Afterward, do you follow the plan that's been laid out for you?

God will help you find your footing amidst life's traumas.

—STEPHANIE KANAK

We Can't All Be Feet

"But God made our bodies with many parts and he has put each part just where he wants it. . . . Now all of you together are Christ's body and each one of you is a separate and necessary part of it."

1 Corinthians 12:18, 27

Sitting around Susan's kitchen table, I listened while she cried. Her family was in turmoil. Family members had turned against her; her husband was indifferent. "They say I'm the crazy one," she explained.

I looked at her and thought how mixed up the world is. Susan has wonderful gifts that bless her family and her friends. Yet, some see her as different, nonconforming, and odd.

Susan bakes bread, organizes vegetable co-ops, shops thrift stores, and homeschools her children. She's a devoted friend, generous, and faithful. It is true Susan does not conform to society's generally accepted ways.

God made His children uniquely different, each with special gifts and purposes. Everyone has a place in his or her immediate family, as well as the family of God. In terms of the parts of Christ's Body, can everyone be a foot? A hand? Our differences complete the body of believers and glorify our Creator! Today let's celebrate that we are not all feet!

You are a unique part of the Body of Christ.

—SHANNON RULÉ

Whom Can I Trust?

"It is not an enemy who taunts me—I could bear that. It is not my foes who so arrogantly insult me—I could have hidden from them. Instead, it is you—my equal, my companion and close friend. What good fellowship we enjoyed as we walked together to the house of God."

Psalm 55:12–14

David actually wonders aloud if God is deaf and undependable in his time of trouble. The Creator cuts His creatures a lot more slack than we would, so don't worry about expressing your anger or frustration or doubts to God. He knows all about it anyway.

More disheartening to David was his good friend who betrayed him. They had spent many pleasant hours walking to the temple and sharing their deep soul and spirit thoughts, in both the good and bad times.

Have you ever been disappointed by a person with whom you had an open and transparent relationship? You have invested both time and emotion. Then a crisis comes and you feel abandoned. I understand. David understands. Jesus understands. "Give your burdens to the LORD, and He will take care of you. He will not permit the godly to slip and fall" (Psalm 55:22).

Though your soul-mates may abandon you in a crisis, God will never leave you nor forsake you.

—KENNETH M. HANSEN

Why'd You Leave Me?

"For you are God, my only safe haven. Why have
you tossed me aside? Why must I wander around
in darkness, oppressed by my enemies?"
Psalm 43:2

Have you ever challenged God when things aren't going
well? Have you ever asked Him, "What are You doing?"
You're in good company because David often wondered the
same thing. We love David, as God did, for transparency in
the good and bad times.

As a freelance project manager for many years I have
often wondered where God was in my life circumstances,
what His plan was, and when He was going to implement
something I could see.

Even our Lord on Calvary asked, "Why have You left
me alone?" The question itself affirms our relationship as
parent-child or close friendship. Honest questions can never
do real harm.

Our struggles are for a season, whether we can see the
path clearly or not. David challenges himself again to "put my
hope in God and praise Him again." Will you join me today?

*In the great crises of life, even the
Lord wondered where His God was.*

—KENNETH M. HANSEN

You Have Been Called

"Therefore I, a prisoner for serving the LORD, beg you to lead a life worthy of your calling, for you have been called by God. Be humble and gentle. Be patient with each other, making allowance for each other's faults because of your love."

Ephesians 4:1–2

In this passage, Paul speaks to us about our calling. Do you have a calling? Of course you do! You may not be a pastor, evangelist, or teacher, but God still has a calling on your life. He has called you to serve Him. We are called to be examples of Christ.

We are told to be humble and gentle, patient with each other. How many times today did you exert those qualities? He tells us to make allowance for each other's faults because of our love. How many times in the past week have you noticed or "picked at" someone else's faults?

We should be careful in what we do, for when people see us, they are not looking at us, but rather the example of Christ that we are setting. Are you showing others who Christ is?

Be like Christ in all you do.

—STORMY NIEVES

MARCH

SECOND CHANCES
—MICHELE STARKEY

"And we know that God causes everything to work
together for the good of those who love God and
are called according to his purpose for them."

ROMANS 8:28

*I*F ANYONE HAD ASKED ME WHAT I WANTED FOR my forty-second birthday, I would have said, "A new brain." Today, at forty-five years of age, I wouldn't change a thing about my life or myself. I like who I am.

In my twenties, I lived in Europe. In my thirties, I had a terrific job, lived in a townhouse just north of Boston, and traveled the world. A typical at-home afternoon would include a jog through my New England neighborhood.

Then my father's illness prompted me to change careers and return home to New York to be closer to my family. I found another good job, another nice home, and Keith, the man I later married. It was almost as if I were being rewarded for placing my family first.

Some months later, Keith and I were relaxing at my home when my life took a turn. My head began to hurt and nothing seemed to help. We waited. We prayed. No relief. Aspirin, ice packs, and rest had no effect. In fact, the pain ominously grew more and more intense. After an hour, the pain was so piercing I began to scream in agony. My legs went numb and I became severely nauseous. Keith frantically dialed 911 as I slipped in and out of consciousness.

Within minutes, sirens were blaring outside of our home. The paramedics rushed in, assessed my situation, and notified the hospital: "Apparent stroke, fortysomething-year-old female. Extreme distress. Unconscious."

Keith told me we were at the hospital only moments when the ER doctor called for a helicopter. I was medevaced to the nearest neurosurgical unit located at Westchester Medical Center in New York. I needed brain surgery as soon as possible.

I woke up for the briefest of moments and asked the surgeons to gather around me for a moment of prayer. Keith and my family stood silently by in the waiting room, stunned by the unfolding events.

More than ten hours after I went into surgery, the doctors let my family know that I had survived the surgery and explained what they had done. A brain shunt had been inserted and the aneurysm clipped successfully. Only time would reveal, they said, how much normal brain function would return.

As the days passed, the nurses would ask me my name, the date, who the president was, and did I know where I was? I really wasn't ever sure where I was. I could not believe what was happening and just wanted to wake up from this nightmare and get on with my life. I would reach up to touch the bandages on my very swollen, misshapen head and cringe in agony if I accidentally touched one of the drainage tubes. The pain was excruciating.

Weeks passed, seasons changed, and I was released only after much coaxing and convincing by my doctors that I would recover more quickly at home. The grotesque scars on my head were nothing compared to the memories that continually flashed through my mind of the sirens of the ambulance, the chopping sounds of the helicopter blades in the cold black skies, the sickening smell of the ICU ward in the darkness of the night. I was haunted by the events. It was unreal to imagine that nearly two months had passed me by. Two months and a lifetime had forever been changed. I would lie awake in my bed at night, staring at the ceiling fan and asking God, "Why? Why me? Why this?"

At home, overwhelmed by my inability to perform even the simplest tasks that I once took for granted, I would oftentimes weep for hours on end. Then my mother would show up.

From the first day that she came to visit me at my home, she tied my sneakers on my feet and took me by the arm and led me outside. I was in such a weakened state that I had to lean on her just to lift each of my feet. My mom would quote Proverbs 3:5, "Trust in the LORD with all of your heart and do not depend on your own understanding."

It was during these walks with mom that my questioning of God turned to thanking God. It was during those walks with my mother that I came to give thanks to God for a second chance at life. I'd made it halfway to Heaven and back.

It has been four years since my brain surgery. Keith and I are married. I take life one day at a time now. It scarcely seems possible that I've been given a second chance at life. A chance to make a new beginning and give God all the glory for the many blessings He has given to me.

I quit my high-powered job and opened a small business with my sister. Life seems a whole lot more precious now. I never leave home without my sneakers in hand as those walks around the block are so much more meaningful now. I owe that all to my mother who showed me that taking a walk around the block can always bring you closer to home.

Frustration and Learning

"This command I am giving you today is not
too difficult for you to understand or perform."
Deuteronomy 30:11

I was one of the last children in my kindergarten class to learn to tie my shoes. The bulletin board listed the names of the students who could, but my name was absent for a long time. My brain understood how to make a loop and wrap the lace around, but my fingers were not coordinated enough to actually tie the bow.

When my father found out how frustrated I was, he showed me a new way to tie a bow by making two loops with the shoelace, which were then tied together in a knot. Within a few minutes, I could tie my shoe.

In the same way, our Heavenly Father guides us in performing tasks we think are too hard, although not always in the way we might expect. We need to be open to his lessons and the possibly unusual forms they might take.

*If you listen, God will guide you in
performing the tasks He has chosen for you.*

—KIM SHEARD

A Pure Perspective

"Everything is pure to those whose hearts are pure. But nothing is pure to those who are corrupt and unbelieving, because their minds and consciences are defiled."
Titus 1:15

My uncle, an artist, sat beside me on Grandma's porch one summer evening long ago. Having recognized a similar ability in me, he decided to share some inspirational thoughts.

"We artists don't see things the way other people do. Others may look at this wall and see bricks. But we notice beautiful designs in the cracks, focus on varying shades of color, and marvel at the patterns formed by shadow," he explained.

Later, I realized that when we become Christians, we are filled with glory and acquire, like artists, a unique perspective on life.

The promise of eternity before us gives us a reason to rejoice. We are content focusing on the simple joy and beauty in life. We enjoy delightful thoughts and cheerful possibilities, look for good in others, and when we stumble, have incentive and strength to go on.

Regenerated by His grace, you can
view life with a clearer perspective.

—DEBORAH R. MCCORRY-NUNEZ

He Hears Us

"Morning, noon, and night, I plead aloud in my distress,
and the LORD hears my voice."
Psalm 55:17

Isn't the telephone a wonderful invention? Isn't it amazing to be able to pick up your phone, press a button or two, and talk to anyone in the world with whom you're longing to communicate? Well, thanks to Alexander Graham Bell, we can do this. Born on this day in 1847, he created one of the world's most important inventions. We remember his famous words: "Mr. Watson. Come here. I want to see you."

Even though this was one great invention, I know a means of communication that can never be surpassed. The King of our universe invented it—prayer! It's mind-boggling to think that at any time, night or day, we can call out to God and He will hear us. Wireless, yes. And there are no bills, only benefits.

Go ahead! Give Him a call!

You can be sure that when you pray, God hears you.

—WENDY ANN DUNHAM

We Are the Seeds

"This is the meaning of the story:
The seed is God's message."
Luke 8:11

Late one night my young daughter was digging through her Scripture box. She carefully copied one, then said, "Here Mommy, I picked this for you."

The note read, "You are the seed that decides the harvest around you. Love Kalaya. P.S. He loves you."

Tears tumbled as I realized the truth behind the words. I am the seed that decides the harvest around me. When I allow God to pour into me daily, I am able to pour out seeds of love upon my family. In turn, the harvest is plenty. However, when I neglect my time with God, I have no seeds of love to offer. In turn, the harvest proves shallow. I am indeed the seed that decides the harvest around me. How about you?

What kind of seed are you?

—MONICA CANE

Happy Song

"For the LORD your God has arrived to live among you. He is a mighty savior. He will rejoice over you with great gladness. With his love, he will calm all your fears. He will exult over you by singing a happy song."

Zephaniah 3:17

My entire life I have approached our Heavenly Father much as Queen Esther approached King Xerxes, with much fear and trepidation. I had always envisioned Him as stern and emotionless; that is until I read this Scripture.

The book of Zephaniah deals with the exile of the Israelites and their return to the Father. Even though they were exiled because of their own sin, the Father drew them back to Him, dancing and singing as they came. (The word "exult" means to skip, dance, make merry, revel, be elated, be exhilarated, be in high spirits, be delighted.)

Hallelujah! This Scripture puts to rest any images I had of the Father as distant and cold. I now approach His throne with great confidence that He not only forgives my sins but sings and dances over me each time I draw near.

What an awesome Father we have!

No matter what you've done,
the Father greets your return with celebration.

—DENARAE CARLOCK

Forever and Ever

"He died for us so that we can live with Him forever."
1 Thessalonians 5:10

Three-year-old Brooke, our youngest grandchild, was spending the day with us. It was lunchtime and we were enjoying one another at the kitchen table.

Brooke looked at her granddaddy and me, and to our astonishment she said, "I am going to stay with you forever and ever."

Jerry replied, "But, Brooke, your mother will be so sad."

That didn't faze Brooke one bit. "I would call her," she stated quickly.

When I spend quality time with God, that is how I feel. At those moments I am anxious for the day when I will go to live in heaven forever and ever. Even though it might leave my earthly family a little sad at the time, the Holy Spirit will comfort them and assure them that all is well.

You can live with God forever if
you accept His Son into your heart.

—MELVA COOPER

Hiding from God

"The LORD God called to Adam, 'Where are you?'"
Genesis 3:9

When I was a young girl, my father was music minister at a small Baptist church. Sometimes, while my parents led choir practice, my brother and I played hide-and-seek under the pews in the sanctuary. We crawled around on all fours, ducking our heads so we wouldn't bang them on the wooden benches above us.

After experiencing a miscarriage, I found myself hiding again. Only this time, I was angry at—and hiding from—God. When I began to have panic attacks during the summer after our pregnancy loss, I realized something was dreadfully wrong. After tests ruled out a physical problem, I sought out a Christian counselor. As she walked me through my grief, I began to realize He wasn't punishing me.

Rather, through my pain, He was calling out to me, "Where are you? I long to heal you. Let's get through this together."

God longs to heal and comfort you.

—DENA DYER

A Better Deal

"That is why he is the one who mediates the new covenant between God and people, so that all who are invited can receive the eternal inheritance God has promised them. For Christ died to set them free from the penalty of the sins they had committed under that first covenant."

Hebrews 9:15

When we lived at home, my sister and I often found ourselves in various conflicts of our own making. These childhood clashes were regular events that involved important issues like who left a towel on the bathroom floor, who ate the final piece of cherry pie, or who forgot to lock the gate. For our parents, the key issue was always the truth.

Since all previous agreements had failed to resolve this integrity issue, my father instituted a new covenant with us siblings. The deal was simple: If we told the truth, there would be no punishment. Our wrong choices still carried consequences, but we were free from any penalty.

Christ instituted a new covenant with his followers as well. It was a better arrangement based on truth, filled with eternal promises, and free from the penalty of sin. The only thing we add is our faith.

When you tell the truth about your sins, God forgives you.

—CHARLES E. HARREL

Eye Showers

"They weep as they go to plant their seed,
but they sing as they return with the harvest."
Psalm 126:6

Recently, I met a friend coming from a movie, dabbing her red eyes. She approached me and threw her arms around me. "It's been a long while since I've had a good cry," she sniffled in my ear, "and it feels just great!"

Tears refresh the eyes of contact lens wearers and noticeably improve the clarity of images. Those afflicted with dry tear ducts must put artificial tears in their eyes. A welling of tears in our eyes notifies us and those around us how deeply we have been moved by sadness or happiness.

The Bible shows us a sequence: first tears, then songs; first sorrow, then joy. We can thank God for the marvelous mixed nature of tears, both for their cleansing release and for their promise of happier days. Eye showers may precede life's flowers.

Tears may signal sorrow but they may also forecast better times.

—JAN SEALE

Church Lights

"You are the light of the world—like a city on a
mountain, glowing in the night for all to see."
Matthew 5:14

My church is on a hill in a rural area. Driving to church for
an evening Lenten service, I topped a hill and suddenly saw
the church glowing like a beacon on the next hilltop. Most
of the year trees full of leaves block the view, but the bare
branches let the light burst from the stained-glass windows,
warm and beckoning.

This is what Jesus tells us we must be—a glowing
beacon of faith, warm and beckoning to those outside the
faith to join us in the light.

How bright is your light?

You must let your light of faith be a beacon for others.

—MERRY E. VARGO

Held in Safekeeping

"I give them eternal life, and they will never perish. No one will snatch them away from me, for my Father has given them to me, and he is more powerful than anyone else. So no one can take them from me. The Father and I are one."

John 10:28–29

My wife and I went to an exhibit in Edinburgh, Scotland, called the Camera Obscura. Over 150 years old, this exhibit uses a parabolic mirror that can be swiveled in a 360-degree circle to see the entire city. The image is shown through a series of mirrors onto a board in a darkened room. You can see real-time images of people and events outside but everything is miniature. When the camera exhibit first opened, people ran screaming from the room thinking they were in the presence of witchcraft.

The operator asked if I would like to "pick up" a pedestrian. I held out my open hand and she adjusted the mirror to place in my palm the image of a person on the sidewalk outside. It looked like I was holding a three-inch man!

Jesus said that He holds us in His hand and that we are eternally secure in His grip. No one—no power, no evil, nothing—can snatch us away from His loving hand. There is a good biblical name for that—it is called grace.

God holds you in His hands.

—DON M. AYCOCK

When the Time of Testing Comes

"But he knows where I am going. And when he has tested me like gold in a fire, he will pronounce me innocent."
Job 23:10

Jesus warned us, "Here on earth you will have many trials and sorrows." All good things, however, come with a price. Few items of value are initially free of imperfections.

In the fires of refinement, gold is repeatedly heated to its melting point so impurities can be skimmed off. The resulting metal is then deemed pure and worthy.

When a loved one succumbs to an illness or a job loss threatens to turn the world upside-down, the temptation to despair or find inappropriate methods of dealing with the test now before us brings us to our melting point.

Still, we have a loving Father, a Master Jeweler whose skill at refining our hidden golden treasure ensures we will become what He desires us to be. The only thing He asks of us is to trust His skill. So surrendered, the end of our journey will find us golden.

God will lovingly accomplish what He wills for your life.

—DAN EDELEN

My Life Belongs to Him

"Then Jesus said to the disciples, 'If any of you
wants to be my follower, you must put aside your
selfish ambition, shoulder your cross, and follow me.'"
Matthew 16:24

When my friend, Kris, faced brain surgery a few years ago, I
learned about faith.

"Are you afraid?" I asked, sitting close to her hospital
bed. She smiled and patted my hand. Soon a nurse would
shave her head, give the pre-op injection, and wheel her to
surgery. Kris wasn't afraid, but I was.

"Whatever the Lord wants to do with my life is okay
because I trust Him," she said. Her words stuck in my heart.

That day Kris followed the Lord into the operating
room with His peace. To her, having a tumor wasn't just a
"cross" to bear; the Cross meant death to an old way of
living—being anxious, worried, or afraid. Her quiet trust
humbled me. Later we rejoiced that the tumor was benign
and had been completely removed.

Carrying the cross may involve pain, but it leads to peace.

—VICTORIA GAINES

Waiting Is Not for Lazy People

"Don't be impatient for the LORD to act!
Travel steadily along his path. He will honor you,
giving you the land. You will see the wicked destroyed."
Psalm 37:34

How people behave in various circumstances has been measured and cataloged. Regardless of your personality profile, we see that responsible people want to take action in a crisis. However, David, the shepherd king, with warrior blood on his hands, says we need to resist our natural "Type A" and "doer" disposition and instead "wait patiently for the Lord."

Waiting is hard work, because for the doer it requires soul discipline. Waiting is not inactivity. It requires a great deal of spirit activity. This is not laziness, lethargy, or indifference.

David says (thirteen times) our highest priority is to be godly. We need to hold back on the "doing" and work hard on the "being." I'm a doer and I like to work on projects with aggressive goals and tight timetables. I'm often impatient. How about you?

Waiting on the Lord is an active expression of faith.

—KENNETH M. HANSEN

Washing Needed

"And since I, the LORD and Teacher, have washed
your feet, you ought to wash each other's feet."
John 13:14

I don't remember how it all started. It may have begun as a misunderstanding, a disagreement, or an unresolved problem. One thing seemed certain; I allowed an emotional hurt to fester in our marriage and now it had surfaced.

My wife and I loved each other, yet neither of us knew precisely how to end this upsetting conflict. Although I cared and tried to help, nothing I said improved the situation.

I left the room to offer a silent prayer and reflect for a moment, when a possible solution invaded my thoughts. Throwing a bathroom towel over my shoulders, I returned to our bedroom carrying a bowl of water. Kneeling in front of her chair I asked, "Laura, may I wash your feet?"

*When you demonstrate a servant's heart,
you avoid conflicts and render healing to the hurting.*

—CHARLES E. HARREL

God Is Watching

"The LORD is watching everywhere,
keeping his eye on both the evil and the good."
Proverbs 15:3

Ever notice how children hide when they are doing something wrong? I recall one afternoon when I was taking care of my nephew who was two years old. I was in the kitchen washing dishes when I noticed silence in the room where Robert was playing. I stepped into the den and saw his toys left in a pile on the floor. I searched the house but he was nowhere around.

My parents had just laid carpet in one of the rooms. A small excess piece was rolled up and laid to the side. I watched as the little piece moved slightly. I walked over to the carpet, gently unrolled it, and found Robert inside eating a tube of lip balm! A frightened look filled his eyes as he realized he'd been caught.

As Christians, we are a lot like my nephew; we think that if we hide we won't get caught. But God is always watching.

God sees your sin and longs to forgive you.

—STORMY NIEVES

A Tool for the Carpenter

"Furthermore, because of Christ, we have received an inheritance from God, for he chose us from the beginning, and all things happen just as he decided long ago."

Ephesians 1:11

One of my husband's best friends, whose passion was to share God's love, passed away recently. He left his mark on my husband. Since then, Mike has felt led more strongly than ever to be a bold witness in sharing his faith. He prays daily for God to bring the lost into his path.

One such occasion was a Sunday morning, before Mike left to sing in the choir. During a rest period in the last service, Mike sat outside. A young Middle Eastern boy, carrying a backpack, walked on campus and sat down right next to Mike.

"Hey, do you know anything about this church?" the young man asked.

"I sure do," Mike replied. "What would you like to know?"

As they talked, Mike was able to share God's love and plan for salvation. The young man couldn't have been more eager. And Mike thought that God's timing, once again, couldn't have been more perfect.

If you make yourself available,
it's amazing how God will include you in His plans.

—SUE RHODES

Glad Rags

"Worship the LORD with gladness.
Come before him, singing with joy."
Psalm 100:2

In a small provincial town in central Texas, an elderly man has made himself famous. When Mr. Munn hears of a person's or group's anger, he pronounces, "Well, they can just get glad in the same clothes they got mad in." People find Mr. Munn's saying quite useful.

We smile at the "glad/mad" rhyme but also at the idea. To change our mood, we need not wait for a new day with fresh clothes. We simply get over our "mad" right now, and become happy.

"Glad" comes from Old German and earlier Latin meaning "bright" or "smooth." Being contented and cheerful shows in a shining, pleasant face. Even pronouncing the word "glad" causes our lips to turn up in a slight smile.

What a marvelous ability God has given us, as we focus on what He's done for us, to change our mads to glads in less time than it takes to change clothes!

Gladness is a frame of mind that you choose.

—JAN SEALE

They Try to Drown Them

"And this is a picture of baptism, which now saves you by the power of Jesus Christ's resurrection. Baptism is not a removal of dirt from your body; it is an appeal to God from a clean conscience."

1 Peter 3:21

We attended a baptismal service at our Baptist church one Sunday evening when several children chose to dedicate their lives to Christ. A Baptist baptismal involves one or more of the church leaders submerging the new believer in water.

Two boys in front of us were talking. One had never seen a baptismal before. He asked, "What will they do to them?" There was a great deal of concern in his voice. The second child answered him in a reassuring manner, "Don't worry, they try to drown them in the water, but Jesus always saves them."

Out of the mouths of babes!

Jesus does always save us. The world may have its way with us, but in the end, if we have faith and trust the Lord, we will be saved.

Jesus does save.

—MICHELE STARKEY

Guilty Party, Grace-Filled Pardon

"Yet now God in his gracious kindness declares us
not guilty. He has done this through Christ Jesus,
who has freed us by taking away our sins."

Romans 3:24

The police officer walked up to my car. I'd been driving over
the speed limit. "License, insurance card, and registration,
please."

I quickly found the first two items but was so shaken I
couldn't locate the registration. The officer saw the panicked look on my face. He suggested I try the glove compart-
ment. There it was. He checked over my information and
told me how fast I'd been going. I knew the ticket was next.

Instead, the officer issued me a warning. I deserved
more. I was guilty yet I received a gift of grace. Since that
incident, I've been aware of my speed and obedient to the
posted signs.

God's law also provides protection and security. Yet, I
often fail. I'm a sinner. I'm grateful for the gift of grace found
in Jesus. My grateful response to this undeserved present is
obedience to Him.

Obedience is the grateful response to God's grace.

—LORI WILDENBERG

He Will Shine the Light

"Whatever you decide to do will be accomplished,
and light will shine on the road ahead of you."
Job 22:28

My son Evan was playing with his toy solar calculator. It didn't take long for him to discover that when he typed in a math problem, he could see the answers only when he held the calculator in the light. When he held it in the dark, his answers could not be seen.

So it is with us. When we face questions or problems and need an answer, we shouldn't keep them in the dark. The place of uncertainty and unanswered problems is not a fun place to be. We need to bring our problems into the light of God, and He will lead the way for us. He will shine His answers.

God will shine His light on you and lead your way.

—WENDY ANN DUNHAM

Press on to Know Him

"Oh, that we might know the LORD! Let us press on to know him! Then he will respond to us as surely as the arrival of dawn or the coming of rains in early spring."

Hosea 6:3

If you had asked me twenty-eight years ago, "Do you know Larry?" I'd have said, "Yes." But now that I've been married to him for over a quarter of a century, my yes means so much more.

How have I gotten to know my husband? By spending time with him, by listening to what he says, by learning about the things he loves. The effect of all this time together is a deeper relationship and a greater appreciation of the man I love.

So it is with God. When we spend time listening to Him, when we get to know His people, when we stop to observe His work, His response is just as Hosea said: certain as the dawn and dependable as rain in spring.

God wants us to know Him. He wants to bless us with His goodness. Press on to know Him!

Each day you can get to know God on a deeper level.

—SHERRY L. POFF

Treading Water?

"Save me, O God, for the
floodwaters are up to my neck."
Psalm 69:1

In the year our first child was born, my father and then my mother died, I lost my job, and my wife was laid off, leaving us with no income shortly after purchasing our first home.

Yet grace holds on when all else fails. It allows for the mistakes we inevitably make as the waters rise. It reminds us that the troubles may be more than we can bear, but they are not unbearable for God. For in the midst of the storm, He whispers His words of life deep into our souls. We may not hear them now, but when the floodwaters inevitably subside, we will.

Friends who are left with no other words can only remind us that God never leaves us. He is unshakable. And because we are in Him, we are as well.

Sometimes when it rains, it pours.
But God is there for you all the same.

—DAN EDELEN

A Simple Truth Revisited

"But God showed his great love for us by sending
Christ to die for us while we were still sinners."
Romans 5:8

"Grandma, do you want me to sing for you?" When I assured my granddaughter I'd love to hear her song, she climbed up on my wooden blanket box and began the song she was practicing for the Wee Wiggler's Choir. She sang "Jesus Loves Me" with her whole heart.

Three small words, so simple a child can understand them, yet they contain so much profound truth. Jesus, the Son of the Almighty God, loves us. The next three words are equally profound, for they say that we can know of His love personally: "Jesus loves me, this I know."

Where would a five-year-old child or a fifty-year-old adult find this knowledge? "For the Bible tells me so!"

If we hear no other truth than the words of this simple song, then we have an immeasurable treasure that will lead us to meet this very same Jesus face-to-face someday.

God's most profound truths can
be learned by the smallest child.

—ELAINE INGALLS HOGG

The Faith Like a Child's

"'I assure you, anyone who doesn't have their kind of faith will never get into the Kingdom of God.' Then he took the children into his arms and placed his hands on their heads and blessed them."

Mark 10:15–16

The three- and four-year-olds in my Sunday school class are precious. One little boy is an exceptionally good listener. As I told the story about Jesus rising from the dead and how the women found his tomb empty, he raised his hand. "What is a tomb?" he wanted to know.

I described it and his brown eyes grew big and round. "Sounds scary to me," he said.

About that time there was an unexpected knock at our classroom door. The little boy stood straight up and shouted loudly, "It's Jesus!" It was only a man coming to count how many children I had in class, but whenever my faith wavers I think about that little boy and the pureness of his faith.

Oh, to be like him and to be aware that at any moment Jesus may knock at the door!

Seek the pureness of a child's faith in order to please God.

—TERESA BELL KINDRED

Love Right Back

"Future generations will also serve him.
Our children will hear about the wonders of the LORD."
Psalm 22:30

My granddaughter Amy is a student at Texas A&M. When she was three years old, God changed the course of my life. My friend Jean said, "John, we are desperate for Sunday school teachers for the children for the summer months. Will you help?"

The Holy Spirit seemed to say, "John, you would be comfortable helping in Amy's class." So I said yes.

Over the ensuing fifteen years, I have felt a childlike joy being with the children. At first, I continued helping with children on Sunday during the summer. Then upon retiring from an engineering career eight years ago, I began helping with three-year-olds in the church's weekday preschool.

Young children are trusting. As they sense your love, they love right back, beginning with the first day of school.

Love begets love.

—JOHN C. WESTERVELT

Daily Detours

"Jesus told him, 'I am the way, the truth, and the life.
No one can come to the Father except through me.'"
John 14:6

When driving the same route to and from work every day, at times we can slip into autopilot mode. The subconscious part of our brain just takes over and sometimes we don't even remember driving home, unless there's something unexpected on the route.

Sometimes life throws us a detour just when we expected to be home in time for dinner. Just when we thought there weren't going to be any obstacles. Just because we thought there might be an easy road home tonight. And then, detour strikes.

The next time you find yourself driving down the highway of life and running head-on into a detour, try turning to the One who holds the map. He knows the way.

Jesus answered, "I am the way and the truth and the life. No one can come to the Father except through me" (John 14:6).

Let Him help you find your way home amid the detours in this life.

*If you follow His map, you will always find
your way through the obstacles in your daily walk.*

—MICHELE STARKEY

Jesus Laughed?

"Therefore, it was necessary for Jesus to be in every respect like us, his brothers and sisters, so that he could be our merciful and faithful High Priest before God. He then could offer a sacrifice that would take away the sins of the people."

Hebrews 2:17

In the four homes my husband and I have shared, there is a picture that has always been hung in a place of honor—an artist's depiction of Jesus laughing. I love thinking that He, even knowing what lay ahead of Him, could laugh.

Many people know the shortest verse in the Bible: "Jesus wept" (John 11:35, NIV). The verse is potent not just because it's a record holder, but also because it shows that this God Man had human feelings.

So if tears, why not the opposite? The Bible doesn't say so, but surely, for instance, He chuckled at the sight of a child's antics. That's human nature, and sharing in it fully, understanding it deeply, was part of His gift to us. Others may say they know how we feel, but He really does.

Jesus shares your joy and pain.

—JANE ROBERTSON

Lather. Rinse. Repeat.

"No one hates his own body but lovingly
cares for it, just as Christ cares for his body,
which is the church. And we are his body."
Ephesians 5:29–30

Lather. Rinse. Repeat. These are simple steps to maintaining a healthy, clean head of hair. It's the same with your body. Every day, you get into the shower, lather up, and rinse. Repeating is optional, as long as you come out clean.

Few would neglect daily hygiene. When circumstances occasionally keep you in the same clothes for days, finally getting to shower, shave, brush your teeth, and put on clean clothes, you are wonderfully refreshed and even say, "I feel like myself again."

The same is true with spiritual hygiene. Skipping time in the Word, avoiding praying, and generally ignoring God for a period of days can leave you feeling in desperate need of a spiritual shower. Just as prolonged neglect of your body will result in serious health problems, prolonged neglect of your spiritual well-being makes you a dysfunctional part of Christ's body.

Keeping our lives clean helps keep His body functioning properly.

Spiritual cleanliness is the only route to true godliness.

—SRC

Clean out the Lint

"So get rid of all the filth and evil in your lives, and
humbly accept the message God has planted in your
hearts, for it is strong enough to save your souls."
James 1:21

Our clothes dryer was dying. I thought I knew how to give it
artificial respiration and keep it going for a while, so I went
to a local appliance parts place and asked for a drying ele-
ment for our model. The lady behind the counter checked
the inventory and announced that she did not carry that
part. As I was leaving she asked, "Have you cleaned out
your vent lately?"

What could the vent have to do with anything? But I
went home, moved the dryer away from the wall, and dis-
connected the vent. It was stuffed with lint! I pulled out
handfuls and then got the vacuum cleaner and sucked out
every trace I could find. I hooked it up and put in a wet load.
When the buzzer sounded I opened the door to find . . .
completely dry towels. We need to keep the channel with
God and others pure as well.

Clean your spiritual "lint trap"
daily with prayer and the Word.

—DON M. AYCOCK

A Welcome Interruption

"So let us come boldly to the throne of our
gracious God. There we will receive his mercy,
and we will find grace to help us when we need it."
Hebrews 4:16

Our family has a "Peeping Tom." At numerous times throughout the day, a red bird presses against the window and takes a good long look at us. We've named him Cecil. Once noticed, he rushes to a nearby dogwood tree and sings to the heavens.

Cecil's visits are as much a blessing to us as I imagine our coming to Him must be to our Heavenly Father. And just as I do for Cecil, my Heavenly Father drops everything He's doing just to say hi! What a joy it must be to God when we humans leave our interludes with Him filled with His Spirit and energized to sing His praises. Like the red bird, we should be so bold!

You never need an appointment with your Heavenly Father.

—MARCIA SWEARINGEN

APRIL

WORTH THE WAIT
—LORI WILDENBERG

"May he grant your heart's desire and fulfill all your plans."
PSALM 20:4

I NEVER THOUGHT MY BODY WOULD BETRAY ME in such a sinister manner. I ate healthy foods; I exercised.

During a routine exam, the doctor discovered a mass. After a few unpleasant procedures, the tissue was identified as endometriosis. Getting pregnant is the cure for endometriosis; the irony is this condition makes it difficult to conceive.

My husband and I had a plan for our family. We wanted four children. Three of them would be our natural children and we would adopt a fourth. We'd be terrific parents and we could provide a loving home to a child who needed one.

Consumed with the goal of conceiving, I became hooked on doctor visits; placing all my hope in the medical field. Nothing was going to stop me from achieving my goal. Not even a traveling husband!

But again and again, for three years, my determination was confounded by disappointment.

God opened my eyes. I realized my hope was misplaced. I needed to place my hope in the Lord. God is so good. He had been reaching for me from the beginning.

My husband and I concluded that instead of relying on medicine, perhaps it was time to pursue adoption. We sensed this was God's will for us. Refreshed with a new and clear vision, I took things back into my own hands and out of God's. I was determined to get this job done as swiftly as possible and hold my baby.

Once again, there were potholes of delay and discouragement. I didn't think I could take much more. At the end of my rope, I cried out to God. I was in my car driving to my job as a teacher, and I felt emotionally driven to my knees. I prayed, "Lord, I can't do this anymore. This is yours. I need you. I'll accept your perfect timing." It was all back in God's hands.

That morning, while teaching my third-grade class, an announcement came over the PA system: "Mrs. Wildenberg, could you please come to the office?" This was a strange request since the office staff never interrupts classtime.

Quickly, I made my way down to the office. "You've got a phone call," said the administrative assistant, handing me the phone with a smile. The familiar voice of the social worker handling our adoption announced, "Your daughter's born."

My husband and I traveled to Bogotá, Colombia, to receive our gift from God—our first baby. Holding her, I knew I needed my daughter more than she needed me.

Today, God has blessed us with four great kids, the last three our biological children conceived without medical intervention. His plan was different, yet much better, than ours. His plan was worth the wait.

In Spite of Faithlessness

"If we are unfaithful, he remains faithful,
for he cannot deny himself."
2 Timothy 2:13

I was around nine or ten years old at the time. We had gone to friends of my parents' for dinner. They had a couple of kids my age. After dinner while the adults sat around talking, the kids went outside.

It was getting dark. They had a new bike and let me take it for a spin. While I had been through the neighborhood in daylight, I really didn't know the neighborhood.

As I came around the last corner of the block the house failed to appear where it was supposed to be! I pedaled a little farther, took another turn thinking this must be it. Nope. I was lost.

"Lord," I prayed solemnly, "help me find my way back to the house and I'll never be bad again." I was serious about finding my way, which I did. But about being good? Well, kinda-sorta-maybe. Fortunately, God remains faithful even when I'm not.

When you finally turn to Him, God is always there.

—SRC

Showing Love

"LORD, don't hold back your tender mercies from me.
My only hope is in your unfailing love and faithfulness."
Psalm 40:11

"Please, Mom, can I keep reading?" my son, Michael, begged. His reading lamp cast shadows across his plaintive face as he clutched a book to his chest.

Keeping his best interests at heart, I said, "No."

"Why?"

"You have school tomorrow and need sleep. Besides, you've already read for an hour. Now, lights out." With great reluctance, Michael surrendered the book and turned off the light.

I knew that although he neither liked nor agreed with my decision, he'd appreciate getting a good night's sleep. Saying no to him showed my love, though he certainly didn't see it that way.

Many times we respond like my son when God says no to our requests. We grumble, fret, and plead for *our* way. Sometimes, later reflection reveals what grace and love we were shown by that no. Sometimes, we don't understand. In those cases, we must trust that God has our best interests at heart.

His way is always better than your way.

—LORI Z. SCOTT

Stay with Me

*"He told them, 'My soul is crushed with grief to
the point of death. Stay here and watch with me.'"*
Matthew 26:38

After a long workday, I take pleasure in tucking my daughters into bed. With a quick cheek peck and hug, two girls are off to slumber quickly. But one, Carly, needs more attention.

"Please stay with me," she requests. In the dark I can feel her little fingers lock tightly around mine, secure in my silent companionship. Neither of us talks as the sun nestles beneath the horizon. We share a quiet moment; my daughter content with me there. Within minutes the little hand relaxes, her fingers unlock, and Carly is finally asleep.

This ritual heightens my distress when reading Matthew 26:38. I see my Savior overwhelmed. Jesus needed a little human companionship and was let down. I think, "Lord, I would have supported you that night."

But I know how often I fail my Savior with my actions, words, or thoughts. I realize that I, too, fall asleep clinging to Him while He watches.

Jesus stays with you.

—THOMAS SMITH

Shelter from the Storm

"Have mercy on me, O God, have mercy! I look
to you for protection. I will hide beneath the
shadow of your wings until this violent storm is past."
Psalm 57:1

Spring thundershowers. Most children dread the violent thunder and lightning, but even in my earliest memories I loved them. As soon as a thunderstorm rolled into the area, my father would set a chair in the patio doorway. He'd pull me onto his lap, and together we'd watch for lightning and count, "One, one thousand, two, one thousand . . ." Those were special times. Snuggled in my daddy's lap, I knew I was safe.

In his attempt to banish my childish fears, my father gave me a wonderful picture of how my Heavenly Father wants me to view spiritual storms. When trouble arises, I can run to my Father and we can watch the storm together until the turbulent times of life pass.

I do not fear the storms that come to oppress my soul. I know my Father will hold me until the winds calm and the sunshine returns again.

God will be your refuge in the midst of life's storms.

—LISA TUTTLE

God's Body Armor

"But let us who live in the light think clearly,
protected by the body armor of faith and love, and
wearing as our helmet the confidence of our salvation."
1 Thessalonians 5:8

My stepson, Ron, wears a bulletproof vest to work. As an armed security guard, it's a necessary part of his equipment. We gave it to him as a gift when he changed from unarmed to armed security. We gave him a hot, heavy vest to wear because we love him and it can save his life.

God gives all of His children even better protection. He gives us the body armor of righteousness that will save our souls. God doesn't promise to save our mortal life, but our eternal one!

But just as Ron's vest won't protect him unless he puts it on, neither will our armor protect us unless we wear it. Put on the body armor of God's righteousness in the morning and remind yourself of its protection as you go through your day. You'll be surprised at how safe you feel!

*You need to take advantage of
all the help God provides for you.*

—MERRY E. VARGO

Led by the Spirit to Be Tested

"Then Jesus was led out into the wilderness by
the Holy Spirit to be tempted there by the Devil."
Matthew 4:1

As I read this verse again, the words "by the Holy Spirit" leap off the page.

Jesus must have spent some time in prayer alone, as was His usual habit. He probably asked His Father for direction for the day before setting out. In answer to Jesus' prayer, His Father led Him by His Spirit into the desert. He led His Son to a dry place, a tortured, hot environment.

Why? God knew His Son; He knows us. Why does He have to test us? Is testing done so that we can know our own hearts? Jesus was alone in His testing, except for the angels. The angels learned a lot from Jesus.

Maybe when we are led by the Spirit and tested, God is trying to impact more than just us. Maybe he wants to impact His church. In times of testing, pray that God would further His Kingdom. Maybe we, too, have something to teach the angels.

God uses tests to teach you more about Him.

—JESSIE ANN MOSER

What to Wear

"Don't lie to each other, for you have stripped off your old evil nature and all its wicked deeds. In its place you have clothed yourselves with a brand-new nature that is continually being renewed as you learn more and more about Christ, who created this new nature within you."

Colossians 3:9–10

I have nothing to wear. There are clothes in my closet, but minutes tick by and the clothing pile on my floor grows. Each item is too tight, too dressy, out of style, or too casual.

It would be fantastic if clothes, perfectly suited to us in every way, were provided with invitations. A holiday party invitation would bring a jazzy red dress or a smart polo shirt and slacks. A hay ride and bonfire would bring a pair of jeans, boots, and flannel shirt.

God has done that. He invites us into his Kingdom, and provides—through Christ—pure, beautiful garments suitable for a royal gathering in his presence. My ill-fitting rags of sin are cast off and replaced with God's robe of righteousness, trimmed with truth, peace, and saving grace.

That pile of discarded clothes on the bedroom closet floor doesn't bother me so much in light of my exquisite eternal wardrobe.

Through Jesus you are worthy to be in
God's presence, perfectly clothed in purity.

—LAURIE WHITMAN

Perfect Timing

"'At last the time has come!' he announced.
'The Kingdom of God is near!
Turn from your sins and believe this Good News!'"
Mark 1:15

I wondered, "Why was the first century the perfect time?" Years later, while researching a project about books, I caught a glimmer of why Jesus arrived when he did.

Centuries before Christ, the Greeks made learning and literacy a priority throughout their culture. Their plays and philosophies were so well known that Greek became the language for communication. When Rome rose to power it adopted the Greeks' language and ideas and then spread them throughout the far-flung empire along Roman roads. Shortly after Christ's resurrection, an innovation, the codex—folded papyrus or parchment secured between sturdy covers—replaced the fragile scroll and made the written word durable and transportable.

At the end of my research I marveled at God's awesome and impeccable timing. A convergence of literacy, an international language, the ability to travel quickly, and the development of the codex provided the ideal setting for the spread of the Gospel.

You can trust God for His perfect timing in your life.

—SARA ROSETT

Why Me, Lord?

"And in human form he obediently humbled himself
even further by dying a criminal's death on a cross."
Philippians 2:8

After six years of full-time caregiving to my parents, raising
two preschoolers, and enduring menopause, I wondered
how much more I could take. One morning I awoke and
groaned, "Lord, what did I do to deserve this?"

To my surprise, the Lord answered, "What did I do to
deserve the cross?" After a brief silence, I heard more. "Will
you lay down your life for your family?"

It's so easy to say yes in the prayer closet. But the same
Lord of the prayer closet walks with me through my difficult
days—and He's only a prayer away. Giving service to others
was His will for my life, and the lives of all His children.

Jesus wants you to be a servant.

—MARY ROBERTS CLARK

God's Daily Planner

"Do not withhold good from those who
deserve it when it's in your power to help them."
Proverbs 3:27

Frail and terminally ill, he lifted his bandaged hand and caressed my cheek. I hadn't expected to be visiting Henry. I'd come to the hospital to wait with a friend while her daughter had surgery, but rules prevented me from going with her. Alone in the waiting room, all I could think was, "What a waste of time."

To my surprise, my dad showed up. He told me he was there to visit our longtime neighbor, Henry, who was dying. After dad left I decided to visit Henry, too. I wasn't even sure if he'd remember who I was. As I chatted with Henry, I talked to him about how much Jesus loved him. He listened intently and tearfully whispered "Thank you" as I left. Three days later, he died.

My time wasn't wasted that day. I was keeping a divine appointment to be there for Henry.

*Divine appointments are all around you every day.
All you need are eyes to see and ears to hear.*

—LINDA KNIGHT

The Redeemer

"He is so rich in kindness that he purchased our freedom
through the blood of his Son, and our sins are forgiven."
Ephesians 1:7

What a beautiful word *redemption* must have been to Lily, an
eighteenth-century slave, when Amos Fortune, a free black
man, paid the ransom and rescued her from a lifetime of
slavery.

Amos's compassionate act toward an enslaved person
reminds us of what Jesus accomplished for us on the cross.

God's justice required a price be paid for our sins.
Knowing we could not offer an acceptable payment for sin,
God sent Jesus to be the ransom.

By accepting God's provision, we are brought back to
God—redeemed!

We now can enjoy a relationship with God as His child
and look forward to a child's inheritance—life everlasting.

Before his death in 1801, Amos, a tanner by trade,
managed to free five people from slavery. Christ did much
more. On the cross He touched the entire world, purchasing freedom for every person—whoever comes to Him
and believes.

*Christ's death and resurrection made it possible for every person
to be redeemed from sin and begin a new life as God's child.*

—JEWELL JOHNSON

Jesus, My Brother

"Anyone who does God's will is
my brother and sister and mother."
Mark 3:35

My friend Marilyn once taught a Sunday school class in which there was a young hearing-impaired boy. On Easter Sunday she displayed a poster showing the risen Christ. It declared in bold print, "Jesus Rose!"

When the deaf boy saw the caption, joy and excitement lit up his face. He signed to his teacher, "B-r-o-t-h-e-r!" Little Timmy Rose thought that "Rose" was Jesus' last name and so they must be brothers.

Marilyn felt a stab of concern and frustration, wondering how she would make this caption and concept clear to Timmy, but she stopped herself when God's truth dawned in her heart. "Timmy, you are absolutely right!" she signed. "Jesus is your Brother."

You are part of His family when you do God's will.

—SUSAN ESTRIBOU RAMSDEN

Second Chances and Sheep Feeding

"After breakfast Jesus said to Simon Peter,
'Simon son of John, do you love me more than these?'
"'Yes, LORD,' Peter replied, 'you know I love you.'
"'Then feed my lambs,' Jesus told him."
John 21:15

Have you ever found yourself thinking that relationships would be much easier if they didn't have to involve other people? Family members seem oblivious to our feelings and friends do things that hurt us for reasons that we can't even understand. Most often our first and strongest impulse when we are hurt is to put up our defenses and distance ourselves from those who have hurt us.

How radically different from this typical human response is the way that Jesus deals with Peter following Peter's denial that he even knew Jesus on the night of His arrest! What I find most interesting about Jesus' dealings with Peter here is that He clearly links the restoration of Peter's relationship with Him to Peter's willingness to give of himself in his relationships with others—"Do you love me? . . . Then feed my sheep."

Lord, When I am hurt, grant me the grace to forgive and restore my relationships with others the way You made it possible for me to be forgiven by dying in my place.

When God forgives you,
restore your relationships with others.

—HEIDI L. JANZ

Why?

"Jesus replied, 'You don't understand
now why I am doing it; someday you will.'"
John 13:7

"Why, Mudder, why?" My daughter's anguished question broke my heart. Her three-year-old tongue couldn't quite wrap around "Mother," but the emotion was genuine.

She was terrified of needles and our pediatrician had prescribed an injection every day for a month. Her worsening allergies had twice led to pneumonia that threatened her life. So, I wept with her, and helped the nurse hold her down for the shots. There was no way to explain immunization to a toddler.

Today she is tall and strong, the mother of a teenager. Recently our family experienced painful times and my heart's cry to the Father reminded me of her long-ago wail: "Why, Mudder, why?" There are things God cannot explain to human hearts. But surely we can trust the One who sent His only Son to die for us.

You can trust in Jesus even if
you don't understand all the whys.

—KATHRYN THOMPSON PRESLEY

We Have a Hope

"He will remove all of their sorrows, and there
will be no more death or sorrow or crying or pain.
For the old world and its evils are gone forever."
Revelation 21:4

It's a fact. Pain, death, sorrow, and despair are all a part of this world. There's no way around it. They are unavoidable.

On April 14–15 in 1912, one of the most tragic and devastating events in history occurred: the sinking of the British luxury liner, the *Titanic*. There was death, sorrow, panic, despair. It's estimated that 1,500 lives were lost.

And this is only one of the tragic events of history. There have been countless more on a large scale, and even on a more individual scale. Perhaps even now you are going through a difficult time.

Still, there is good news even in the midst of trouble. Our lives on earth are temporary; a mere blip on the timeline of eternity. God promises that, when we reach our heavenly home, there will be no more sorrow, or death, or crying, or pain. All of it will be gone forever!

You have something wonderful to look forward to.

—WENDY ANN DUNHAM

He Provides

"It is the LORD who provides the sun to light the day and the moon and stars to light the night. It is he who stirs the sea into roaring waves. His name is the LORD Almighty. . . ."

Jeremiah 31:35

The job I'd had for two years suddenly evaporated. Despite my sending out dozens of resumes and going on several job interviews, nothing was jelling. What little money I had was dwindling fast and my fridge was pretty empty. I felt like I was teetering on the brink of homelessness.

I was on the train heading into New York City for yet another interview. At one of the stops along the way, Jack, the singles pastor from the church I attended, got on. He worked in the city and was taking one of his daughters in for the day as well.

We sat together and chatted. At the last station as we parted, Jack grabbed my hand, said "God bless you, brother!" and took off. Slowly I realized that I was holding something. I looked at my hand and there was money. Near tears, I unfolded three twenty-dollar bills. I could eat this week.

God provides for your needs just in time.

—SRC

Coping with Stress

"Be still in the presence of the LORD, and wait
patiently for him to act. Don't worry about evil people
who prosper or fret about their wicked schemes."
Psalm 37:7

An office can be a noisy place. The shrill ringing of the telephone, the beeping of the fax machine, the dinging of the computer's e-mail program, the shrieking of the paper shredder, and the demanding voice of one's boss all contribute to on-the-job tension. Some days the administrative assistant, be it secretary, receptionist, loan processor, title researcher, or clerk, becomes the recipient of criticism and complaints from customers and supervisors alike. These days, one needs a break.

A few moments with God are a wonderful stress reliever. Whether one takes a walk, hides in the lunchroom, or rests one's head on a cluttered desk, a quick, quiet prayer puts everything back into perspective. The knowledge that God is always there soothes like a deep, refreshing breath. A hundred years from now, it won't matter how many folders were filed today. But God will still be there.

The stress of modern-day life is no match for quiet faith.

—ROBIN BAYNE

Pussy Willows and Pinecones

"Jesus Christ is the same yesterday, today, and forever."
Hebrews 13:8

When I was small, my sister told me that umbrellas grew in the rain—that they bloomed into large, fully grown umbrellas. The closed-up ones had to get wet before they got bigger. It made sense to a five-year-old who also believed that pinecones turned into porcupines when watered, pussy willows grew to be cats, and lightning was God taking a picture of me. I used to look up at the sky and grin from ear to ear so He could get a good shot of me!

My perception of the world had an innocent patina that faded as I grew older, except for one belief that remained steadfast: My Aunt told me stories about Jesus—a man who came to save the world and loved me so much He died for me so that we could spend eternity together. He walked on water, healed the sick, and rose from the grave—these truths have never lost their luster.

Perceptions change but God's faithfulness is steadfast.

—S. (SHAE) COOKE

No TV Day

"I will be careful to live a blameless life—when will you come to my aid? I will lead a life of integrity in my own home. I will refuse to look at anything vile and vulgar. I hate all crooked dealings; I will have nothing to do with them."

Psalm 101:2–3

I decided to conduct my own experiment—no TV, no secular books, no secular magazines for thirty days. The first week was tough, almost like withdrawal. I would twiddle my thumbs wondering what I could do with all my extra time. I hadn't even considered myself an avid TV fan.

Before I knew it, projects that I had procrastinated on were completed. I wrote letters and sent cards. I read my Bible and really enjoyed it. I meditated and enjoyed the silence. I exercised more and met with friends. I sang in the car and danced to praise songs in the living room. My anxiety level went down. My thoughts were pleasant.

One day I chanced to pass a TV in a store. It was showing one of those crime programs I had watched for years. It was stunning to see what had once entertained me. My thirty-day experiment became forever.

Purity and integrity lead to peaceful
and productive lives in your own home.

—SHANNON RULÉ

In God We Trust

"But when I am afraid, I put my trust in you.
O God, I praise your word. I trust in God, so why
should I be afraid? What can mere mortals do to me?"
Psalm 56:3–4

David would have culture shock overload were he to time-travel to any contemporary Western society. I believe after a few days here, his deepest sadness would be over the actions being taken to eliminate all references to God in the public forum.

Here we see one of the greatest and most courageous individuals and kings in history confess transparently both his fear and unshakable trust in God. While for most men, increasing fear diminishes all confidence, taking them toward fatalism and suicide, David's confidence increases as the pressure mounts. He "lets go and lets God" as you can see from the verse above.

While your circumstances may not seem so earth-shaking to those around you, God sees how much they are affecting your heart. The Lord is able to "keep your feet from slipping" off the path. He wants you to have all the Light you need in a dark world.

God desires your confidence in
Him to grow as life's pressures mount.

—Kenneth M. Hansen

Fearfully and Wonderfully Made

"Listen to me, all of you in far-off lands!
The LORD called me before my birth;
from within the womb he called me by name."
Isaiah 49:1

When the doctor placed my son on my chest after the delivery, I breathed in his exhaled breath and the sweetness of it overwhelmed me. My emotions became supercharged as the reality of this new life—of creation—overwhelmed me. Tears fell as I embraced my new little one, and it was all I could do not to hug him too hard.

Did the angels feel the same way as they witnessed their Master create man on the sixth day? For, everything they saw Him create up until then, He created for this being. Did they sense that this creation was going to surpass all they had yet witnessed?

I imagine one could hear a feather drop, as the angels watched the Lord select the clay and shape it into a being in His own image. Oh, to be a dove on an olive branch, and witness the Master breathe life into the limp form. Hosanna! No doubt, God received a thunderous heavenly applause.

I gazed at this "clay touched by God" snuggling next to me, and clapped for joy.

God's touch was on you before you were born.

—S. (SHAE) COOKE

The Art of Casting

"Give all your worries and cares to God,
for he cares about what happens to you."
1 Peter 5:7

When I was five years old, I decided that if I could learn to handle a fishing rod, my brother might take me fishing with him. My cerebral palsy complicated this simple task.

My dad cast the line for me the first time. I coaxed my spasmodic hand to hold the reel lever and jerkily reel in the line. When it was time to cast out again, I could hold down the release lever, swing the rod over my shoulder, and thrust it forward, but I was never able to let go of the lever to release the line. Reeling in was difficult, but casting seemed impossible.

Our fear and doubt can make our hearts seize in spasm so that we're unable to release our anxieties and cast them upon Him. We need to learn the art of casting our cares onto Jesus and reeling in His promises.

*It's one thing to bring your worries and cares to God.
But it's a totally different thing to leave them with Him.*

—HEIDI L. JANZ

129

Can't Clean the Closet!

"And, 'LORD, in the beginning you laid the foundation of the earth, and the heavens are the work of your hands. Even they will perish, but you remain forever. They will wear out like old clothing. You will roll them up like an old coat. They will fade away like old clothing. But you are always the same. . . .'"

Hebrews 1:10–12

Fifteen years of watching my closet full of suits and "dry clean only" apparel take a backseat to casual, washable "mom" clothes left me feeling unsettled. I couldn't bear to part with my exquisite suits. I simply shuffled them from one rack to another. Examining skirts and jackets closely, I found frayed hems, lost buttons, and remnants of stains.

Was it my clothing that carried me through a successful professional career that gave way to motherhood, birthday parties, and PTO activities? Of course not! My faith carried me through all those changes.

No matter how much I wished those lovely clothes could retain their savvy appearance, I realized that only God is unchanging. Our garments lose their luster, appeal, and shape. God's love for us, however, is unceasing, unconditional, and undeserved.

Even though the earth perishes, God remains God forever!

—KARLA R. JENSEN

What Are You Worth?

"For even I, the Son of Man, came here
not to be served but to serve others,
and to give my life as a ransom for many."
Mark 10:45

My husband and I collect antiques and often argue about their value. He'll say, "This is worth five hundred dollars." And I'll reply, "It's not worth anything unless someone is willing to buy it!" Worth, just like beauty, is in the eye of the beholder.

An appraiser may place high value on an item, and a dealer may ask any price he or she chooses, but if nobody buys it, the antique is virtually worthless to the seller. Nothing is worth more than what someone's willing to pay for it.

Even your worth and mine are determined by how much someone would pay for us. There is someone who values us enough that He paid an outlandish price for our purchase. Jesus paid the ultimate price by giving His own life for ours. God values us so much that He gave up His own Son to redeem us.

*The Creator of the universe was willing
to give His life in exchange for yours.*

—MARSHA JORDAN

Know the Truth

"Give your burdens to the LORD, and he will take care of you. He will not permit the godly to slip and fall."
Psalm 55:22

"God helps those who help themselves" is an oft-heard "biblical" phrase you will have trouble finding in Scripture because it isn't there. It's just a common saying.

What does the Bible say? "Give your burdens to the LORD, and *he* will take care of you."

The myth that God helps those who help themselves drives us to try to do God's job. We pray, pray for change. Change in anything. Change in our lives, our career, our children, our spouse, those nasty neighbors down the street. The list goes on and on. But nothing changes since we're the ones applying all the "fixes."

As long as we are trying to do God's job, He won't. God will stand back and wait until we stop trying to do what we've asked Him to do. Yielding to God brings marvelous results!

God will sustain you when you lean on Him.

—Nancy F. Revie

God's Overwhelming Reassurances

"This promise is to you and to your children,
and even to the Gentiles—all who have been
called by the LORD our God."
Acts 2:39

"This promise is to you and to your children. . . ." I cherished these comforting words, praising God for our baby daughter. And to add to our joy, my husband and I would be blessed with another child; I had just discovered I was pregnant!

We were on our way to fellowship one rainy Sunday morning, the church steps wet and slippery. Hurrying in from the rain, my husband, together with my daughter in tow, took a nasty fall. Audrey, a nurse, came quickly to our side.

"You had better get to the emergency room," she advised.

My daughter suffered a skull fracture and I began to show signs of miscarriage. As I prayed, God's words came back to assure me: "This promise is to you and to your children. . . ."

He healed her and after my daughter recovered, I carried her new brother to term. I know that God's words of reassuring comfort saw us through safely.

When you need His care, God's reassuring
promises are always there to comfort you.

—KIM JONN

Band Jam

"When I am with those who are oppressed, I share their oppression so that I might bring them to Christ. Yes, I try to find common ground with everyone so that I might bring them to Christ. I do all this to spread the Good News, and in doing so I enjoy its blessings."

1 Corinthians 9:22–23

As a youth worker, it's a challenge to break the ice with the kids. At one church, I had a tough time building relationships with some of the "cool" senior high teens.

I tried everything, including sports nights, elaborate activities, and day trips to local events, but still made little headway. Then I realized many of these kids were budding musicians, so I instituted Thursday night band jam.

It was a no-holds-barred session with guitars, drums, and cranked-up amps. The sound shook the dust off the ceiling of that little church. Over time, those sessions led to several youth worship teams, lives committed to Christ, and spiritual growth in all who came.

The joy and blessings I received from this sharing of common ground still reverberates today.

Joy in serving God is absolutely electrifying when you roll up your sleeves and share yourself and share Christ.

—THOMAS SMITH

God's Word

"The grass withers, and the flowers fade,
but the word of our God stands forever."
Isaiah 40:8

Twenty-five years ago our home was one of three in our county that was flooded. The water was chest-deep in the backyard when my husband waded through to turn off the gas. I could visualize what this might look like on the evening news.

After the water receded, we began the long, slow process of cleaning our home and determining what had been ruined. Compared to that of the other two homes in the county, our loss was small. A few items, such as the stuffed dog my brother gave me before he died, were irreplaceable and their loss brought sadness.

One discovery, in the midst of all of the mess, surprised us. There on the floor lay a perfectly dry Bible. It was a little thing, but the symbolism was great. God was with us even in the flood.

God's Word will stand forever.

—LINDA ROBERTS

Wisdom of the Foolish

"Instead, God deliberately chose things the world considers foolish in order to shame those who think they are wise. And he chose those who are powerless to shame those who are powerful."

1 Corinthians 1:27

Chris and Carl are a couple of amazing guys. They are twin brothers who share an overflowing capacity for joy and love.

Often they play off of each other's humor. Their boisterous laugh booms throughout the room as they share a joke or tell a story. It is not hard to fall in love with them and their distinctive personalities.

God has given them as a gift to all who meet them. But it is a gift that is sometimes hidden from those who think they are so wise. You see, they are mentally challenged. Some people would call it retarded. That label certainly doesn't fit them. They seem to have a better understanding of love and compassion than most people I know, including me.

God calls us to love our neighbor. How much simpler could His command be? Why do we make it so hard?

Don't despise the wisdom of what seems foolishness.

—JAY D. ROHMAN

Planting Trees

"Then Abraham planted a tamarisk tree at Beersheba, and he worshiped the LORD, the Eternal God, at that place. And Abraham lived in Philistine country for a long time."

Genesis 21:33–34

Surely planting a tamarisk or any other tree is a curious thing for a landless wanderer to do.

For owners of property of any size, planting trees is an investment that adds value and character. Let's suppose that Abraham planted his tamarisk as a courtesy to the friendly neighbors who granted him passage and valuable grazing and water rights for his flocks and herds.

Such an action on Abraham's part returned something to his neighbors. This gesture and others like it account for the courtesy he received later at Hebron when he needed a burial plot.

Pioneers throughout our nation planted trees by investing themselves in service and generosity. They often began by founding or supporting schools and libraries. Their legacy continues to enrich our nation by nurturing new leaders.

Abraham planted a tree. So, what are we planting for the benefit of our neighbors?

Honor God by acknowledging blessings
received and passing them on to others.

—RICHARD S. BARNETT

MAY

SEEING HIM
—CHARLENE CLAYTON

"And let us run with endurance the race that God has
set before us. We do this by keeping our eyes on Jesus,
on whom our faith depends from start to finish."

HEBREWS 12:1–2

*I*T WAS A REALLY HARD DAY. MY MOM HAD reached what appeared to be the end of her two-year battle with Lou Gehrig's disease without much physical distress, but suddenly she began to have spasms in her throat that would stop her breathing instantly. Her husband and children gathered around her bed and attempted to calm her as we watched her turn darker colors of blue. Repeatedly, I bowed my head and asked God to help, then opened my eyes confidently, and yet nothing changed.

After several hours, a breakthrough came, her symptoms abated, and she rested comfortably once again. For that I was grateful, but there was a nagging question in the forefront of my mind: "Lord, why didn't you stop her suffering right away? You have never failed me . . . what happened today?"

I spent another night at Mom's bedside, reassuring, medicating, and making sure she was comfortable. I talked to my Heavenly Father. I felt so weary and sick inside. I could feel my foundation being tested and wondered if it would hold. The next morning the Lord spoke quietly to me and reminded me of an account in the Bible. It was the one of Peter walking on the water with his eyes fixed on the Lord. He was in the midst of the storm doing things that he never imagined he could do, and then it happened. Peter saw the storm and realized that he was in the midst of a very bad situation, with very real waves churning under his feet. He began to sink because he took his eyes off the Lord and became caught up in the storm.

A burden lifted from my heart and was replaced by renewed, simple trust as I turned the eyes of my soul toward my Lord. And then, with redeemed emotion, I recalled what had occurred during Mom's episode just prior to her calming.

At a loss of what to do for my mom, Dad had asked me to call our pastor. He and others from the church came and we gathered around Mom's bed. One woman had come to sing some hymns. I told her that she would need to come back later. She brushed by me to my mother's bedside, opened her worn hymnal, and began to sing. Others joined in, but I couldn't even choke out a note. "Turn your eyes upon Jesus / look full in His wonderful face. / And the things of earth will grow strangely dim / in the light of His glory and grace."

I looked at my mom and was amazed. There she lay, peaceful and serene, breathing normally. She could not open her eyes or move a muscle in her body because of the disease, yet her spirit had laid hold of the Master's hand.

The praise continued for a long time and we were refreshed. How faithful He is to test our foundation and to give us what we need.

Second Chance

"Choose some men from each tribe who have
wisdom, understanding, and a good reputation,
and I will appoint them as your leaders."
Deuteronomy 1:13

The son of sharecroppers, his path was not easy. Born to poverty, life was often hard. Indeed, graduating from college took this future principal two tries. God gave him a second chance that not only changed his life, but it would eventually impact the lives of every child he encountered.

It was his calling to help children. He understood the obstacles they faced. He refused to give up on a single one. Blessed by having both family and teachers who believed in him, Leroy Helire knew that they had made a difference in his life. Now it was his turn.

And so, with God's guidance, Leroy started Northdale Magnet Academy in 1986. The first diploma-bound alternative high school in Louisiana, Northdale and Mr. Helire have offered hundreds of young people a second chance for a dream once forgotten, the dream of earning a high school diploma.

God offers you many opportunities to give back.

—Pat Friedrich

Much

"When Abram was ninety-nine years old, the
LORD appeared to him and said, 'I am God Almighty;
serve me faithfully and live a blameless life.'"
Genesis 17:1

Rex introduced himself to me one day when I visited his church. He looked well wrinkled and slightly bent, but his warm smile and good humor made me feel welcome. As we conversed, he talked about his life.

"I used to work at the university. Now I'm too old," he said with a light chuckle. "I don't do much anymore."

But I discovered otherwise. One day I stopped by the church nursery and spotted him. Dressed in a baggy shirt and a crooked baseball cap, he scooped up a ball and rolled it to a squealing two-year-old boy. They both giggled.

"Rex," I exclaimed, "how wonderful of you to help out."

He grinned like sunshine. "Well, I can't change diapers," he said, "but I can play."

Despite Rex's age and physical limitations, he still found a way to serve God.

No matter how seemingly little the task, serve God faithfully.

—LORI Z. SCOTT

Our Awesome God

"And the very hairs on your head are
all numbered. So don't be afraid; you are more
valuable to him than a whole flock of sparrows."
Luke 12:7

I regularly think of this verse as I shower, watching strands of my long hair flow down the drain as I rinse out the shampoo. I find them all over the house, too, on the furniture and the rugs. I'm constantly shedding old hairs and growing new ones, yet God is so great that He knows how many are on my head—and on every person's head—at any moment of any day.

With a little research, I found that the average number of hairs per head is 100,000, and most people lose strands at a rate of 50 to 100 per day. With 6 billion people on His earth, all tracked—what an illustration of how awesome God is!

Is there anything He can't do? No. Is there anything we can't trust Him with? No. There's no need for us to worry with someone so awesome paying such close attention to us. Praise the Lord!

God is so awesome and so caring that you need not worry.

—KIM SHEARD

Hearing Voices

"I know that you sincerely trust the LORD,
for you have the faith of your mother, Eunice,
and your grandmother, Lois."
2 Timothy 1:5

I hear voices, now and then. I grew up in church in a time when you sang out of hymnals and not from projection screens. I still have one of the old, worn hymnals from my childhood church, rescued from the trash bin.

When do I hear voices? On those rare occasions when one of the hymns illuminates the screen on Sunday morning. Amidst the strains of "The Old Rugged Cross," "Just Over in the Glory Land," or "Just a Closer Walk with Thee," I hear the tremulous voice of my mother.

Her name was Grace. While not perfect, she was a godly woman, and, man, could she sing! She instilled in me both the joy of singing and the power of God's Word that was laced through the lyrics of those hymns.

When I sing an old hymn, I feel both the love of God and of a godly mother.

Live to leave a legacy of faith for those around you.

—SRC

Sprinkle Your Day with Prayer

"For what great nation has a god as near to them as the
LORD our God is near to us whenever we call on him?"
Deuteronomy 4:7

The other day, I lamented to my mother-in-law how my
prayer life has evaporated since I gave birth to my children.
I never seem to have a quiet moment.

She smiled knowingly and said, "Sprinkle your day with
prayer."

"What do you mean?" I asked.

"Mothers usually don't find many uninterrupted
periods of time for prayer," she said. "Instead, you have to
utilize small chunks of time throughout the day. Pray in the
shower, or while driving to pick up the kids from school.
Pray while you chop the carrots for dinner. Whatever time
you find works for you, even if it's only for a minute, pray."

I tried her advice, and found success, especially during
my morning run. I lace up my shoes and literally have a
"running conversation" with God. It's refreshing to feel the
nearness of Him again.

If you're having trouble finding time to pray, try sprinkling your day with prayer.

Let prayer be the glue that holds your day together in Him.

—LORI Z. SCOTT

A Selfless Nurse

"The LORD nurses them when they are
sick and eases their pain and discomfort."
Psalm 41:3

The Lord, who is King of all, alleviated the pains of all those
who needed Him and did not limit Himself to people who
were accepted in society. He aided outcasts such as lepers
and even cured people on the Sabbath day when it was considered sinful to work. He took the time to care for the forgotten. He nursed people and eased their discomfort while
proclaiming the message of God.

Nurses are living expressions of Christ's compassion.
They, too, care for the ailing in desperate need. Working
faithfully and selflessly, nurses exemplify the love of Christ.
Today the Lord can also ease your pain if you place all your
trust in Him.

He performs miracles. Just open your eyes and heart.

—LINDSAY OBERST

Training Wheels

"Teach your children to choose the right path,
and when they are older, they will remain upon it."
Proverbs 22:6

When I was six years old, my grandfather bought me a shiny new bicycle. After riding the bike for several months with training wheels installed, I one day demanded that my mother remove them. She did, and I immediately climbed on and rode off on two wheels as though nothing had changed.

Riding with the training wheels had helped me learn to pedal, brake, and balance. I knew what it felt like to ride. It never occurred to me that it would be harder to keep my balance on only two wheels. I simply got on and rode as usual.

Likewise, the training wheels of faith—church attendance, Bible reading, making right decisions—can be provided to our children from an early age. Then, later, when they begin to make their own decisions—when the training wheels come off—it is natural for them to choose the right path.

*Training children in the faith early
makes it easy for them to remain faithful.*

—KIM SHEARD

Give Us This Day

"God blesses those whose hearts are pure,
for they will see God."
Matthew 5:8

Living on a widow's allowance, my husband's tiny, four-foot-eleven-inch grandmother didn't have much. But what she lacked in wealth and stature, she made up for in heart. Whatever Grandma Lesperance had in her cupboards, she shared—with neighbors, family, strangers, you name it; always serving a feast fit for a king. When you finished eating she'd pack up the leftovers and give them to you, refusing any help with the cleanup. "I'll do it tomorrow, so I can remember today," she'd announce.

One day I asked her, "Grandma, how do you do it? You're always smiling and happy, always giving people anything and everything you have." Grandma turned to me, opened her arms wide, and said, "I just love everybody."

Grandma's long since passed away, but the Jesus in her lives on in each of us, every time our arms are opened wide.

Wherever you are, God can use you.
Whatever you have, God can bless it.

—LINDA KNIGHT

My Hero: Mom

"Her children stand and bless her.
Her husband praises her."
Proverbs 31:28

My mom has never run a marathon—but she has run to the store at midnight for medicine for sick kids. She has never held public office—but she knocked on doors so my dad could win a political office. Mom has never climbed the corporate ladder—but she often climbed into our tree house with us. My mom has never worked outside the home, but she always worked at making the inside of our home an oasis. That's why she's my role model.

My mom dried hundreds of tears when I had boy troubles, comforted me when I had nightmares, and prayed thousands of prayers for me.

I've told my mom many times that she is my hero. And I smile when people say I remind them of her—because there's no one else on earth I'd rather be like.

Moms with godly priorities are their children's heroes.

—DENA DYER

The Master's Touch

"... give generously to those in need, always being ready
to share with others whatever God has given them."
1 Timothy 6:18

After a rich, full life, my ninety-one-year-old grandmother
found herself felled by a stroke and confined to a wheelchair
in a nursing home. I visited her often and she would smile,
but it was very hard to see her there.

One day when I came, she was radiant. I had to
know why.

She smiled the most amazing smile and spoke with
luminous hazel eyes: "I've learned the secret," she
exclaimed. "We're to give ... give ... give ... and keep on
giving! And some days when I'm feeling down, I just decide
to make it my mission to roll myself out in the hall and find
somebody else to cheer up. It always makes my day, and
theirs, too."

It was then I knew she'd been healed. No matter what
constraints her body might be experiencing, her spirit was
soaring. And not long after that, she went home to heaven.

It is never too late to give yourself to others.

—MARCIA SWEARINGEN

Wrenches and Chainsaws

"You didn't choose me. I chose you. I appointed you to go and produce fruit that will last, so that the Father will give you whatever you ask for, using my name."

John 15:16

"What does a wrench and chainsaw have to do with Jesus?" asked Sean, one of my Vacation Bible School students. Puzzled by his question, I thought back over the week and asked God for wisdom.

"I know!" he exclaimed a moment later. "The words of the song are 'riches in Jesus' not 'wrenches and chainsaws'!" God cleared up Sean's confusion.

Still, I continued to ponder Sean's confused lyrics. Actually, wrenches and chainsaws have a lot to do with the riches we have in Jesus. A chainsaw prunes and cuts away the unwanted growth and the wrench's job is to grip and turn.

God continues to develop my character through pruning and then He gently holds and turns me so I may follow His lead in order to do His will.

A wrench, a chainsaw, and Jesus; I learned a lot at VBS!

When you allow God to work in you,
He can also work through you.

—LORI WILDENBERG

My Inheritance

"All those listed above include fourteen generations from Abraham to King David, and fourteen from David's time to the Babylonian exile, and fourteen from the Babylonian exile to the Messiah."

Matthew 1:17

My mother is my mentor. When she emigrated from Holland at the age of nineteen, her desire to know God intensified. Despite adverse circumstances, she became a godly woman of tremendous wisdom and strength. When I was young, she helped pastor a small church.

It wasn't until I married and became a parent that I began to truly appreciate my mother. I've endeavored to pass on to my sons the heritage she has given me in her faithfulness to Christ, her unwavering integrity, and her courage. My sons are blessed to be nurtured by their grandmother's legacy.

Legacies live a long, long time. My children will bequeath this beauty to their children. And to their children's children. I wonder if my mother realizes the great gift she is to generations she will never know.

Pass on a godly heritage to your family and friends.

—RACHEL WALLACE-OBERLE

Need a Lift?

"So don't get tired of doing what is good.
Don't get discouraged and give up, for we will
reap a harvest of blessing at the appropriate time."
Galatians 6:9

It feels good when someone pays us a compliment or commends our efforts. Our spirit feels uplifted by such acknowledgments. It also feels good to give out commendations, compliments, and kind gestures. The ripples of kindness can go on and on.

Consider this scenario. You are in the grocery store checking out and a man comes up behind you visibly agitated and in a rush. You offer to let him go ahead of you in line. Though amazed, he accepts and his demeanor shifts.

Because of your act, he heads home in a more pleasant and relaxed mood. He greets his wife and kids with warm affection instead of the usual gripe of the day. The next day, each family member goes out into the world with a slightly more positive outlook and that touches others.

By acting on daily opportunities to lift up others, many are blessed, including ourselves.

Be an encourager to all you meet.

—ELAINE BRITT

A Perfect City

"And I saw the holy city, the new Jerusalem,
coming down from God out of heaven like
a beautiful bride prepared for her husband."
Revelation 21:2

The day after our church sponsored a free community carnival, our Sunday school lesson was on the New Jerusalem—that beautiful city coming down out of the clouds. One of our questions was: "What would a city without evil be like?"

We brainstormed and one response likened it to the previous day of fellowship and fun . . . without the pony poop! Lots of wet wipes and volunteers had been needed to clean the children's shoes. But working at the exit gate handing out goody bags, I got to see the smiles as kids were leaving.

I believe that after bathing that night, they fell asleep with visions of the moonwalk still bouncing in their heads and the memory of cotton candy melting in their mouths. Once we get to the Holy City, we'll feel clean, too, and the good will be so great, all the bad will be forgotten.

God daily prepares you to be the bride of Christ.

—MARCIA SWEARINGEN

All in the Family

"And now, it has pleased you to bless me and my family so that our dynasty will continue forever before you. For when you grant a blessing, O LORD, it is an eternal blessing!"

1 Chronicles 17:27

Mother Teresa was born Agnes Gonxha Bojaxhiu, on August 26, 1910, in Skopje, Macedonia. She traveled to India in 1928, and it was while in Calcutta that she was moved by the presence of the sick, poor, and dying on those city streets.

At one time, she said, "There is a terrible hunger for love. We all experience that in our lives—the pain, the loneliness. We must have the courage to recognize it. The poor you may have right in your own family. Find them. Love them. Put your love for them in living action."

Start your own family mission. Reach out to someone who is lonely, poor in spirit or finances, even hard to love. Write a letter, cook a meal, or send a care package. Is there someone you haven't spoken to in a long time? Call or visit. In loving them, you are loving God himself.

You must put His love in action.

—S. (SHAE) COOKE

Potholes in the Pavement

"You have allowed me to suffer much
hardship, but you will restore me to life again
and lift me up from the depths of the earth."
Psalm 71:20

"Life is difficult." So begins the best seller *The Road Less Traveled* by M. Scott Peck. Once the teen years slip behind us, the reality that life doesn't always go the way we anticipate becomes increasingly clear.

My ideal was to grow up, marry once, have a wonderful life. I am enjoying a good life and a wonderful family, but the path has been bumpy. There were some big potholes. My response once the pain of each fresh tragedy has dissipated with time and prayer, is always, "So what?"

So what if from time to time my life has been sideswiped by someone else's hurtful choices or by my own willful detours? Who hasn't suffered, or caused suffering? The bigger truth is that life is not one-dimensional. On the flip side of sorrow, loss, and failure there are joy, success, and fulfillment.

Everything that comes into my life is a gift from God. The negatives teach me how better to appreciate the positives.

Even when life hurts, God is always good.

—SRC

No Response Required

"He is the God who made the world and everything in it. Since he is Lord of heaven and earth, he doesn't live in man-made temples, and human hands can't serve his needs—for he has no needs. He himself gives life and breath to everything, and he satisfies every need there is."

Acts 17:24–25

Our daughter Kelsey rushed into the house to change clothes and leave again to attend the Labor Day fireworks. "We need to talk to you before you leave," her father said. Gently, we told her that her birth mother had been found. Suddenly her day's priorities changed drastically.

"How? Who is she? How can I contact her? This is so exciting!" she said, sobbing with joy.

"You can write her a letter, but she does not promise to write you back," we explained. "This is quite a shock for her. I know that's disappointing to you."

"Yes, but better than nothing!" she quickly responded.

Just like Kelsey writing to her birth mother, God has sent us numerous letters without requiring a response. He continues to shower blessings on us as well as making His Word readily available. How disappointing to Him when we do not respond! But He remains faithful throughout.

God speaks to you constantly in a variety of ways.
You must respond to Him.

—LANITA BRADLEY BOYD

Wake Up and Pray!

"'LORD, help!' they cried in their trouble,
and he rescued them from their distress."
Psalm 107:6

"Where is Tanzania?" Mary Jo woke me with her query, and my sleepy brain had no answer.

"I don't know; why do you ask so early in the morning?"

"I've been awake since 3 o'clock this morning with that one word on my brain—'Tanzania.' I don't know where it is; I haven't read or heard anything about it lately—but I believe God woke me to pray."

The next day we read a description in the newspaper of a train wreck in central Tanzania that occurred at the approximate time of Mary Jo's awakening. The last lines of the account read: ". . . Survivors from the morning crash described how most of the 1,200 people on board were praying—some quietly, some loudly—while others screamed as the train swayed from side to side."

We believe that God heard the frightened prayers of people on a runaway train in Africa and woke someone on another continent to pray!

God uses His people in a process of prayer to help others.

—VIRGINIA DAWKINS

A Few Choice Words

"A truly wise person uses few words; a person with under-standing is even-tempered. Even fools are thought to be wise when they keep silent; when they keep their mouths shut, they seem intelligent."

Proverbs 17:27–28

I blew it, and I knew it.

There I stood, laughing with a friend about one of my husband's faults. Suddenly, he turned the corner and heard my remark. As his face fell, my heart sank.

I had wounded him deeply and I felt ashamed. Later, I apologized to my husband, and I asked the Lord's forgive-ness. Both forgave me, but I never forgot that my words caused a rift—however temporary—in two of my most pre-cious relationships.

That day, I learned the truth of what the Bible says in Proverbs 12:18: "Reckless words pierce like a sword, but the tongue of the wise brings healing."

As I've pondered the often-rash remarks that flow out of my mouth and studied Scriptures pertaining to words, I've discovered I need to pray daily for providential patience. There is no way I can use words the right way without God's help.

You need God's help to use your
words to encourage and not hurt.

—DENA DYER

Forget Me Not

"I said, 'Plant the good seeds of righteousness, and you will harvest a crop of my love. Plow up the hard ground of your hearts, for now is the time to seek the LORD, that he may come and shower righteousness upon you.'"

Hosea 10:12

While leaning on my shovel one hot afternoon, I surveyed my landscaping project and checked off a mental list to myself: Grass planted. Peat moss mixed with soil. Still, something wasn't quite right—the plants were stiff and regimental.

My sculpted, uptight garden needed a kick in the plants. Forget Me Not were the ideal companion. Through spring and summer, the Forget Me Not tirelessly filled my garden with vibrancy, chaos, and a definite style of their own!

I want to be remembered as one who had a definite style. I hope family and friends will chuckle as they recall the resilient lady who willingly ventured onto the rocky, less traveled path, seeding the love and hope of Jesus Christ.

How will you be remembered? Will you leave a spiritual legacy? Sow the seeds of righteousness—a genuine Forget Me Not.

Leave a spiritual legacy filled with promise and hope.

—CHARLENE FRIESEN

Comfort Is Conditional

"The LORD is my shepherd; I have everything I need. He lets me rest in green meadows; he leads me beside peaceful streams. He renews my strength. He guides me along right paths, bringing honor to his name."

Psalm 23:1–3

The Great Shepherd offers great comfort to the troubled soul. However, there are conditions that need to be met. One must first confess, like David, that He is "my shepherd."

Unemployed and financially strapped frequently over the last fifteen years, I have learned to affirm His leadership and my dependence on Him. David testified to the results of his surrender to the Lord: "I have everything I need . . . He leads me . . . He renews my strength . . . He guides me."

Life's storms catch us all at some time, of that we can be certain. What is uncertain is whether we choose to depend on ourselves or on the Lord.

Have you chosen Him as your Shepherd in your current crisis?

To receive the Shepherd's care,
obediently submit to his leadership.

—KENNETH M. HANSEN

Lesson from a Tree

*"For I am like a tree whose roots reach the water,
whose branches are refreshed with the dew."*
Job 29:19

When I think of my friend, who is a new Christian, I'm reminded of a scene in the forest of a misshapen tree clinging to rocky soil. Ruth wasn't born into a nurturing home and until recently has had little opportunity to experience God's love.

Often at first, she wasn't facing in the same direction as the older Christians in our church thought she should be. Like the clinging tree, her roots needed time to bend around the rocky patches in her life and to dig into the rich soil of the Word of God in order for her spiritual growth to be supported.

Over time, as she learns and lives Scripture, she is growing tall and upright. Like the tree that bent around the rock and grew toward the light, Ruth's life is becoming a testimony to the strength of her roots, anchored in the Word of God and growing toward the light of God.

All new Christians need time to grow.

—ELAINE INGALLS HOGG

All God's Benefits

"Praise the LORD, I tell myself, and never
forget the good things he does for me. He
forgives all my sins and heals all my diseases."
Psalm 103:2–3

"You'll be an asthmatic all your life," the doctor said.

"It can't be!" I cried. "Who'll care for my children?"

It is strange where your mind goes in times of crisis. Besides the children, I also thought of my garden. If I can't breathe properly, how can I seed and tend the plot of ground behind our house?

As I pondered the doctor's diagnosis, five words came to mind: *He heals all your diseases.* That phrase gave me courage to ask for God's help.

Before my feet touched the floor each morning, I asked God to heal me. When I fed my family, I asked again. When I took medicine, I asked for His touch.

Healing didn't come immediately. Rather, it came imperceptibly, like the growth of plants in my garden. I don't understand how they sprout beneath the soil's surface. Neither do I know how God healed me. But He did.

God can work healing in your body, mind, and spirit.

—JEWELL JOHNSON

You Are Never Alone

"And do you remember God's reply? He said,
'You are not the only one left. I have seven thousand
others who have never bowed down to Baal!'"
Romans 11:4

In the days following my son's death, then again during the lengthy months when I felt even God couldn't repair my damaged marriage, and even later in the excruciatingly sad months following retirement, I felt hopelessly alone. These were the winters of my soul.

At each of these times it seemed I couldn't connect with my Maker or His people. Yet I would recall the story of the lonely prophet, Elijah, in 1 Kings 19. God told Elijah to stand before Him at a mountain, but did not appear to him there, or in the wind, fire, or earthquake. He came to Elijah in a gentle whisper.

In facing my own mountains, or winters, I often was not quiet enough to hear His voice. When I was, I discovered I also was not alone. Thankfully, spring followed winter and new people entered my world. If you are hurting today, be still and hear what He is saying: "You are not alone."

God is right beside you, right now.

—ELAINE YOUNG MCGUIRE

Wings of Comfort

"He will shield you with his wings.
He will shelter you with his feathers.
His faithful promises are your armor and protection."
Psalm 91:4

A few weeks ago, my son Matthew and I visited the duck pond at the local park. One mother duck was shepherding a flock of seven offspring. Matthew squealed in delight at the baby ducks' antics as they would swim away and then quickly scuttle back to the protection of mama's wings.

Matthew is like those ducklings. Having just learned to walk, he will toddle away, only to be back again in a matter of seconds, checking in to show me the toys and other things he has found on his travels. He will look to me for direction and seek comfort if his unpracticed feet give out from underneath him.

God promises the same comfort. He is always there, waiting for us to seek shelter, companionship, and guidance.

God wants to provide the refuge you need each day.

—MICHELLE PETERS

The Empty Nest

"And the very hairs on your head are all numbered."
Matthew 10:30

After our children left for college, my sleep was often disturbed with visions of drunk drivers, rapists, sociopaths. Fortunately, I had memorized many of the Bible's "seed promises," and found comfort in Isaiah: "I will pour out my Spirit on your offspring and my blessing on your descendants" (Isaiah 44:3, NIV), as well as, "I will contend with those who contend with you, and your children I will save" (Isaiah 49:25, NIV).

But it was Matthew 10:30 that finally brought the "peace that passes understanding." I laughed aloud at the thought of our Heavenly Father patiently counting my children's thick red hair. Much as I love them, I never counted all that hair.

Now, when tempted to fret, I thank God for His watch and care over the smallest details of our existence. Then, while He inventories hair, I can go to sleep, like a child resting in my Father's arms.

You can trust the Heavenly Father to care for your dear ones.

—KATHRYN THOMPSON PRESLEY

Grow Deep Roots

"But blessed are those who trust in the LORD and have made the LORD their hope and confidence. They are like trees planted along a riverbank, with roots that reach deep into the water. Such trees are not bothered by the heat or worried by long months of drought. Their leaves stay green, and they go right on producing delicious fruit. 'The human heart is most deceitful and desperately wicked. Who really knows how bad it is?'"

Jeremiah 17:7–9

I don't know about you, but many days I find myself putting my "roots" down into the world. I find myself worrying about my kids, my husband, and my finances. I think of the future, without spending enough time thinking of the One who holds us in His hands.

When I place my trust in this world, I place it in things that will not last. My roots are planted in shallow ground. When I place my trust in the Lord, and make Him my confidence and hope, my roots are secure for eternity.

God doesn't promise to be with us *if* we have troubles in this life, but *when* we have them. If we will root ourselves in Him and His Word, we will have the strength to face the troubled times and those periods of drought.

When you plant your roots deep in the Lord,
you can withstand life's trials.

—SUE RHODES

Which Way

"I will search for my lost ones who strayed away, and I will bring them safely home again. I will bind up the injured and strengthen the weak. But I will destroy those who are fat and powerful. I will feed them, yes—feed them justice!"

Ezekiel 34:16

The Indianapolis Children's Museum is a four-story structure full of gadgets and gizmos, computer screens and carousels, slides and stars. As our rambunctious group of eleven perused through the exhibits, a game station distracted my son. He was so caught up in the display that he took his eyes off me and strayed away.

A museum worker led him to an area designated for lost children where I claimed him. Frightened and teary-eyed, he clung to me until he calmed down.

We can have a similar experience in our spiritual life. Like my son, we can become so engrossed in the world that we take our focus off the Father and stray away.

Or, like the museum worker, we can serve as a reconciling guide. Things like prayer, hospitality, and assistance bring backsliders to a place where God not only reclaims them, but binds and strengthens them as well.

Help someone find their way back to the Father.

—LORI Z. SCOTT

Tuning In

"Why can't you understand what I am saying?
It is because you are unable to do so!"
John 8:43

These two little walkie-talkie radios—one for me here in the house, homeschooling the kids; one for my husband out in the barn—have been one of the best gifts I've ever received.

With the press of a button, we enter the other's day—to cheer each other on, to be a listening ear, to be part of each other's emotional world.

But there are days when Darryl comes in from the barn, locates my radio, and, with a chuckle, shakes his head.

"You're on the wrong channel! I've been paging you but to no avail!"

"That explains why you seemed so quiet all morning!"

I wonder how many times My Father has been trying to get ahold of me today. He's been speaking, but I've been on the wrong channel. Instead of being on His wavelength, I've been tuned in to my to-do list, the ringing telephone, the endless errands. Time to get tuned in!

Stay tuned to God's channel
so you can hear His every word.

—ANN VOSKAMP

Sunrises and Sunsets

"From the time the world was created, people have seen the earth and sky and all that God made. They can clearly see his invisible qualities—his eternal power and divine nature. So they have no excuse whatsoever for not knowing God."

Romans 1:20

"Wow," said my daughter, staring at the horizon, "Look, Mom!" We stood watching the pinks and reds mingling together until the beautiful sunset gave way to night.

"Why does it have to end?" asked my daughter.

I had to think about that one. I stood outside and looked at the stars and realized how little I appreciated their beauty. I went back inside and gave my daughter the answer.

"It's a reminder," I said. "The sunset is a reminder that God is all around us and He will take care of us through the night."

"I like that," she said.

"And the sunrise is a reminder that He will be with us through the day as well."

"Can we watch the sunrise tomorrow?" she asked.

And we did. That day, and every day since, we started our day together—my daughter, God, and me.

You can find God every day in sunrises and sunsets.

—SHELLEY WAKE

Just Like Joseph

"As they discussed who should be appointed for the job, Pharaoh said, 'Who could do it better than Joseph? For he is a man who is obviously filled with the spirit of God.'"
Genesis 41:38

I pray often that my husband and sons will be like Joseph wherever they go.

Many years ago my husband Jay hired a new employee. They were at a job late one night installing carpet tiles in an office. Jay spread adhesive over sections of the floor before putting down the tiles. Later his employee said, "You're different than other guys; that glue is expensive and most of them cheat by applying it only at the seams."

Jay's business has prospered. To his clients he's known as a man of integrity. Our oldest son now has a part-time job after school. I've noticed his work ethics are the same as his dad's.

Every day we're given countless opportunities to demonstrate righteousness in our choices. Sometimes we're unaware of being watched. When we heed the call to holiness, our lives become beautiful blueprints of Christ's character that rub off on others.

Living a life of holiness impacts those around you.

—RACHEL WALLACE-OBERLE

JUNE

THERE WAS LIGHT
AND IT WAS GOOD
—SHANNON RULÉ

"Do you know how God controls the storm and
causes the lightning to flash forth from his clouds?"

JOB 37:15

"I'M GOING TO BED NOW," MY HUSBAND hollered. "The weather report said storms could be bad tonight."

"Okay. I won't be long." On the kitchen table sat the sewing machine where I had just finished making new kitchen curtains. I remember thinking, "Hope nothing happens to my new curtains." A short while later, I went to bed.

At four o'clock the next morning, there was an explosion. It had begun to rain. Steadily it grew louder and harder. I awoke and was heading into the bathroom when the house jolted and I was knocked to the floor. Then in an instant it was quiet, and the rain was falling gently on my face. That was when I realized the roof was gone.

Struggling to stand, I looked toward the bedroom. I screamed my husband's name but there was no answer. The bathroom door jammed. I clawed to open it. My husband ripped the door from the hinges and threw it aside. We moved toward each other, still not sure what had happened.

Quietly I said, "I smell gas." He pulled me back toward the bedroom where he grabbed a pair of jeans left neatly folded on the dresser.

"Get some clothes. We have to get out," he said, as I stood there wet and shaking in my nightgown.

Looking around, I said, "There aren't any clothes." There was the bed, the built-in dresser, the jeans, but no ceiling, no closet doors, and no clothes.

"Come on, we have to go. Let's go." We made our way down the hall and through the living room. The walls were ripped away; insulation hung out of gaping holes. I couldn't recognize anything. Opening the front door, I stalled again: "The steps are gone."

"You'll have to climb down," he said. Nothing looked the same. I finally spotted the car and ran for it. I glanced behind me to see my husband going in a different direction. He headed for the propane gas tank from where we both heard the gas spewing.

The car keys were in my hand. I don't remember how they got there. I can't imagine how I would have found them. I started the car, my husband jumped in, and I took off for my parents' house down the road. Would it be there? Whatever had happened, did it happen to them, too?

We careened into the yard; I jumped out and ran for the front door. My yelling and beating on the door woke my dad. He unlocked the door and we tumbled inside, telling him our story. He had heard nothing of the storm.

I pushed past him to the phone, called 911, and reported that we had been hit by a tornado. I must have realized it by then. The operator verified everyone was okay and then dispatched the fire department. We were asked to go back to the scene.

My mom gave me a raincoat and some shoes and we went back to our house. Fire trucks arrived. It was still dark and I couldn't see. I was standing next to a fireman. He was shaking his head. At that moment I remembered my wedding rings. Every night I took them off and laid them on the counter in the bath-room. My rings were gone!

I turned to the fireman and frantically said, "I've got to go back inside and get my wedding rings!"

He looked at me aghast and said, "You can't, ma'am. It's not safe."

I grabbed the arm of his coat and said, "You don't understand. I have to have my wedding rings."

He must have felt sorry for me because he agreed, but he'd go with me. I dashed for the door, climbed into the hole with him behind me, and journeyed back down the hall and into the bathroom, his flashlight lighting my way.

Again, I don't remember how I put my hand on two tiny rings, but I did. I started for something else and he said, "No. We have to get out now. It's not safe."

Agreeably I followed him. Once outside he said, "It will be easier when daylight comes. Then we can see." At that moment I looked around and saw that the headlights of the fire trucks were the reason we could see. Otherwise, it was pitch-black. This would be significant days later.

Neighbors came from everywhere. There was a flatbed truck and men were loading appliances onto it. People were taking things to safe, dry places. Some people I recognized and some I didn't.

That first week after the storm, my husband and I were in the car when it hit me. I asked, "Was the light on in the yard the morning of the storm?"

"No, don't you remember? All the lines were broken and dangling."

"Well, if there were no lights and the firemen couldn't see when they got there, how do you explain that we could see each other perfectly and we could see how to get out?"

He thought for a while and then said, "A miracle, I guess."

It was a miracle. It was a miracle that we were alive. Besides the direct hit of the tornado, there were live wires dangling and the gas spewing, but we suffered no injury, not one. Not even a cut or a scratch from debris or broken glass when we escaped barefooted. God's hand had covered our lives, and His light had guided our way to safety.

Survivor

> "And the LORD replied, 'I will personally
> go with you, Moses. I will give you rest—
> everything will be fine for you.'"
> Exodus 33:14

"I knew God was sending me a message when I was diagnosed with prostate cancer," said Deacon Lerory Helire. "Surgery was recommended as my best chance for survival. I prayed, read my Bible, and trusted God to guide my life."

"I faced surgery with peace of mind and peace in my heart. Although the road to recovery was slow and is ongoing, God had given me a second chance. What good is life without a mission? It was time to give back," Deacon Helire explained.

With the help of his church, he started a support group. The purpose is to share information and prayer with other men who face this same killer.

Although there's always the possibility that the cancer will return, Deacon Helire chooses to live his life as a survivor, putting his faith in God and gaining strength from the obstacle placed in his path.

Look to the Lord for guidance and strength.

*By turning over your life to God,
you can be free to carry out His mission.*

—PAT FRIEDRICH

Precious Gems

"God has made everything beautiful for its own time. He has planted eternity in the human heart, but even so, people cannot see the whole scope of God's work from beginning to end."

Ecclesiastes 3:11

Sand in your shoe. People in your family. Coworkers in your office. All these things can be a source of irritation. We want to put things right, now. Sometimes we can. Other things take time.

God has all the time in the world. He is willing to wait for fruit to ripen, for light to dawn, for promises to be fulfilled. He knows we are just dust, but He puts us in tight places to make us shine. Sometimes we feel like the oyster, constantly trying to smooth over life's irritations. But He wants us to know deep down we're really His pearls. And He won't stop polishing until we're perfect!

Jesus hung on a cross to pay for our deficits. He'll help us hang in there with each other until the process is complete.

Not everything can be fixed in the click of a mouse.
Really good things take time.

—Marcia Swearingen

Call to the Wilderness

"Then Moses gave them this command from the LORD: 'Take two quarts of manna and keep it forever as a treasured memorial of the LORD'S provision. By doing this, later generations will be able to see the bread that the LORD provided in the wilderness when he brought you out of Egypt.'"

Exodus 16:32

My friend said, "We have to go to the wilderness." She walked away prepared to draw her family close for forty days, no outside influences, no activities.

"We need to evaluate who we are and where we are going as a family," she said. "We'll walk, we'll talk, and we'll take time for one another."

"I wish you the best," I called out. "I'm praying."

Forty days seemed like forever, but when she returned, she was smiling; she was lighter. "God dealt with me in places I didn't even know I had. Our supplies didn't last the forty days but neighbors showed up with bags of milk, bread, and other groceries. They told us, 'I have no idea why I'm bringing you this, I just felt impressed to do it.'"

My friend smiles a lot now, the wilderness guided her home.

It is in quietness and solitude that
you can most vividly see the hand of God.

—SHANNON RULÉ

Light My Fire

"Give freely without begrudging it, and the LORD your God will bless you in everything you do. There will always be some among you who are poor. That is why I am commanding you to share your resources freely with the poor and with other Israelites in need."

Deuteronomy 15:10–11

On a recent camping expedition in the Adirondacks, we encountered a family with a half-dozen children who were setting up their tent. I overheard the father telling his older boys, "Go on up in the woods and gather some firewood for the campfire." It was beginning to rain and I looked at our stack of camp wood piled high next to our trailer. I knew we would be sleeping in a warm bed tonight, sheltered from the storm, while this family would be sleeping in their tent. I turned to my beloved with that "we need to help them out" look that only your mate can understand.

After we finished unloading our wood at their campsite, we returned to ours. Watching them in the distance, their campfire glowing warmly in the night, I turned once again to my beloved: "Honey, go on up in the woods and gather some firewood, will you?"

Are you giving freely that which was given to you?

—MICHELE STARKEY

Uncle Al

"Those who shut their ears to the cries of the
poor will be ignored in their own time of need."
Proverbs 21:13

"Uncle Al" was my dad's best friend from high school. Every
time we went to my dad's hometown, we went to see Uncle
Al. Uncle Al had multiple sclerosis.

These visits were uncomfortable for me as a child.
Uncle Al lost his ability to talk. He was moved from his
family home to a nursing home. My dad faithfully visited
and told us with his words and actions that this friendship
was too important to be forgotten.

When I was in high school, my dad was diagnosed with
Lou Gehrig's disease. As his condition deteriorated, I prayed
that my dad would not be forgotten by his friends. God was
faithful. Dozens of people from our church visited Dad during
his illness. They were faithful friends up until his death.

God honored my dad's commitment to his friend by
providing friends in his own time of need.

God provides help to those who have helped others.

—MARY J. BAUER

Trash to Treasures

"'Now gather the leftovers,' Jesus told
his disciples, 'so that nothing is wasted.'"
John 6:12

"What are you going to do with that?" I asked my husband.
He loves to find things that others have discarded and put
them to use. I often refer to him as my "trash collector."

He is quite handy. So many times, with just a little
fixing, he can make something as good as new. Although I
am not usually impressed with the item he brings home, by
the time he has finished it I can see the vision he had from
the beginning.

I am glad we have a God who treats us the same way.
He doesn't trash us just because we are cracked, chipped, or
broken. On the contrary, He takes the fragments of what is
left over in our life and makes us as good as new. Christ
doesn't look at what we are; instead He sees what we can
become.

In Christ your life is never wasted.

—ANNETTEE BUDZBAN

Wisdom's House

"A house is built by wisdom and
becomes strong through good sense."
Proverbs 24:3

"What's that?" my husband exclaimed when he saw the doghouse I'd built. Really, the word "house" is a stretch; I've seen better engineering in a game of pick-up sticks.

I have no building experience, followed no plans, and did no research into the art of doghouse construction. I haphazardly nailed boards together, self-assured it would be a strong, sensible shelter for my pooch. But to call what I'd built dilapidated would be polite. It ended up in the scrap pile.

At times I have gone about building the structure of my life the same way, without wisdom or good sense. As a result, I have experienced times of instability and loss. It's only as I seek the wisdom and the plans of the Master Architect that my life is built on a foundation strong enough to weather the storms of time.

Build your life on the foundation of God's purposes.

—DENARAE CARLOCK

Future, Not Failure

"Their disagreement over this was so
sharp that they separated. Barnabas took
John Mark with him and sailed for Cyprus."
Acts 15:39

Mark failed in his call as a missionary, but his uncle didn't give up on him. In fact, Barnabas chose to take a chance on Mark when Paul refused to deal with him again. Although Mark returned after deserting Paul once before, the great evangelist wasn't convinced that this young man wouldn't betray the ministry again.

What happens when we fail? Some One does not give up on us! Both God and Barnabas saw something in Mark worth hanging on to. Nothing can cancel the call of God on your life.

At the end of his life, Paul asked for Mark, calling him "profitable to his ministry." Though it took many years, Paul saw what Jesus had seen all along—not temporal failure, but eternal success!

No one can stop you from fulfilling God's purpose but you.

—MARILYNN GRIFFITH

Talking to Yourself

"Why am I discouraged? Why so sad?
I will put my hope in God! I will praise him again—
my Savior and my God!"
Psalm 42:11

Have you ever seen people talking to themselves? I have even caught myself doing it and I looked around to see if anyone saw me or, worse, was laughing. David talked to himself. It was actually his spirit chastising his soul: "Why am I discouraged? Why so sad?"

Our spirit-soul interface is where the greatest battles are fought. Our spirit needs to continually monitor our soul (the seat of our ego, will, intellect, and emotions). Many people can discipline their sensual or physical appetites. But the old man, the inner self, wants its own way.

David tells his soul what to do: "I will put my hope in God! I will praise Him again!" Saying the right things to yourself is healthy, growing, and disciplined. Have you challenged your soul today?

*Your spirit needs to keep your soul in line;
the critical Christian battleground.*

—KENNETH M. HANSEN

One Saturday Morning

"But God is so rich in mercy,
and he loved us so very much . . ."
Ephesians 2:4

Saturday morning presented two tasks—a chore for me and a project for Dad. My job was to remove a pile of wood slats blocking the road by throwing them over the hedge and into our yard below. Dad's project consisted of hanging a new screen for the front door. The old screen had rusted out long ago and even the patches needed repairs.

To ease my boredom, I turned my chore into a game by tossing the pieces of wood high into the air and watching them stick in the lawn below. Meanwhile, my father worked diligently to finish his project. When he stepped back to admire his job, a piece of wood pierced through the new screen and landed between his feet.

I should have been grounded for weeks, but instead I received his mercy. On that Saturday I discovered how much my father loved me.

Love shows favor and favor releases mercy.

—CHARLES E. HARREL

That's What I Do!

"And anyone who calls on the
name of the LORD will be saved."
Acts 2:21

Of the houses I recall being raised in, my favorite was the first one. But it was also the birthplace of many nightmares that plagued my sleep for years.

At bedtime, I would demand that my father check under the bed and in the closet. The boogie man raced to another room in a split second when he heard me call my father. My dad never minded—he simply explained his search and destroy mission as, "That's what dads do." When I became a father, I likewise told my sons that, "This is what daddies do."

In my walk with God, I find myself repeatedly calling upon my Heavenly Father to drive out real demons whenever I feel beset by them. Then comes a time of peace and I can detect His presence and softly hear, "That's okay. That's what I do."

*It's in God's job description to protect
you from all evil—it's what He does.*

—MICHAEL HERMAN, SR.

Let It Shine

"In the same way, let your good deeds shine out for all to see, so that everyone will praise your heavenly Father."
Matthew 5:16

When I tripped and hit the sharp corner of a metal table, a small chip fell out of the opal ring my husband gave me for our anniversary. It broke my heart. For many years I was afraid to wear it because it was "less than perfect" and it might crumble some more. Finally God helped me see that I had to wear it because, even though it wasn't perfect, it was too beautiful to hide.

"Trust me with the flaws," he seemed to say. "I won't let it fall apart. Because of the flaws, my light will shine through even more beautifully."

I knew he meant more than just the ring. And wearing the imperfect ring, I found the courage to accept a personal and professional challenge that was a stretch for me. I didn't have to be perfect. I could just be me. With God that was enough.

God will use you despite your flaws.

—MARCIA SWEARINGEN

How to Make Friends with Your Sandals

"For forty years I led you through the wilderness,
yet your clothes and sandals did not wear out."
Deuteronomy 29:5

"Today is the day you'll make friends with your sandals!" I informed my fourteen-month-old son. Previous attempts to put on the dreaded sandals resulted in his refusing to put his feet on the floor and, of course, lots of tears—from both of us!

This day was going to be different. And it was! He actually stood up in the things. Victory! There was my son standing in his sandals and not crying. And there he stood defiantly in the same spot for seven minutes and twenty-three seconds. Eventually, I prevailed and while they aren't his most favorite things in the world, he does wear his sandals.

I wonder how many times I've stood defiantly in the same spot when Jesus was urging me to do something. Thank goodness he's not a new mommy who gets frustrated and worn down and tired. His patience is never ending.

God is patient even when you are stubborn.

—STEPHANIE KANAK

Rallying to the Flag

"Moses built an altar there and
called it 'The LORD Is My Banner.'"
Exodus 17:15

In biblical times, a banner or flag was used as a rallying point. As they wandered in the desert, each family of the Children of Israel had a unique banner. These banners helped keep them organized and focused.

In battle, the flag is used to rally the troops and lead them into battle, as well as to mark won territory.

As school children we pledge our allegiance to the flag. Politicians campaign in front of large banners bearing slogans and promises. We adorn our homes with seasonal flags as entertaining decorations.

Throughout our lives, banners and flags declare our interests, intentions, concerns, promises, loyalties, and more. While some come and go, one remains above all others.

Unlike the failed slogans of politicians, God's promises and love remain steadfast. Song of Solomon 2:4 states about God, ". . . his banner over me is love." He is both rallying point and covering.

*Flags and banners declare your allegiances
and serve as inspiration and encouragement
as you face the challenges of life.*

—SRC

Awesome Faith

"Be glad for all God is planning for you.
Be patient in trouble, and always be prayerful."
Romans 12:12

Corrie Ten Boom and her sister, Betsy, were amazing women of faith. The Ten Boom sisters were over fifty years old when they began hiding Jews in a secret room in their home during the Holocaust. Eventually they were found out and sent to a concentration camp.

Corrie managed to smuggle pieces of a Bible into camp. The two sisters held secret prayer meetings and cared for other prisoners, never giving up hope. Once they even gave thanks for fleas (that's right, fleas!) when their barracks became so infested that the guards refused to enter.

Betsy never tasted freedom again, but Corrie survived and went on to tell her story in one of my favorite books, *The Hiding Place.* Their joy in hope, patience in affliction, and faithfulness in prayer never fail to encourage me.

There is hope to be found, even in the midst of affliction.

—TERESA BELL KINDRED

The Separation Notice

"And I am convinced that nothing can ever separate us from his love. Death can't, and life can't. Our fears for today, our worries about tomorrow, and even the powers of hell can't keep God's love away. Whether we are high above the sky or in the deepest ocean, nothing in all creation will ever be able to separate us from the love of God that is revealed in Christ Jesus our LORD."

Romans 8:38–39

It wasn't a sorry-to-see-you-go or thanks-for-the-memories letter. There wasn't even a hastily scrawled "We'll miss you" sticky note. The required form, from the Labor Department, arrived with my last paycheck, and it was totally unexpected. The separation notice ended twenty-three years of "service."

The reason given for the separation was neatly filled in in the appropriate blank: "Personal decision, disability," it read. Even as I cried, I laughed at the ludicrous wording. Who, in their right mind, would make a personal decision to become disabled?

Then I recalled God's assurance, in Romans 8, that nothing can ever separate me from His love. I felt entirely at peace, knowing that He will never leave me, and, as 2 Corinthians 12:9 teaches, even in my disability, He will still enable me to work for Him.

Earthly ties are easily broken, but God's love is eternal.

—ELAINE YOUNG MCGUIRE

Broken Windows

"For the angel of the LORD guards
all who fear him, and he rescues them."
Psalm 34:7

While I pastored a church in a small town, a rash of vandalism took place. Our children were fearful that our home or church would be vandalized. We emphasized to our children that if we serve Him, the Lord will watch over us and protect us.

One morning my daughter ran into our house as we were finishing breakfast. She excitedly told us to come outside, we had to see something. As we went outside, we looked up and down the street seeing that all the cars on both sides of our street had their front and back windows smashed.

She said, "Look, do you see?" She pointed frantically at our car. It was the only one on the street with no broken windows. What a lesson our children learned that day about God's protection to us.

If you are in God's will, He will protect you.

—BEVERLY HILL MCKINNEY

Temptation

"Do not steal."
Exodus 20:15

Standing on tiptoe, I could see over the counter. There, just inches from my nose, was a chocolate candy bar. It was my birthday and I yearned for chocolate. My mouth watered with longing, but as a family surviving the Great Depression, we didn't buy candy.

With the storeowner busy elsewhere, I could grab the chocolate bar, dash out the door, and run home. I gazed at the candy with sweating palms and knocking knees.

Recently, I had memorized God's Ten Commandments and now they flashed through my mind, especially number eight. Certainly by stealing candy, I would be a sinner, a thief. With flowing tears and empty hands, I turned and ran.

Mother saw me coming and opened the door, saying, "Surprise, it's your birthday!" At my place on the dining table was a chocolate candy bar, exactly like the one that had tempted me at the store.

Virtue is rewarded.

—PAT CAPPS MEHAFFEY

Real Freedom

"He gave his life to purchase freedom
for everyone. This is the message that
God gave to the world at the proper time."
1 Timothy 2:6

President Lincoln issued the Emancipation Proclamation on September 22, 1862, but it wasn't fully implemented for two years. On June 19, 1865, slavery in the United States finally ended as the last remaining slaves were freed. That day of liberation is known as Juneteenth.

Liberty. Freedom. We love these words and what they mean. We cherish the right to live and believe as we choose.

Civil liberties are wonderful but an even greater freedom is available to us. In Christ, we can be free from the deadly bondage of sin and chilling separation from God.

Thousands died in the Civil War to bring freedom to the slaves. Nearly 2,000 years earlier, one died for all, making eternal liberation possible.

Just as no one should be a slave to anyone else, none need be a slave to sin. Tell another about Christ's love and lead him or her from slavery into the family of God!

*True freedom is available to everyone
through Christ's death and resurrection.*

—SRC

Father's Day Every Day

"And this is the promise:
If you honor your father and mother,
'you will live a long life, full of blessing.'"
Ephesians 6:3

Sonora Smart honored her father.

William Smart was a veteran of the Civil War. His wife, Sonora's mother, died while giving birth to their sixth child. Mr. Smart became a single parent. He raised all six children by himself.

Later, Sonora Smart married and became Mrs. John B. Dodd. In 1909, she proposed the idea of a day to honor fathers. This was her way of honoring her own dad. The first Father's Day was celebrated June 19, 1910, in Spokane, Washington. The idea gained presidential support from Calvin Coolidge in 1924. In 1966, Lyndon Johnson signed a proclamation making the third Sunday in June Father's Day.

What a wonderful way to honor her earthly father!

As God's children, every day can be Father's Day! We can show Him honor and respect by living holy lives, exhibiting integrity in all we do, and showing kindness and compassion to others.

Just as you celebrate your earthly father, it's also important to show honor and respect toward your Heavenly Father.

—SRC

Our Nourishment Comes from Christ

"I am the true bread from heaven. Anyone who
eats this bread will live forever and not die as your
ancestors did, even though they ate the manna."
John 6:58

During my morning walk around a neighborhood park,
I enjoy the tranquility of watching the ducks lazily glide
along the pond. One particular morning, I nearly jumped
out of my skin as a zealous duck all but broke the sound barrier, zipping across the pond with a humorous, but very
determined, run-and-flap motion. I quickly realized that this
fowl was missile-locked on generous handouts from a father
and son. He knew his source of nourishment and wasted no
time in getting to it.

Jesus Christ refers to Himself as our Bread of Life . . .
our source of nourishment. Are you weary of the daily grind?
His outstretched arms offer life-giving strength and solace.
Are you haunted by the past or fearful of the future? His
tender hands extend life-changing forgiveness and hope. Do
you crave significance and purpose? His very heart cries out,
"I am your Creator, your Lover, your Savior. Your sustenance
is in Me."

Run to Him. Let Jesus, the Bread of Life, nourish your soul.

—BROOK CHALFANT

Great Things from God

"For the sake of your promise and
according to your will, you have done all
these great things and have shown them to me."
2 Samuel 7:21

When David was a very young man, God told him he would
be king. Many years passed in which God's promise seemed
impossible.

David found himself running for his life, feigning
insanity, and camping with the enemy before he was finally
installed as King of Israel.

When the promised kingdom was at last a reality and
God reiterated His promises of eternal blessing, David
offered words of thanksgiving and praise.

May we, like David, realize that when God carries out
His plan in our life, the results will be "great things" that
only our loving and powerful Lord can accomplish.

*Your success in life comes from God,
who keeps His promises.*

—SHERRY L. POFF

Boys, Dogs, and Snake Tales

"No, the wisdom we speak of is the secret wisdom of
God, which was hidden in former times, though he
made it for our benefit before the world began."
1 Corinthians 2:7

Three young boys antagonized my dogs while I was working in the yard. I tried repeatedly to make them leave, but they came right back. Finally, I tried a different approach.

I joined them outside my fence and we began to talk about dogs and their function as protectors. Somehow, we wandered to the subject of snakes. Each boy had a snake story to tell. I brought out a reference book with pictures of the different kinds of snakes. By the time the boys left, we were friends.

That incident reminded me of the need we all have for attention, love, and respect. Eventually, that led me to reach out to my neighbors' children and begin teaching Bible studies in my home.

God can use anything to get our lives on track—from barking dogs, to troublesome boys, and even to snakes. His wisdom is expressed throughout His creation if we pay attention.

God will work through you in many ways to reach others.

—LINDA ROBERTS

Feel My Muscle

"So encourage each other and build
each other up, just as you are already doing."
1 Thessalonians 5:11

One night while listening to a radio broadcast, the speaker was talking about men and boys and their need to have someone feel their muscle.

His message was specific to the male gender, but isn't that true of everyone? We all need a word of encouragement to get us through the day. After hearing those words, I pondered them throughout the following week and noticed time after time the truth of those three little words.

The same week a man at the copy shop turned and showed me the document he had made for his mother. He was a total stranger to me and yet he desperately wanted me or anybody to "feel his muscle." Because of the awareness of the message I had heard, I did. I watched as he left the shop beaming. It had cost me nothing. It had paid me much.

Everyone needs daily encouragement
and acknowledgment of their stronger points.

—SHANNON RULÉ

Don't Just Preach

"And remember, it is a message to obey, not just to listen
to. If you don't obey, you are only fooling yourself."
James 1:22

"Ready?" asked my son, Michael. He whizzed around the driveway. I rose on unsteady feet and wobbled after him. The rollerblades felt strange on my feet.

"Wear protective gear," I growled.

"But you're not!" he quipped.

"I'm older than you. I don't need that stuff."

Sighing, he complied. Things went well until the first hill.

"Be careful, Mom," Michael said.

Harrumphing, I barreled past him. As I sped down the hill, I suddenly remembered I never learned how to use the brakes. With a spectacular somersault, I wiped out, and then scraped down the hard pavement for several feet. I ended up with a broken wrist, eight stitches, third-degree abrasions on my knee, and a bruised head.

I scolded myself as God reminded me of the wisdom in James 1:22. My injuries could have been avoided if I had done just what I demanded that Michael do.

Teach by example and do what you teach.

—LORI Z. SCOTT

Penny-Wise

"Then a poor widow came and dropped in two pennies. He[Jesus] called his disciples to him and said, 'I assure you, this poor widow has given more than all the others have given. For they gave a tiny part of their surplus, but she, poor as she is, has given everything she has.'"

Mark 12:42–43

My generation cherished the penny! We collected them in jars and wore them on our loafers. We offered a penny for your thoughts and dreamed that we had hit the lottery if we found a penny heads-up on the sidewalk. Over the years, the purchasing power of the penny has diminished and you can't buy even a gumball with one anymore.

Just when I thought that the penny had lost its appeal to the younger generation, our five-year-old placed a penny in the offering plate on Sunday. I looked at her in disbelief as she smiled and she said, "It's my lucky penny and I want God to have it."

Pennies may go the way of the rotary dial phone and the two-dollar bill. Generation X-Y-Zers don't want to be bothered collecting pennies anymore. Except for one certain five-year-old who still believes in lucky pennies. Lucky for us that God is penny-wise.

Your smallest gift is priceless in God's eyes.

—MICHELE STARKEY

Reach Beyond Your Expectations

"For I can do everything with the help
of Christ who gives me the strength I need."
Philippians 4:13

Most of us feel as though we know her—the little blind and deaf girl. A historical symbol of triumph over adversity, Helen Keller was born on this date in 1880.

At nearly two years of age, illness left her blind and deaf. At age seven, she began to learn to communicate through sign language. Despite her lifelong disabilities, Helen went on to accomplish great things. She completed her schooling, graduated from college with honors, became a speaker, wrote books, and made lasting friendships with great national and international figures.

Is there something holding you back from accomplishing great things? Don't let it stop you. Ask God for His strength, and you can do anything! Isn't that what He promised?!

*With the strength of Christ, you can rise above
your circumstances and accomplish great things.*

—WENDY ANN DUNHAM

Errors in Judgment

"Stop judging others, and you will not be judged.
Stop criticizing others, or it will all come back on you.
If you forgive others, you will be forgiven."
Luke 6:37

For a long time I was annoyed by the behavior of a manager in my office. John never worked late and he never seemed to care that much about his job.

"Where's he off to?" I grumbled as I watched him leave one Monday morning.

Our secretary, Jane, heard me. "His wife called; he's just taking the wheelchairs home."

"Wheelchairs?"

"Yes," Jane said. "For his boys."

"His boys have wheelchairs?"

"Don't you know? They have this weak bone condition; they both can't walk anymore."

"I didn't know. I'm sorry. That's so sad."

I suddenly realized that John didn't work late because he went home to spend time with his boys. And for two years, I'd been judging him as a poor worker for it. The dangers of being judgmental have never been clearer to me. Now, I choose to be understanding instead.

Seek understanding, not judgment.

—SHELLEY WAKE

My Father and I

"Don't be afraid, for I am with you. Do not be dismayed,
for I am your God. I will strengthen you. I will help you.
I will uphold you with my victorious right hand."
Isaiah 41:10

On my wedding day twenty years ago, I sat with my dad in
the pastor's study as we waited for our cue when he would
walk me down the aisle.

I was extremely nervous and said to him, "What if I
cry?" I do not cry prettily.

He smiled and said, "You won't." There was such confidence
and tender assurance in his voice, I remember feeling
strengthened and thinking, "He's right; I won't."

The music began and we entered the sanctuary.
Trembling, I took my dad's arm and we walked to the altar. I
didn't cry.

There are many, many moments like this with my heavenly
Father. He sets a task before me, and looking at it fearfully,
I say, "What if I fail?" He smiles and says, "You won't."
And I take His hand and we walk toward it together.

Your strength comes from Christ.

—RACHEL WALLACE-OBERLE

Asked and Answered

"I prayed to the LORD, and he answered me,
freeing me from all my fears."
Psalm 34:4

Dad called it an explosion in his chest. The doctor called it a heart attack. Following the appointment, my dad mentioned concern over an upcoming procedure.

"Pray specifically about what troubles you." Dad's a pharmacist and he likes formulas. So I suggested, "Use the ACTS model—Adoration, Confession, Thanksgiving, and Supplication—when you pray." He went to his bedroom and talked to God.

A few moments later the phone rang. A caring relative was on the other end of the receiver. At the conclusion of the call, my dad seemed at peace.

"An angioplasty isn't so bad. She described the process. I'd forgotten she's experienced this, too." He was comforted and reassured.

The Lord knew my dad's concerns. He was waiting to be asked to help. Working through regular circumstances and people, God answered a heartfelt prayer. The Father of us all quieted my father's fears.

Peace, comfort, and reassurance is found in the Lord.

—LORI WILDENBERG

JULY

ON BUTTERFLY WINGS
—S. (SHAE) COOKE

"You alone are the LORD. You made the skies and the heavens and all the stars. You made the earth and the seas and everything in them. You preserve and give life to everything, and all the angels of heaven worship you."

NEHEMIAH 9:6

*T*HE HAWAIIAN SUN GLINTED OFF THE WINDSHIELD of the helicopter as it prepared for takeoff. I fastened the seat belt snugly around my waist, tugging it a little tighter than I had to.

"All belted in?" the pilot asked. I nodded.

Seconds later, we took off. My head swirled with the sudden vertical ascent into the cloudless sky. White-knuckled and clutching the edge of the seat, I muttered the twenty-third Psalm. We flew higher. I stammered the Lord's Prayer. The pilot banked the craft sharply left. So help me, I thought I was going to fall out of the helicopter.

I cried out in my most desperate voice, *"God, help me!"* I wanted to live to see my eighteenth birthday. He must have heard, since we leveled off, allowing my heart rate to level off as well. Feeling a tad braver, I opened my eyes—and saw heaven.

"Wow, oh wow!" I blurted mindlessly. We soared over the Pacific Ocean and headed toward a lush and verdant valley. We skimmed the treetops, traveling over palm trees and pineapple fields. The helicopter descended and we arrived at the base of a waterfall. The water cascaded over cliffs and rocks while we hovered alongside of the falls like a hummingbird. Water fell like dew on the windshield. We ascended slowly, observing the flora and fauna growing up the steep incline.

My heart leapt as we reached the top of the falls. Before me was a scene of incredible artistry. We lingered, taking in the scenic wonder. From that vantage point, I could see for hundreds of miles. Shades of azure blue, aqua, and indigo framed the portrait. An endless patchwork quilt of vibrant greens blanketed the canyons and hills. A light, smoky mist drifted out of a rain forest. Rainbows arched like porticos over groves of mossy trees. In the distance, snow-capped peaks crowned the tropical paradise. I viewed the palette of nature and saw God's face.

"My Daddy is quite the artist, ain't He?" quipped the pilot. I nodded, fixing my gaze at the vivid panorama. "It's just like riding on the wings of a butterfly," I thought.

We swooped down from our "perch" and into the fertile valley below. Mossy canopies sheltered the rain forests.

As we headed west, into the sunset, and home, my thoughts turned to my uncertain future, without my mother—a victim of smoke inhalation in a fire just that past Christmas.

God seemed so close. In fact, I felt His presence in every glorious gift of nature I witnessed. The incredible detail of His creation gave me confidence that He cared about every facet of my life. I reveled in the glory and beauty of His nature.

As we touched down on the landing pad, I felt elated. My spirit praised God, for I finally grasped the magnitude of His love for me, through nature.

A Quiet, Ordinary Faith

"And so I tell you, keep on asking, and you will be given
what you ask for. Keep on looking, and you will find.
Keep on knocking, and the door will be opened."
Luke 11:9

Recently there was a miracle in my mailbox. It arrived in a smudged envelope with my name and my husband's scrawled across the front. There was no stamp or return address. It was stuffed with $700 in cash.

When my husband opened the envelope and counted the bills in disbelief, I started laughing. I couldn't help it. For years I'd been praying for a mighty faith that would move mountains, and there, right before my eyes, an enormous mountain had definitely been moved.

In response to our pastor's appeal to pay off the church's substantial mortgage, my husband and I prayerfully made a pledge; we didn't have the funds but believed God would provide.

The deadline grew closer. The money we had promised did not materialize. And then on an ordinary morning, God quietly stepped in and provided the exact amount we had pledged. We had asked and He answered. The following Sunday, our congregation burned the mortgage papers.

God answers when you seek to build His kingdom.

—RACHEL WALLACE-OBERLE

In the Presence of God

"Don't hide your light under a basket! Instead, put it on a stand and let it shine for all. In the same way, let your good deeds shine out for all to see, so that everyone will praise your heavenly Father."

Matthew 5:15–16

My eleven-year-old son stood by my side and asked me a question I couldn't answer: "Mom, why do some people not believe in God?"

All I could do was answer, "I don't know," and hug him close.

I wonder the same thing. How can someone look at the ocean and not feel small in the presence of God? Or look up at the endless blue of the sky and not give thanks for the creation of our universe? Or feel a summer breeze and not know that it's God's touch? How can anyone look at a baby and not know that God's greatest blessing is the miracle of life?

God is merciful and loving and He wants everyone to come to know Him. I want to shine my light so that others see Him living in me.

In order for others to see God living in you,
you have to shine your light brightly by doing His will.

—TERESA BELL KINDRED

God Loves a Birthday Party

"And if God cares so wonderfully for flowers
that are here today and gone tomorrow, won't he
more surely care for you? You have so little faith!"
Luke 12:28

My friends Dave and Tina met with numerous pastor search committees while anticipating Dave's seminary graduation. One church near Denver was particularly interested in them. Dave and Tina loved the church, but they wanted Dave to start work immediately after his May graduation.

"We always go to Six Flags on our son's birthday in July," Tina told me. "He's too young to understand if we have to skip the tradition this year." But she felt silly asking for a delay in the moving date.

During a committee meeting, talk turned to the rapidly growing area of Colorado surrounding the church. Then one of the ladies blurted out, "We even have a Six Flags now!"

Dave and Tina just looked at each other, their mouths open. Then they began to laugh and wonder why they had ever doubted that God knew their concerns—even for a seven-year-old's birthday party.

God cares about all the details in your life—
even birthday parties!

—DENA DYER

On the Shoulders of the Father

"Moses said this about the tribe of Benjamin: 'The people of Benjamin are loved by the LORD and live in safety beside Him. He surrounds them continuously and preserves them from every harm.'"

Deuteronomy 33:12

At our small town's parades there are always toddlers hoisted up on daddies' shoulders to get a better view. From that height, the child is not afraid of the horses or clowns or even the fire engines. She has confidence in the safety of her father's shoulders. His firm hand reassures her.

As an adult with worries of a different sort, I need the support and comfort of my Father. I can tell Him my problems and know He will shield me all day long.

Challenges diminish when I am resting on His shoulders, reassured that He is in charge. Like the child at the parade, I gain the proper perspective in the Lord's presence. Shielded by His shoulders, I see that my concerns are really quite small.

You can gain perspective on life's situations
when you rest on your Father's shoulders.

—LANITA BRADLEY BOYD

What Kind of Sub?

"And I pray that Christ will be more and more at home in your hearts as you trust in him. May your roots go down deep into the soil of God's marvelous love."
Ephesians 3:17

At a recent parade, I was surprised to see a contingent carrying a banner that read "Sub Vets." What could that mean? Substitute veterans? A second banner carried the fuller meaning: "Submarine Veterans." Of course! Why didn't I think of that?

In contemplating the two meanings of "sub," I was reminded of my Christian life as well. Which kind of Christian am I—the substitute for the real thing, or the submarine that goes deep and is effective in my missions? Do I take my turn at the homeless shelter or appear at church to get "Christian credit," or to glorify Christ?

I want to go deep in my study of Scripture, to go deep in my conversations with both believers and seekers, to go deep in my understanding of my family members. I want to be a Submarine Christian!

*Christians can bring depth to
conversations with family and friends.*

—LANITA BRADLEY BOYD

Fireworks

"The voice of the LORD strikes with lightning bolts."
Psalm 29:7

Last night a lot of fireworks were set off by local governments to celebrate our nation's festival of freedom on the Fourth of July. As burst after burst lights the sky, everyone utters collective ooohs and aahs! No one shouts "Glory!"

No one shouts "Glory!" for a flash of lightning either. We don't hear God's voice in the crack of thunder, just a frightening noise. Some people are so terrified by lightning and thunder that they scream and tremble in fear.

Yet, unlike fireworks, which are meant only to entertain, God's summer fireworks usually accompany rain that cools us and waters our dry lawns. All God's deeds are done for a purpose.

The next time there is a lightning storm, why don't you try answering "Glory!" to the voice of God?

God's fireworks reveal His power and His bounty.

—MERRY E. VARGO

Protection Against Potshots

"Be careful! Watch out for attacks from
the Devil, your great enemy. He prowls around like
a roaring lion, looking for some victim to devour."
1 Peter 5:8

My dad was a teaser. All my childhood foibles were fodder for his jest. I wanted ammunition of my own. I went to my grandmother and asked, "Tell me something my dad did as a kid." She laughed and told a story.

They lived on a farm, where, among other things, they planted corn by hand. Dad got tired of planting one day, but still had seed left. He dumped it all in a hole at the edge of the field, went to the house, and declared he was done! In a few weeks his indiscretion was visible to everyone. He got a whoopin' for that one. Finally, I had something on him, I thought.

Satan, the enemy of our soul, is looking for ammunition to use against us, too. His goal is not to tease, but to steal, kill, and destroy (John 10:10). But through vigilance and repentance, his accusations are meaningless.

*Through daily prayer, Bible reading,
and repentance, your soul can be safe.*

—SRC

A Refuge from the Storm

"But to the poor, O LORD, you are a refuge from the storm. To the needy in distress, you are a shelter from the rain and the heat. For the oppressive acts of ruthless people are like a storm beating against a wall. . . ."

Isaiah 25:4

One summer heavy downpours flooded a large area near my childhood home. The storms were followed by blazing heat, making cleanup miserable. Tears filled my eyes as I saw pictures and read news stories that described the devastation. Then I read that area churches—and some from far away—had provided temporary shelters and food for those whose homes were ruined. What blessed relief it was for these hurting people to have some respite from the forces of nature beyond their control.

God is such a shelter. Like a welcome shade in the summer heat or a strong wall of protection against storms, He is there for us when life is overwhelming.

Whether our distress comes from physical troubles, inner conflicts, or difficulty with other people, we can rest in God's strength. He will see us through.

God is stronger than the fiercest storm
and greater than any enemy you face.

—SHERRY L. POFF

Swollen Feet

"For all these forty years your clothes didn't wear out,
and your feet didn't blister or swell."
Deuteronomy 8:4

One summer I studied Moses and the Israelites in the wilderness with a group of second and third graders at church. To simulate wandering, dependent upon God's direction, I took them on a "penny" hike through the neighborhood. When we would get to an intersection, we would flip a penny and walk left for heads and right for tails.

The simulation worked better than I had anticipated. After just twenty minutes of walking, my cheap sandals wore blisters on my feet. I was reminded of how God miraculously provided for His people. They had no foot problems after forty years of walking. I couldn't walk without pain after only twenty minutes.

Although the wilderness wandering was a result of the Israelites' unbelief, God gave them evidence of His involvement in their lives. He still does this today.

*God stretches even the smallest
resources to provide for His people.*

—MARY J. BAUER

Heart Gifts

"'No, please accept them,' Jacob said,
'for what a relief it is to see your friendly smile.
It is like seeing the smile of God!'"
Genesis 33:10

There at my back door stood my four-year-old grandson holding a vase full of sun-bright dandelions. "I picked these for you, Grandma." Kyle smiled proudly as he handed them to me. Kyle and my daughter-in-law, Michelle, had walked two miles in the summer's heat to give me this gift. My heart felt like it was going to burst with happiness over the joy of it all.

I wonder if I ever make God's heart feel like it's going to burst with happiness. How often do I go out of my way each day to be with him?

Just as we experience joy in being loved by others, just think of the joy God experiences in being loved by us.

God loves to see your face in His presence.

—LINDA KNIGHT

More Than a Sparrow

"What is the price of five sparrows? A couple of pennies?
Yet God does not forget a single one of them."
Luke 12:6

My husband and I discovered our minivan wasn't worth fixing. It was finished. We were overwhelmed by the thought of searching for another vehicle and adding to our debt load. We began to pray.

My parents found a car for us that was a great deal and decided to pay for half of it. Close friends contributed another $500. Then a check arrived unexpectedly.

The car salesman who delivered our new car was going through a difficult time. We prayed with him at our kitchen table and a friendship began to form.

Clearly this was not just the purchase of a vehicle; it was a beautiful demonstration of how much the Father loves and cares for His children. How could I have worried? Indeed His eye is on the sparrow and I know He watches me!

God does not ignore or forget your needs.

—RACHEL WALLACE-OBERLE

Asleep in Church

"As Paul spoke on and on, a young man named
Eutychus, sitting on the windowsill, became very
drowsy . . . and fell three stories to his death below."
Acts 20:9

When Paul's extended sermon lasted until midnight,
Eutychus, whose story is found in Acts 20:7–12, fell asleep
and toppled three stories from his seat in the window. They
found his lifeless body in the courtyard below. Paul went to
him and brought him to life—a marvelous ending to a tragic
situation.

This one act determined how Eutychus is remembered
in history. Anytime after that when someone met him, the
response was probably, "Oh, yes, I heard about you down at
the synagogue. You're the one who went to sleep during
church. Were you really raised from the dead?"

Eutychus's name means "happy" or "fortunate." He was
truly fortunate that of all days to have a fatal accident, his
fall came on the day when a Spirit-empowered apostle was
present.

Eutychus will be remembered for the time he fell asleep
during church. What will you be remembered for?

One act can make your reputation for life.

—STEPHEN D. BOYD

Word from the Lord

"Confess your sins to each other and pray for each other so that you may be healed. The earnest prayer of a righteous person has great power and wonderful results."

James 5:16

The people of Jeremiah's day were very much like people today. None of the people "paid any attention to the words the LORD had spoken through Jeremiah the prophet" (Jeremiah 37:2, NIV). Yet at the same time, King Zedekiah sent word to Jeremiah, "Please pray to the LORD our God for us" (Jeremiah 37:3, NIV).

How often do we ignore the Lord's will, and yet continually pray to Him for help? And like the people of Jeremiah's day, we may believe in God but not admit it publicly. King Zedekiah sent for Jeremiah to ask privately, "Is there any word from the LORD?" (Jeremiah 37:17, NIV).

Jeremiah was persecuted, and we may be also. He remained true to the word of the Lord and so can we. Let's not be people who pray only in times of crisis, but let's be Jeremiahs—people of faith who do not hesitate to share God's message.

You must remember to live for God as well as pray to Him.

—Lanita Bradley Boyd

Mind over Body

"I know perfectly well that what I am
doing is wrong, and my bad conscience
shows that I agree that the law is good."
Romans 7:16

"I'm not going to tell you again," I told my son. "You are not
to hang out on neighbors' doorsteps. You don't need
someone to play with every minute." Our home was in a
neighborhood teeming with children. Casey felt that anytime he wanted a playmate, there just had to be someone to
play with.

After a moment, Casey said, "My mind tells me not to,
but my body just takes me there!" I tried not to laugh as I
explained that even if his body tries to take him the wrong
way, his mind needs to win the battle.

I, like the Apostle Paul, can identify with Casey,
knowing but not always choosing the right thing. Many
believe that it's okay to always follow whatever feels good.
But thoughtlessly following anything that takes you away
from God and His will for your life is going in the wrong
direction.

God equips you to overcome
temptations and make right choices.

—AMY CARR

Refreshment

"Day and night your hand of discipline was heavy on me.
My strength evaporated like water in the summer heat."
Psalm 32:4

For nine months children in school desire summer! One season folds into the next, the days lengthen, the skies get bluer. Then the final bell rings, the kids scream and run for the doors out into sunshine and freedom!

Through June and July, it's not too bad. It's great to be outside playing baseball, riding bikes, lying in the grass just watching the clouds float by. But the dog days come in August. Growing up in Indiana without air-conditioning, the heat and humidity could be oppressive, day and night.

We are called to live godly lives. No exceptions. God's "hand of discipline" when we misstep can feel oppressive. Avoiding repentance drains our spirits of joy.

But getting right with God through confession of sin is like getting out the lawn sprinkler on the hottest day of August and playing in the cool, refreshing water.

God's discipline is intended to yield repentance.
Repentance restores and refreshes your soul.

—SRC

Because He Promised

"But the Scriptures have declared that we are
all prisoners of sin, so the only way to receive
God's promise is to believe in Jesus Christ."
Galatians 3:22

Not long ago I had one of those nights when sleep wouldn't come, no matter how many sheep I counted. My heart was troubled and I couldn't let go of my worries no matter how hard I prayed.

Late the next day the heat and humidity exploded in a summer thunderstorm. After the storm passed I went outside to enjoy some cooler air. What I saw took my breath away. It was the most beautiful rainbow I had ever seen. Each color was as vivid as if God had hand painted the rainbow in the sky just for me.

"God's promise," I said softly, and the rainbow is just a reminder of one of His promises.

God promised that He would answer my prayers. It may not be soon. It may not be the answer I want, but it will be the answer I need.

I know because He promised.

God keeps His promises.

—TERESA BELL KINDRED

God's Rod Is His Comfort

"Even when I walk through the dark valley of death,
I will not be afraid, for you are close beside me.
Your rod and your staff protect and comfort me."
Psalm 23:4

"Ms. Bauer, Gabe won't sit down on the bus!"

I was supervising the students as they went home on their buses for the day. Gabe, one of my first graders, who constantly tested limits, was refusing to cooperate with his driver. A group of students was eager to come tattle to me.

The minute I entered the bus, Gabe sat down and grinned at me. "I knew you'd come," he said.

Just as Gabe knew I would be there to enforce the limits of his behavior, we can know that God will be there to enforce the limits of ours. God's rod is His discipline. It is one way He protects us. It demonstrates that we are His well-loved children.

God's limits are a sign of His care for you.

—MARY J. BAUER

The Woman Who Touched Jesus

"Jesus turned around and said to her, 'Daughter,
be encouraged! Your faith has made you well.'
And the woman was healed at that moment."
Matthew 9:22

Two summers ago, neighbors rushed me to the hospital with a potentially life-threatening illness. My husband was away on a business trip and I was alone. The prognosis wasn't good, and there were important decisions to make.

As I lay on the gurney, my thoughts turned to the woman in Scripture, who bravely pushed her way through a huge crowd to touch the hem of Jesus' garment. The moment she touched the Savior, she felt something change, and so did Jesus. "Who touched me?" He said. For He knew someone touched Him in faith.

That night, I decided to do as that woman did. I pushed through the fear and anxiety that crowded my mind. I reached out to Jesus in a way I never had before, with faith and expectation. My fear and anxiety fled.

Touch Him, and He'll touch you back.

—S. (SHAE) COOKE

His Strength Is Yours

"They will continue to grow stronger, and each
of them will appear before God in Jerusalem."
Psalm 84:7

One of our family's favorite pastimes is watching the
Olympic games. Yes, every four years we're taken in by a
mad rush of adrenaline, experiencing the thrill of victory
and the agony of defeat as we cheer on our favorite athletes.
We're amazed at the training, endurance, and skill of these
young men and women. They become Olympic athletes
because, even in their weaker competitions, they remain
steadfast and focused.

The moment we become Christians, we are grafted onto
a supernatural power source. Our trainer and teammate is
the all-powerful God of the universe. Sure we have our
weaker games, but we're never helpless or inadequate. As we
tap into God, with steadfast reserve, we will move forward.

*Be faithful, press on, and be
confident in your position in Christ.*

—BROOK CHALFANT

Listen, God Whispers

"And after the earthquake there was a fire, but the LORD was not in the fire. And after the fire there was the sound of a gentle whisper. When Elijah heard it, he wrapped his face in his cloak and went out and stood at the entrance of the cave."

1 Kings 19:12–13

My cat Spooky loves to curl up in my lap, purring loudly. It takes him a while to get settled. He walks over me and turns around a couple of times before lying down. Even then, he is not still, switching his tail back and forth, something still agitating him. Then, as I repeatedly stroke his silky head, he becomes content.

I seem to be a lot like Spooky when I pray. It is hard for me to begin. I usually think of something that needs to be done first—add something to the grocery list, check to be sure the trash is out, and so forth. Finally I sit, after circling around several times, just like Spooky. Even then, I find myself metaphorically swishing my tail, have-to-do's agitating me. But at last, I focus on the One to whom prayer is directed. I listen, God whispers. Comfort and answers come.

He is found in stillness and silence. Listen, He whispers.

—NANCY BAKER

The Carnival Mirror

"Now we see things imperfectly as in a poor mirror, but then we will see everything with perfect clarity. All that I know now is partial and incomplete, but then I will know everything completely, just as God knows me now."

1 Corinthians 13:12

"Mom!" my children shouted as we moved through the Fun House, "Come see how funny we look!" Approaching from behind, I saw their perfectly shaped bodies in front of the curved mirrors with distorted images staring back at them.

"Is my head really that long? How come my hands reach down to my sneakers but I can't feel the floor?" asked Evan.

Then Erin said, "Mom, I know I'm shorter than normal, but do I really look that short?" I had to laugh as I explained how the mirror worked, and why their image was distorted.

How often do we see things only as they appear, but later discover the truth? Isn't life like that? So often we think we have answers to the deep questions in life. But soon, when God reveals all to His children, we will see everything with perfect clarity—not through the funny mirror of life.

What you don't understand now
will be made clear in heaven.

—WENDY ANN DUNHAM

Negotiating with God

"How long, O LORD, will you look on and do nothing? Rescue me from their fierce attacks. Protect my life from these lions! Then I will thank you in front of the entire congregation. I will praise you before all the people."

Psalm 35:17–18

Have you ever negotiated with God? You tell Him, "If You do that, then I will do this." Like the prayer of a soldier in a foxhole, our prayers have this tone. The crisis is so intense you'll promise almost anything. David makes lots of promises through the Psalm. I've made promises.

While on a maritime Mediterranean Shipping Cruise, anchored in Villefranche's deep-water bay, my roommate and I decided to swim from the shore the one mile out to the ship—at night. The darkness, the depth of the water, the unknown creatures swimming around us, and the cramps in both legs brought me to a "foxhole moment." I made several promises to God as I struggled to reach the ship.

Whether your circumstance is the result of a foolish decision, as mine was, or the actions of others, or society's pressures, God will hear your cry for help, and because of His compassion, He will deliver you.

God loves to help His children, especially in crises.

—KENNETH M. HANSEN

Seeking the Lost

"And I, the Son of Man, have come to
seek and save those like him who are lost."
Luke 19:10

That afternoon, after helping Dad pitch the tent, I headed out from the campsite for the fishing hole. Although I was only seven, I had walked this trail a dozen times and never experienced a problem, but something felt different this time—I was lost. I knew better than to keep walking. My father always said, "If you ever get lost, stay where you are, wait, and I'll be there directly." So I sat down by a post and waited. I was still waiting when the sun dipped low on the horizon.

Before the darkness closed in, I noticed someone rushing up the path. It was Dad. He came looking for me just like he said he would. My father only grinned when he saw me sitting by a signpost that said, "Campground This Way."

When you feel spiritually lost, stop for a moment and wait. God will be there directly.

The Good Shepherd always comes looking for his lost sheep.

—CHARLES E. HARREL

His Plan for Me

"For God is working in you, giving you the desire
to obey him and the power to do what pleases him."
Philippians 2:13

"God had bigger plans for me than I had for myself," a character in a movie once said. I've been thinking about that line ever since.

When I look at the tapestry of my life, I can see God's hand weaving the threads together. Over the years I have made many mistakes, but there aren't any flaws in His weaving. Jesus' death on the cross unraveled my mistakes and knit the single strands back together into the unique design He has in mind for me.

When you are discouraged and feeling insignificant . . . when things don't go the way you think they should . . . when life seems unfair . . . when the good guys don't win . . . when suffering and pain seem beyond what you can bear . . . remember that even when you don't understand, God always has a plan for you. In fact, His plan is likely much bigger than the one you have for yourself!

God's plan is better than any other.

—TERESA BELL KINDRED

Telling Mr. Sims

"The LORD is a shelter for the oppressed, a refuge in times of trouble. Those who know your name trust in you, for you, O LORD, have never abandoned anyone who searches for you."

Psalm 9:9–10

Mr. Sims, a family acquaintance, isn't a nice man. He hasn't led an exemplary life. Over the years his behavior destroyed his family and his days are now spent alone, weeping in a nursing home.

A few weeks ago I sensed God urging me to visit Mr. Sims. It's been fifteen years since I saw him and I wasn't eager to go. But the feeling persisted; I knew he needed to hear about God's love. And so I went.

I nervously entered his room. He was delighted to see me, but the moment I asked how he was doing, he started to cry. When I asked him if he wanted to accept Christ as his Savior, Mr. Sims said yes immediately.

How needlessly I worried. God's grace went ahead of me that afternoon to arrange a miracle.

God responds to those who reach out to Him.

—RACHEL WALLACE-OBERLE

Circles of Influence

"You are to influence them;
do not let them influence you!"
Jeremiah 15:19b

A favorite summer pastime for my grandson is to go to the lake and throw stones into the water. Last summer, as I stood beside him, I observed the ever-widening circles in the clear blue lake that grew after the pebble he had thrown landed in the water. Although only one pebble was thrown into the lake, the circle it made became larger and larger, and, as we watched, I thought of the ever-widening circles made by each individual's influence.

Often our society doesn't give the homeless person the same respect that it does the leaders of our countries. But, according to the Bible, God doesn't move away from anyone, but will take the contributions we give, the choices we make, and the influence we have and use them in an ever-widening circle to reach our world, for, you see, God loves us just the way we are.

God accepts you, rich or poor, just the way you are.

—ELAINE INGALLS HOGG

Do You Have a Piece Missing?

"You will keep in perfect peace all who trust in you,
whose thoughts are fixed on you!"
Isaiah 26:3

My sons love to assemble puzzles. It's fun to watch as they twist pieces around trying to make them fit. Sometimes they get the right piece in the right spot. Other times they try to wedge pieces together even though they don't actually fit. And sometimes they get to the end of a puzzle and a piece is missing.

Every day we encounter puzzles. We wrestle with daily activities, relationships, and situations. We work hard to fit all of them together just right so they make sense. Sometimes, at the end of the day, we discover a "peace" missing; we've left Christ out of the equation.

There is no need to search frantically for the missing peace. We need merely to turn the remains of the day over to Him and His peace will stay our minds.

Fix your mind steadfastly on Christ and you will not be troubled. He is your peace. Do you have a peace missing?

The Lord has offered you His wisdom and His peace,
which can soothe your frustrations.

—STACY DECKER POOLE

Life Buoy

"But I trust in your unfailing love.
I will rejoice because you have rescued me."
Psalm 13:5

I watched in sympathy as little Matthew struggled against the swim teacher's instructions to lie on his back in the pool.

"Put your head back, your tummy up, and relax." Miss Bowman smiled her reassurance at my little friend. "Trust me. If you don't fight the water, it will hold you up."

But each time, Matthew tensed his little muscles, gave way to fear, and then began to sink. "He's trying too hard," I thought.

Finally, with Miss Bowman's patient coaxing, he began to let go of his mistrust and anxiety. Later, she was able to release Matthew to the buoyancy of the water and, in triumph, he floated on his own.

In the same way, when we put our complete trust in God and surrender ourselves to Him, heart, mind, and will, we are buoyed on the sea of His unfailing love.

When you surrender to God you will find peace and security.

—SUSAN ESTRIBOU RAMSDEN

For His Own Glory

"Whatever you eat or drink or whatever you do,
you must do all for the glory of God."
1 Corinthians 10:31

"Laquindra, why did God make you and all things?" I asked the five-year-old in my lap. "For Him's own glory," she answered.

We love to hear the mispronunciations of little children and to pass them on to others. Do we also love to pass on the truth of our Father's Word?

Laquindra was right. God made us for His glory. Just think of that! Our entire purpose in life is spelled out for us even before we are born. He gives our life purpose. We don't have to perform or do anything to get it.

Laquindra had learned the words to say. I pray that her life, and ours, will only add to our reason for being. May our actions and words, as well as our very existence, be always to His glory.

Everything you do should fulfill His purpose for your life.

—LINDA ROBERTS

How Does Your Faith Grow?

"Let your roots grow down into him and draw up nourishment from him, so you will grow in faith, strong and vigorous in the truth you were taught. Let your lives overflow with thanksgiving for all he has done."

Colossians 2:7

I remember spending Sundays in the yard with Grandma, as she taught me the secrets of a healthy vegetable garden.

"You have to plant the vegetables well," she said. "Plant them in good soil and give them a firm base."

"Don't they need water, too?" I asked.

"Yes," she said. "But unless they've got a firm base, even the perfect amount of water won't be enough."

"What about sun?" I asked. "Don't they need good sun, too?"

"Good sun helps," she said. "But unless they have a firm base, even the perfect amount of sun won't be enough."

Years later, I looked back and realized how right Grandma was. And not just about plants. Everybody needs a firm base. That firm base comes through faith in God. And with that base, you'll always find nourishment, no matter what the conditions.

Let your faith in God be your firm base
and you'll find the nourishment to grow.

—SHELLEY WAKE

Out of the Darkness

"Your word is a lamp for my
feet and a light for my path."
Psalm 119:105

On vacation my husband and I toured a cave. The tour guide briefly turned out all the lights, plunging us into a blackness I had never before imagined. "What if the guide just left us here alone?" I worried to myself. "We would never find our way without a light!"

As Christians, we are blessed to have a Light that will shine for us always, a Lamp for our feet that will show the path ahead of us. Our lives will never be without direction, and we don't need to fear being left behind in darkness.

My experience in total darkness lasted only moments, but the darkness of the world around us never ceases. How comforting that the Word of God is our guide and leads us safely through.

You can depend on the Word of God
to light your path and lead you to safety.

—ADRIAN WARD

AUGUST

SEND ME
—ELAINE L. SCHULTE

"Then I heard the LORD asking, 'Whom should I
send as a messenger to my people? Who will go for us?'
And I said, 'LORD, I'll go! Send me.'"

ISAIAH 6:8

I T WAS AN EXCEPTIONALLY BEAUTIFUL SOUTHERN California morning, and I praised God with all of my heart. The prophet Isaiah's words from my morning meditations, "Here am I, send me," filled my mind and, hoping to be used, I joyously prayed, "Here am I, send *me!*"

At ten o'clock I was working in my home office when the doorbell rang. Jon Nolan, a distant neighbor, stood on the steps and extended a parcel to me, saying, "This was delivered to my house by mistake."

As I thanked him, I noticed how unhappy he looked, and I felt prompted to ask about his wife, although it was a mere matter of politeness since we scarcely knew each other.

"How is Pat?" I asked. "I haven't seen her for months."

His eyes closed as he lowered his head to answer, "She's terribly depressed. She's had a nervous breakdown."

Astonished, I finally managed to respond, "I didn't know. I'm so sorry."

Then after a moment of uneasy silence, I offered, "Perhaps I can help her. I went through a terrible depression myself years ago."

Despite a surge of self-consciousness, I shared how God had removed my depression and changed my life into one of joy, adventure, and enthusiasm. His eyes filled with hope. "Why don't you come out to the car and tell her?" he suggested.

Grabbing my arm, he hurried me out toward their car in our driveway. "She's just been out of the hospital for a few days . . . actually, the psychiatric ward. I have her ride around with me when I do errands so she can get out of the house."

"Just out of the psychiatric ward?" my mind repeated. I'd once visited a psychiatric ward and unnerving reminders of that hour whirled through my mind. What had I gotten myself into?

Jon unlocked the car doors and lowered the power window next to his wife. Although I'd been fore-warned, it was saddening to see Pat, her head drooping so low her chin nearly touched her collarbone. Normally a competent businesswoman, she sat in the car like a dejected child.

"Hello, Pat." She didn't look up. Her long dark hair hung around her face, and she appeared so coiled up in her misery that I knew she was not cured. I sent up a frantic prayer: "Please, Lord, tell me what to say!"

Impatient as usual when I'm nervous, I didn't wait for His answer and plunged in. As eager as I was to help, my words didn't touch her. Her blue eyes darted toward mine momentarily. They seemed clouded and she looked down quickly, ignoring me and my reassurances.

Finally I ran out of words and stopped. What a bungler I was—first asking God to use me and then ruining it all by not waiting for guidance. "Oh, Lord, forgive me and help me," I prayed. An instant later I knew precisely what I was to say. I asked her, "Pat, do you know Jesus?"

Taken aback, she blinked as if no one had thought to mention Him to her lately, and that she hadn't thought of Him herself. Her interest was piqued, but she didn't answer. I asked, "Do you love Him?" Her eyes sparkled for an instant and she nodded.

"The Lord doesn't want you to be depressed," I assured her. "He loves you. He wants you to be full of joy!" She smiled for a moment, then just as quickly looked down, dejected, again.

"Would you like to come into the house and talk more about it?" I offered. She looked down and didn't respond. My spirits plummeted. "What else can I say, Lord?" No answer came.

After some time, Jon said, "I think we'd better be going home." He started the car and added, "Thanks anyhow."

I nodded. Near tears, I remembered to thank God and praise Him even though matters did not appear to be working out well. I prayed for Pat and sent a cheerful card, as well as a little booklet that explained how to live nearer to God. On the card I wrote, "This booklet helped me so much that I thought you might like to have it too." I mailed it and continued to pray for Pat.

A week later, the doorbell rang again. When I opened the door, Pat stood there smiling joyously. Her blue eyes glowed and a wondrous radiance surrounded her as she handed me a bouquet of pink roses. "Thank you. Thank you so much for helping me. You're the first one who mentioned Jesus. And thank you for sending the card and that booklet."

Thrilled at her joy, I caught Pat in my arms. While I embraced her, I said silently to God, "Thank you for using even a bungler like me."

Insightful Seniors

"Wisdom belongs to the aged,
and understanding to those who have lived many years."
Job 12:12

Have you ever sat down and had a discussion with a grand-parent or other elder? Their astuteness never fails to amaze me. Because they have experienced so much, they are over-flowing with stories and advice.

My great-aunt never seems to cease talking. Most of the time I tuned her out, but, upon listening to her, I realized that she has gained a comprehension from her countless experiences. She talked to me about her relationships as a young person, and I realized that she was not that much dif-ferent from teens today.

Seniors deserve to be listened to; their tales can be interesting and instructive, and can help you in your own life. Today we should all hug a senior and take the time to listen to his or her insight.

*Older people possess wisdom and understanding
that come with age and that should be respected.*

—LINDSAY OBERST

Hugged or Mugged?

"Greet each other in Christian love.
Peace be to all of you who are in Christ."
1 Peter 5:14

I was not sure if I had been hugged or mugged. I was visiting in a nursing home and walked through the lobby on my way out. One of the residents was standing there laughing. I stopped to see what was so funny. She was giggling at me!

She said through her chuckles, "You look just like my old man!" That made me laugh. Then she said, "I sure wish I could hug you." I took a step forward and said, "Go ahead." That lady latched onto me with a hug I thought would send me to the chiropractor. She hugged and kissed me and laughed all the while. Finally she let go, waved goodbye, and chuckled as she shuffled off down the hall.

Being hugged and sharing a laugh in a nursing home lasted no more than five minutes, but it was something I will never forget.

Everyone is your neighbor and deserves your love.

—DON M. AYCOCK

Action Speaks the Truth

"Dear children, let us stop just saying we love
each other; let us really show it by our actions."
1 John 3:18

There is an adage that says, "actions speak louder than words." Are we talking about body language here? In a way, yes, because when you put your thoughts into acts, you have to move your body.

You can tell people that you love them, but without showing them, the message of love won't be received. Giving a hand to your spouse, offering your service to the community, being generous to the needy, being willing to listen attentively, hugging someone in grief, patting somebody on the back who did a good job, and smiling at all times are actions and gestures of love. I can go on and on, but the point here is, love should be incorporated with action. And of course, when you say something pleasant, be it a greeting or compliment, be truthful and be sincere.

Put your love into action with gestures that are clear.

—ESTHER B. JIMENEZ

The Right Word

"Timely advice is as lovely as
golden apples in a silver basket."
Proverbs 25:11

A heated debate developed on an Internet discussion list I was a part of, and members of the "loop" on both sides were certain they were correct. There was no right or wrong answer, and I knew it wouldn't be long before members got hurt and started to drop out in anger. Because I've seen this happen before, I decided to gently intervene.

I posted a message that thanked all for respecting one another's feelings and opinions and for handling the discussion like courteous professionals. The discussion took an immediate turn for the better, and many members sent me private messages to say thanks.

God knew we would have conflict among us, and provided His advice for maintaining civility. The imagery in Proverbs 25:11 serves to display the beauty of its wisdom.

Godly advice is a blessing to others.

—ROBIN BAYNE

The Indecisive Squirrel

"But Jesus told him, 'Anyone who puts a hand to the plow
and then looks back is not fit for the Kingdom of God.'"
Luke 9:62

As I was driving down the road, a squirrel ran out in front of
my car. I was far enough from him that I started braking,
trying to miss him. He went one way, then he turned and
ran back, then he turned and went back the other way
again. I managed to miss him, but he was the most indeci-
sive squirrel I've ever seen!

Indecision is a dangerous thing.

As Christians, if we don't know what we believe and
why we believe it, people will see through us. If we say we
are a Christian but don't act like one at home or at work,
people won't respect us.

In our faith, we can't be like the squirrel in the middle
of the road. We have to make a decision about which way
we are going and then follow through!

You have to commit yourself to Christ and stay committed.

—TERESA BELL KINDRED

Mystery of Life

"I was chosen to explain to everyone
this plan that God, the Creator of all things,
had kept secret from the beginning."
Ephesians 3:9

We have a great appetite for mystery! *Perry Mason, Murder She Wrote,* and *Matlock* were some of the most popular television programs ever, and have been in reruns for years. Alfred Hitchcock still sets the standard for mystery movies. Mary Higgins Clark's mystery novels are favorites of many.

But the Christian is involved in a unique mystery. Paul wrote in Ephesians 3:3, "That by revelation there was made known to me the mystery, as I wrote before in brief" (New American Standard Bible).

The mystery is revealed in Ephesians 3:6, ". . . that the Gentiles are fellow heirs and fellow members of the body, and fellow partakers of the promise in Christ Jesus through the gospel" (NASB). This mystery is an open secret—that God has acted to accept all people who will know Him and follow Him, and they have the assurance that salvation provides.

In Christ life is not a mystery.

—STEPHEN D. BOYD

The Prayer God Would Not Answer

"For they loved human praise
more than the praise of God."
John 12:43

As soon as I prayed and even before all the words departed my lips, I knew that God would not answer this prayer.

I had prayed, "Lord, let people see you in me, empty me of myself, and let people not see me as offensive or abrasive."

As the word "abrasive" left my lips, I heard the Holy Spirit whisper, "Some people found Jesus offensive and abrasive."

I then realized what my true heart's prayer had been: "Lord, please let people like me."

Sure, I want people to like me, but if it costs me my desire to put God first, then it costs too much. I prayed again.

"Lord, I desire obedience to You. Be in and around all my relationships. As I love You, let me love others. Your name be praised! Amen."

God's praise is more important than people's praise.

—SHANNON RULÉ

God's Special Gifts

"Since you are so eager to have spiritual gifts, ask God for those that will be of real help to the whole church."
1 Corinthians 14:12

My son Alex has been diagnosed with mental retardation. But he can tell you, in his own special way, that Jesus lives in his heart. And when he comes home from school, he eagerly tells me that God helped him today with his class lessons. When he says it, it's almost as if he saw God standing right next to him, guiding him along.

His special gifts may not be as evident as they are in others. I sometimes wonder if his simpler way of looking at life is not a gift in itself. He isn't hindered by what others think, nor is he affected by the world's views. He sees God in a way that's maybe more real and close than I do some days.

God tells us we should all be like little children. Alex's innocence may be just that special gift that allows God's light to shine through.

You have been given special gifts to use for God's glory.

—SUE RHODES

Living in the Shadow

"The LORD himself watches over you!
The LORD stands beside you as your protective shade."
Psalm 121:5

As I traveled the expressway one day here in the southern tip of Texas, I noticed two cars—one a policeman's—parked on the shoulder. Yet neither driver was readily visible. It seems the two had agreed to walk several yards away to take advantage of the shade of a large billboard.

When the sun is high and hot, we place a high premium on shade. Drivers vie for shady parking spots. Walkers carry umbrellas. Animals retreat to the coolness of rocks and bushes.

Like the wind, shade cannot be touched but most certainly can be felt. The dark patches in our lives may not be as welcome as the protection of a leafy tree on a hot day. Still, we might ask ourselves which shadows are God's ways of providing needed rest, comfort, and a cooldown from our feverish endeavors.

A dark spot in life may be God providing shade to your soul.

—JAN SEALE

The Song of the Day

"Then you will sing psalms and hymns
and spiritual songs among yourselves,
making music to the Lord in your hearts."
Ephesians 5:19

"What's the song of the day, Fred?" my mother asked my father each morning. And every day, in reply to her question, my dad would break out singing the hymn that still played around inside his head from the night before.

The Bible says to speak to each other in songs and spiritual songs. My parents did and in this little example to me, they demonstrated the meaning of these verses and set the tone in our household. A song to God made for a happy conversation and immediately put the focus of the day on God, where it belongs.

When I'm wishing my own home would hold more joy, I pray for God to give me a song at night. I believe that if I do this, He will give me a song in the morning. And then I will give it back to Him.

God's grace can put a new song in your heart every day.

—JESSIE ANN MOSER

Wonderfully Made

"You made all the delicate, inner parts of my body,
and knit me together in my mother's womb."
Psalm 139:13

It's so easy to look into a mirror, and find all of my flaws. I see wrinkles, gray hairs, and all the signs of aging that become more apparent each year. And whenever I compare myself to other women, I almost always come up short. That's not hard to do in Southern California. Many times it's a struggle to appreciate that God made me exactly as He intended.

My son has some developmental delays and doesn't always "measure up" to other kids by the world's standards. I try to encourage him to focus on all the gifts that God did give him. He is physically strong and athletic, and has a warm and loving heart. He is truly God's workmanship from the inside out.

God does not make mistakes. He has made each of us in His image. Be thankful that you are fearfully and wonderfully made.

You need to try and see yourself from God's perspective.

—SUE RHODES

Auto Focus

"Yes, dear friends, we are already God's children, and we can't even imagine what we will be like when Christ returns. But we do know that when he comes we will be like him, for we will see him as he really is."

1 John 3:2

We had one television connected to cable when we inherited a vintage console model. The new arrival was placed in an extra room for my husband and me to watch when our daughter and her friends were using the other one. But the first night we tried it, we could bring in only snowy white static.

We attached some unused rabbit ears and the result was instantaneous. As my husband raised the antennae and spread them apart, the gray squirming sea of static became a sharp, clear, colorful picture with intelligible speech.

"It's like prayer!" I exclaimed.

"What are you talking about?"

"Praying. It brings things into focus!"

My husband smiled and shook his head. Maybe my analogy was a little unorthodox, but it was true.

Prayer helps you see Christ more clearly at work in your life.

—MARCIA SWEARINGEN

Double Heaven

"Instead of shame and dishonor, you will inherit
a double portion of prosperity and everlasting joy."
Isaiah 61:7

A short while ago, my seven-year-old son and I went through some troubled times. Each evening at bedtime, we worshipped the Lord together, and then talked to Jesus about our problems because we knew He would lighten our burdens.

One morning, my son came downstairs and told me about a dream he had. "I saw Jesus walking, and He was getting lots of love and hugs from people."

"Did He get the love and hugs we sent Him last night?" I asked.

"Oh yes, Mom, and He hugged me back!" he said as he snuggled into my arms.

"How did it feel to be hugged by Jesus?"

"It was double heaven, Mom!" he replied.

Jesus gave my son a double portion of His love that night—right when he needed it most.

And it warmed my heart to know that the Lord brought comfort to him when I couldn't.

When it all seems hopeless, God gives you a double measure.

—S. (SHAE) COOKE

Choose God Now

"'Because you trusted me, I will preserve your life
and keep you safe. I, the LORD, have spoken!'"
Jeremiah 39:18

When Blackout 2003 hit New York, my daughter, who works in Manhattan, was away from her desk speaking with a colleague. They held hands, groped toward the stairs, and made it into the streets.

Her friend led the way through the crowds to her brother who was waiting for her where they planned to meet should such a calamity occur. He drove them to New Jersey.

My daughter was safe, though her situation was not perfect. She was far away from her home in upstate New York, without money, bank card, or cell phone. Yet she was relaxed and even grateful because she was with a friend she trusted.

What a difference it makes if we are in fellowship with Jesus when disaster strikes and our day suddenly turns into night. We can face the challenge with faith, not fear.

*God is in control of your life
when circumstances are out of control.*

—DORA ISAAC WEITHERS

Beautiful Feet

"And how will anyone go and tell them without being sent? That is what the Scriptures mean when they say, 'How beautiful are the feet of those who bring good news!'"

Romans 10:15

I was having a rough time and the self-help books instructed, "Do something special for yourself." A pedicure is what I settled on.

I approached the nail technician with fear and trembling: "I would like to have a pedicure, please. My first time. My feet are ugly."

She looked up and said, "Everyone's feet are ugly," as if this would somehow make me feel better. "Sit down."

When she finished I couldn't believe my eyes. My feet were beautiful. Immediately I bought jeweled flip-flops, a toe ring, and an ankle bracelet.

Only days later my troubled life would hit me again. I curled in the fetal position, as I often did when in intense pain. I opened my eyes and looked at my feet, my beautiful feet. They became my reminder. I stood up, smiled, and went on my way. Today was a new day.

God reminds you that you are
beautiful to Him even during tough times.

—SHANNON RULÉ

A Cheerful Giver

"Remember this—a farmer who plants only
a few seeds will get a small crop. But the one
who plants generously will get a generous crop."
2 Corinthians 9:6

My nephew was with me one Sunday noon at the church. During collection, I saw him putting five dollars in the basket. After church, I asked him why he gave his allowance. He told me, "I want to give more but I don't have enough; God gives a lot and everything comes from Him."

What a beautiful virtue of generosity, especially coming from a child. It is not the amount, it's not the number of times, it is the depth of your heart that counts in giving. When I hear somebody say, "I always give from the bottom of my heart," I just ponder for a moment how deep the bottom of that heart is. It is figuratively said, but the real meaning contains the idea of sincerity and generosity. So, remember the blessings of giving generously.

God loves a cheerful giver.

—Esther B. Jimenez

Following the Instructions

"Those who listen to instruction will prosper;
those who trust the LORD will be happy."
Proverbs 16:20

One of my father's favorite dishes was breaded pork chops. One day, while left at home alone, he spied some defrosted pork chops in the refrigerator, so he decided to surprise us with dinner.

However, in the preparation of this meal, my father tried to take a shortcut. Instead of dipping the pork chops in egg batter and then rolling them in the breading, he put the breading in the bowl with the egg batter. He was perplexed when the breading wouldn't stick. Because he didn't prepare them according to the instructions, we all missed out on the blessing of breaded pork chops that day!

Whether we are making breaded pork chops or wanting to please our heavenly Father, the principle of following the specific instructions in His Word applies. It's the only way we can receive the blessings that are in store for us.

When you follow the ways of the Lord, you will be blessed.

—ANNETTEE BUDZBAN

Warts

"You fathers—if your children ask for a fish,
do you give them a snake instead?"
Luke 11:11

When I was about ten or so, our church held a revival. Revivals were pretty common throughout the year in my little church.

During this revival, we were being especially challenged to believe God for healing. I had an ugly wart on one of my fingers. It was embarrassing. The daily applications of wart remover weren't doing the trick. I wanted it gone.

My mother encouraged me to go up for prayer with the evangelist. He took me aside, heard my heart's cry, and we prayed. The next day it was still there. I went up again. The evangelist encouraged me, saying, "Sometimes you just have to keep believing and praying."

"How long?" I asked.

"As long as it takes!" he replied.

After about the third night of prayer, the wart vanished. I knew God had healed me because we had stopped using the wart remover. I was amazed and learned perseverance in faith.

If at first you don't receive, pray again.

—SRC

The Lord Almighty Is in the House

"So we will not fear, even if earthquakes
come and the mountains crumble into the sea."
Psalm 46:2

Fear is both a motivator and a demotivator. We have only two possible responses: We will act or we will freeze. David neutralizes the standard fear formula by saying, "So we will not fear!" What arrogance! He can't be in touch with reality! He's being Pollyanna.

Remember how many times Jesus said to His followers, "Do not be afraid." With both we see a voiding of the power of fear.

I have awakened for workdays, week after week, and been wet with sweat before getting out of bed. Why? Because I was anticipating another day of intense conflict and stress. Are you prone to stress headaches? Do you have persistent phobias?

The Lord is called the Prince of Peace. He is available to banish the power of fear. His name is Emmanuel, God with us! Shalom.

The Lord Almighty, who is over all
natural and human forces, keeps you from fear.

—Kenneth M. Hansen

Pure Honey

"They are more desirable than gold,
even the finest gold. They are sweeter than
honey, even honey dripping from the comb."
Psalm 19:10

Two summers ago, an out-of-town beekeeper knocked at my door. He was selling a recent batch of honey, discounted for that day only. Supermarkets usually sell the same amount for twice the price.

I noticed, however, his containers looked used and the color of the honey appeared darker than normal. Being somewhat cautious, I purchased just one jar. The salesman suggested I buy more at this price, but I declined. After he left, I sampled the product and discovered his honey had the best flavor that I've ever tasted. I should have purchased more.

Likewise, I was hesitant to read God's Word at first. I didn't realize its value. But now, the more I read it, the better it becomes. Like pure honey, the Scriptures taste sweeter each time we taste them. Even God's laws, commandments, and judgments are desirable and just. We should savor their goodness and apply their principles daily.

*God's Word is sweeter than
honey and provides more benefits.*

—CHARLES E. HARREL

A Fat Soul

"If you give, you will receive. Your gift will return to you in full measure, pressed down, shaken together to make room for more, and running over. Whatever measure you use in giving—large or small—it will be used to measure what is given back to you."

Luke 6:38

I came from our garden, my arms loaded with sweet corn and tomatoes. Under a willow tree I began to shuck corn for my family's lunch.

As I pulled the silk from an ear of corn, a verse flashed into my mind: "The liberal soul shall be made fat" (Proverbs 11:25, King James Version).

Glancing at my watch, I noticed it was time to start lunch. The verse returned: "The liberal soul . . ." Then the meaning struck! I filled a bag with corn and tomatoes and instructed our son to deliver the produce to a family that didn't have a garden.

I smiled as I dropped our corn into boiling water. "You thought my soul needed some fattening up, Lord? You're right. This full-to-the-brim feeling that comes from sharing is definitely a fat-soul feeling and what I needed to make a good day even better."

He wants you to share what you have,
no matter how small it is, to bless the lives of others.

—JEWELL JOHNSON

The Stones Praise God

"And now God is building you, as living stones, into his spiritual temple. What's more, you are God's holy priests, who offer the spiritual sacrifices that please him because of Jesus Christ."

1 Peter 2:5

"Where do all these stones come from?" my husband yelled.

With perspiration dripping from his face, Lee was mowing our new lawn for the first time. Every few minutes the power mower sputtered when the whirling blade hit a stone.

"They come from the ground!" I retorted teasingly.

Stones are significant despite their nuisance. Little boys throw them. We kick them out of the way, stumble over them, or walk on top of them. And we complain if they hamper our mowing efforts!

Yet, as part of God's creation, stones, by their very existence—without heart or mind—offer praise to God. If we don't praise aloud, they will.

Peter compares believers to stones. Our task? To praise God. We, who have voices, souls, hearts, and hands, who know the redeeming power of Jesus, can join with all creation—even stones—to extol the majesty of our mighty God.

You are created to give praise and worship to God with your body, soul, spirit, and mind.

—JEWELL JOHNSON

Listen to Me!

"But I called on your name, LORD, from deep within the well, and you heard me! You listened to my pleading; you heard my weeping! Yes, you came at my despairing cry and told me, 'Do not fear.'"

Lamentations 3:55–57

As these words comforted Jeremiah, the weeping prophet, long ago, they comfort me when I struggle, feel lost, cry out, and feel afraid. On dark, damp days, when sunlight appears to be only a pinprick of distant light, I crawl toward God and am confident He hears and understands.

We all seek to be heard by others. We inwardly, but sometimes actually, scream, "Listen to me!" We aren't asking for "fixing." We aren't seeking to "trade spaces" or woes. We simply desire the gift of time and open and compassionate hearts. No judgment or analysis, no second-guessing, no opinions needed or wanted.

"Listen to me!" my heart laments. Job reminds me, in chapter 22, verse 27, "You will pray to Him, and He will hear you. . . ." God always answers these cries of my soul. I am blessed abundantly when a few of His children do, too.

Your loving God always hears your cries.

—ELAINE YOUNG MCGUIRE

The Gift of the Fishing Pole

"If you sinful people know how to give good gifts
to your children, how much more will your heavenly
Father give the Holy Spirit to those who ask him."
Luke 11:13

Jason and his mom were having a very bad day. Jason was being disobedient and Mom had grown weary. Jason went to the garage declaring, "I'm going fishing." Mom thought, "Good!"

Jason couldn't find his fishing pole. Reluctantly he asked his mom for help. As they looked, she thought of the new pole she had hidden in a closet for Jason's birthday. She thought, "I could give him the new pole now, but he doesn't deserve it." The Holy Spirit whispered to her, "If I waited until you deserved good gifts . . ."

She brought out the new pole and shared her thoughts with Jason. He confessed he didn't deserve it. Together they wept.

Years later, the main memory she has about that day is of her son calling out, "I love you!" as he headed out the door to go fishing. Our Heavenly Father loves us even more.

*Like your Heavenly Father, you are to
give good gifts willingly and unconditionally.*

—SHANNON RULÉ

A Blocked View

> "He tried to get a look at Jesus,
> but he was too short to see over the crowds."
> Luke 19:3

You've been there before. We all have. Whether at a concert, play, movie, or game. We choose a spot from which we have the perfect view. No sooner do we get settled in than someone sits in front of us. Someone tall, with big hair, or who continually moves from side to side, blocking our view.

It must have been a lot like that for Zacchaeus. I wonder what was blocking his view most that day. Was it merely the stature of those around? Or was it the height from which they had fallen? Was it their lack of love and compassion for those who had not yet met the Transformer? Was it their love of self, their choice of words, their pride? Was it their tolerance for mediocrity, or their lack of excitement and wonder at what the Lord had done for them?

Regardless, Zacchaeus was determined to see the Lord and let nothing stand in his way.

Keep your life clear of anything
that gets between you and Jesus.

—MARLENE MECKENSTOCK

Give God the Remote

"But you are not controlled by your sinful nature. You are controlled by the Spirit if you have the Spirit of God living in you. (And remember that those who do not have the Spirit of Christ living in them are not Christians at all.)"

Romans 8:9

We love control. He who holds the remote controls what's on TV! The same is true of our hearts and minds. Are you focused or just channel surfing through life?

Rendering control to God is no small feat. When God holds your life's "remote," He controls the programming. He will stay with you through it all—the best and worst of times—even when the viewing is uncomfortable.

Once you hand Him the remote, your life is rated DG, for Divine Guidance. You trust that the Father will provide parental intervention and guidance, and that everything you view in life under all circumstances will be touched by Him.

With God in control you're always on the right channel.

—MICHELE STARKEY

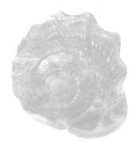

Overnight Delivery!

"Jesus looked at them intently and said,
'Humanly speaking, it is impossible.
But with God everything is possible.'"
Matthew 19:26

Our military daughter was confined to quarters with pneumonia far away from home. Since childhood, sickness meant the two of us on the sofa watching *Anne of Green Gables*. It was better than chicken soup.

"I've already watched the videos, Mom, but I've heard they have a sequel!"

Outside the video store, I got a strong internal nudge to pray: "Lord, this isn't life and death, but I know you know it is incredibly important to me and someone I love. Please let this store have the set of videos I need."

I entered the store. There, on the counter, beside the register, was *Anne of Green Gables Part 2*.

"This is exactly what I came for!"

"Did you call ahead?" asked the clerk.

"No, I prayed!"

"This is really unusual. We carry these only at Christmas, and then we pull them off the shelves."

I overnighted the videos to my daughter.

God cares about all your needs.

—MARCIA SWEARINGEN

Rainbow

"The real children of Abraham, then,
are all those who put their faith in God."
Galatians 3:7

Sarah came running home from her friend's house in tears. "Ina called me 'white'!" she sobbed. I didn't understand why my five-year-old was upset. She is white. When I explained, she retreated to her room, returning with a box of crayons.

"No, I'm not. I'm peach. See, Mama?" she exclaimed triumphantly, matching the peach-colored crayon to her arm.

I smiled with pride. The "black" or "white" label of adults was blurred by my child. She saw the world as God intended, a beautiful rainbow of different shades and colors.

Sarah is now twenty-two years old. She continues to live her life in a multicolored world, making her experiences rich and diverse. Rejoicing in the similarities and celebrating the differences, Sarah surrounds herself with people who don't judge by the color of skin but by the content of character.

We are all God's children.

—PAT FRIEDRICH

No Need Too Small

*"And if we know he is listening
when we make our requests, we can be
sure that he will give us what we ask for."*
1 John 5:15

"Dear Jesus, please find my ball," my son prayed one night. His ball had rolled down our long, hilly street, and though we searched the neighborhood, it was not to be found.

The next morning Matthew bounced into our room. "Dad, Mom, Jesus brought my ball back!" There on the lawn lay a big red ball. How did it get there? Though we thought we'd never see it again, Matthew knew. The mighty God of the universe is not too busy to listen to a child's request.

It's often easier to see God working in the world than in my daily, ordinary life. But the God who hung the stars and directs the nations is the same God who cares about your child's flu, the hot water heater that died, or the search for a new job.

Go to your Father with the simple faith of a child. He cares about each of your needs and provides you with His best.

God hears all of your prayers.

—DORIS SCHUCHARD

The Words of a Bird

"For you are great and perform great miracles.
You alone are God."
Psalm 86:10

After an early divorce and years of loneliness, my friend Diana found Glenn. They had been married only a few years when Glenn died unexpectedly, leaving Diana immobilized by doubt and depression.

One morning she decided to sweep the breezeway. Maybe if she moved about a bit—did something, anything—she'd feel better. Sweeping was a practical matter because Glenn and Diana's parrot Mordecai regularly made seedy messes there.

Mordecai was quiet in his cage, eyeing Diana's droopy demeanor and watching the repetitive motion of her broom. He'd never talked much, and when he did, it was mostly a solitary word like "Eat!" Small company he was in the face of her loneliness!

Suddenly, out of nowhere, came Glenn's voice. With all Glenn's tender inflections and in his unique accent, Mordecai sang out, "I love you, Diana." And her healing began.

Count on God to surprise you.

—JAN SEALE

Running with Scissors

"A vast crowd was there as he stepped from the boat, and he had compassion on them because they were like sheep without a shepherd. So he taught them many things."
Mark 6:34

"Don't run with scissors. You could hurt yourself or someone else." This is good parental advice. If our child runs with scissors, he's likely to cut another person or pierce himself.

I've realized that holding on to scissors while running is a lot like holding on to anger while living. An unforgiving heart's hurtful to others and to me. Recently I saw a picture in the newspaper of a man embracing a husband and wife. The couple he was comforting were the parents of a boy who had brutally slain his son.

This image struck me—how many times do I become angry or offended over relatively small offenses? My self-righteousness and pride often take the place of compassion. I need to remember that the Lord looked down on the multitudes and had compassion. Because God loves and forgives me, I need to put down the scissors and walk in love for Him.

Show compassion to those around you.

—LORI WILDENBERG

SEPTEMBER

THE COMPETITORS
—LAURIE WHITMAN

"As iron sharpens iron, a friend sharpens a friend."

PROVERBS 27:17

*A*S THE NEW THIRD GRADER IN SCHOOL, Monica, the popular class leader, immediately sensed a rival. She initially kept me firmly at arm's length and blocked my access to peer acceptance. Still, a sort of competitive friendship grew and lasted for years.

During our middle and high school days, Monica and I became closer friends, although the rivalry continued in full. We competed academically and vied for top grades. We competed physically as sprinters for the high school track team. We seemed to alternate as the victors from meet to meet.

Occasionally we teamed up and worked together. One year, our algebra teacher announced a day prior to a test, "Anyone who can recite the Greek alphabet will receive an automatic A."

"Meet me in the library during study period," Monica whispered to me after class.

The next day the teacher was incredulous as we recited the Greek alphabet from memory; no one had ever taken his pretest words seriously.

The dance of competition for Monica and me sometimes crossed the line, generating feelings of jealousy. But in retrospect, I know that overall, the rivalry was a catalyst for achievement and improvement.

As valedictorian of our class, Monica gave a speech that was calm and assured. I knew our friendship was also assured. I knew, too, that she would achieve great things. She was a winner.

After high school, as expected, Monica earned a doctorate in pharmacy and had a wonderful career and marriage.

Twenty years later, at our class reunion, I saw Monica looking her competent self in a black dinner dress and pearls. I asked about her family and life.

"I'm a stay-at-home mom," she said with a smile. Because I also stayed at home with my three children, and loved it, I could relate. We began discussing schools and education; then her next words astounded me.

"Two of my children are autistic."

She went on to explain about her research into the latest methods for helping her children so they could grow emotionally and physically. Monica was staying home to personally work with this new challenge, so different from pharmaceutical work, but so like Monica, who never turned away from a worthy challenge!

Monica has been in my thoughts many times. She is a story for my children as they navigate their way through childhood relationships.

People, rivals and friends, are divinely allowed in our life's path as part of the bigger picture of life. I've been doubly blessed with a rival who prodded me to do better, and who also became my friend.

The God of Tomorrow

"'If you keep quiet at a time like this, deliverance for the Jews will arise from some other place, but you and your relatives will die. What's more, who can say but that you have been elevated to the palace for just such a time as this?'"

Esther 4:14

Many years ago I was asked by a neighbor if I would watch her children while she worked. It was a paying job and since our children already played together anyway, it seemed like the perfect fit. Two weeks later, unexpectedly, my husband was laid off. God had already made provision to meet our needs even before they appeared.

The book of Esther is a story of God going before His people to prepare the way, and because of Esther's obedience to her calling, the Jews were saved. I was willing to be obedient to Him based on his advance provision.

Even though life sometimes catches us off guard, it never catches God unawares.

With God you can face tomorrow without fear.

—LINDA KNIGHT

A Continuing City

"For this world is not our home; we are looking
forward to our city in heaven, which is yet to come."
Hebrews 13:14

I was a sophomore in college and feeling the stress of moving from home to the dorm and back again each year. Happening upon this verse in Hebrews one night, I was overwhelmed with peace and assurance that my home in heaven would be permanent.

Years later, when faced with uncertainty about job prospects and unsure of where I would be living the next week, God again comforted my mind with his promises of a secure future.

Now, having lived in the same place for fifteen years, I still need to remember that my real home is in heaven. The troubles of this world are unrelenting, but so is God's peace.

One version of the Bible states the verse this way: "Here we have no continuing city, but we seek one to come" (King James Version). What a blessing to know where we will live for all eternity!

*When the changes of life become discouraging,
it is good to remember that your future is settled.*

—SHERRY L. POFF

Just Grand

"May you live to enjoy your grandchildren.
And may Israel have quietness and peace."
Psalm 128:6

Every time our grown son Avrel came home, he sat right down at "his" piano and played. We offered the piano to him and his wife, Kirstin, for their new home 300 miles away. Avrel was delighted. It was several weeks before the piano mover called to say he could transport it.

By then Avrel and Kirstin had just become parents. Shouldn't we delay the piano a few weeks? Wouldn't it be an addition to the confusion? The eager new father thought differently. "Oh no, Mother, send it on. Perfect timing!"

"How's that?" I asked.

"Well," he said, "we've just given you a grandbaby and you're giving us a baby grand."

What music, our grandchildren! God assigns us the role of enjoying them. Grandchildren play new chords in our hearts and put new tunes on our whistling lips. They are God's music for our remaining days.

Enjoyment and love are the grandparents' job.

—JAN SEALE

Hugs from God

"Everyone enjoys a fitting reply;
it is wonderful to say the right thing at the right time!"
Proverbs 15:23

The music was lively inside the banquet hall as we celebrated my grandmother's seventy-fifth birthday. We'd found out only recently that she'd never had a birthday party before, having been orphaned at age twelve.

"Happy birthday!" we yelled as she arrived. "And many more!"

Several times during the evening, I saw my mother hugging her. Later, I approached my mother and asked about the hugs.

"Her parents died of tuberculosis," she explained. "What I hadn't known was that her last memories of her mother and father were of being kept away from them to keep her healthy. Her parents were contagious. They loved her but they couldn't touch her. So," Mom said, then took a deep breath and smiled at me, "along with the party, I wanted to make up for some of the hugs she missed, to help her make do until she meets them again in Heaven."

Love and care for all the members of your family.
You never know all they have been through.

—ROBIN BAYNE

Remembrance

"Remember the days of long ago; think about the
generations past. Ask your father and he will inform you.
Inquire of your elders, and they will tell you."
Deuteronomy 32:7

As I rummaged through old family files, I discovered a
treasure. Years ago, as a young wife, I had flown to meet my
husband, a submariner, at the halfway point of a six-month
deployment. To share with our families the wondrous sights
of this trip to Hong Kong and the Philippine Islands, I had
written pages and pages describing the great adventure. I
closed with a reference to celebrating my twenty-seventh
birthday twice, crossing the International Dateline.

Time melted away as the vivid images of that memo-
rable trip jumped off the pages in my grandmother's hand-
writing! She had meticulously copied that long-lost letter!
Her home now is in heaven, but her thoughtfulness lives on
in the gift she returned to me that day . . . twenty-seven
years after it was given.

I am thankful for the foresight of grandparents and the
legacy of recycled blessings.

Each generation brings many gifts to the table.
A blessing shared is a blessing doubled.

—MARCIA SWEARINGEN

Working for God

"Be sure to do what you should, for then you will enjoy the personal satisfaction of having done your work well, and you won't need to compare yourself to anyone else. For we are each responsible for our own conduct."

Galatians 6:4–5

Have you ever watched a biography about someone who has done amazing things for humanity with little resources? Have you ever felt more discouraged than encouraged by it? Sometimes we look at people busy starting up charities or volunteering in food kitchens and are overwhelmed by what others are doing and what we aren't.

God expects us to labor in His Kingdom. He also expects us to use our own talents and do what we are able to do. But in Galatians Paul tells us not to compare ourselves with others. Work to the glory of God in the capacity that *you* are able.

Sometimes, simple things like a kind word, a card, or a phone call from someone when I needed it are what have encouraged me the most. Look for opportunities to serve God in every way. God uses people through all these small gestures.

Be accountable for the talents God has gifted you with.

—Maryann Breukelman

Take This Job and Love It

"Work hard and cheerfully at whatever you do, as though you were working for the LORD rather than for people. Remember that the LORD will give you an inheritance as your reward, and the Master you are serving is Christ."

Colossians 3:23–24

With this verse, God used Paul to encourage all of the common men and women who toil in cubicles, who empty the trash in high-story buildings, and who put up with frustrated, angry shoppers in the checkout line at Christmastime.

This verse dignifies the work that men and women do from nine to five. God says, "Hey, work for me, not for that supervisor who takes my name in vain or even the manager who is fair. You work in the Kingdom of God and for the living God."

No matter what we do, God says, do it unto Him. Don't do your work with a bad attitude, with boredom and dissatisfaction. Do your best for God! As you move and have your being in Him, you are in His tabernacle, and all of life becomes holy when lived to the fullest for and in front of your Lord.

Work at your job as if you work for God. You do!

—JESSIE ANN MOSER

A Crooked Smile

"Laughter can conceal a heavy heart;
when the laughter ends, the grief remains."
Proverbs 14:13

I flew over lower Manhattan one evening about a year after the 9/11 attacks there. I could clearly see where the twin towers of the World Trade Center had been. The city was lit up but the tower site was dark. From 30,000 feet it looked like a smiling face with two front teeth missing—a crooked smile that will never be quite right.

Our lives are filled with grief. The loss of anything significant to us can produce an inner pain that is hard to describe but easy to recognize. We have all had it. A personal tragedy like a death in the family, or a national disaster like the terrorist attacks, can send us into a tailspin while we cry out, "Where is God in all of this?"

Whatever the explanation, we live in a world filled with grief. The only genuine relief is from the loving embrace of our Heavenly Father. The writer of the proverb was right— when the laughter ends, the grief remains.

Through the grace of God, grief is never the last word.

—DON M. AYCOCK

I Don't Know about Tomorrow

"So don't worry about tomorrow, for tomorrow will bring its own worries. Today's trouble is enough for today."
Matthew 6:34

In the middle of a news program replaying the scenes of devastation from New York City on September 11, I received a phone call asking me to play for a service at the local seniors' home.

During the hymn-sing an attendant asked if anyone had a favorite. A lady in the back asked for number 558. "It's my favorite," she said.

Soon cracked voices filled the room. I recognized the song my mother used to sing to me when I was a child, and paid close attention to the words: "Many things about tomorrow, / I don't seem to understand, / But I know who holds tomorrow / and I know who holds my hand."

What a beautiful message. Those seniors knew a God who had been there for them through every trial in their past, and they knew He was still there holding their hand now.

Despite the threat of terror you are secure in Him.

—ELAINE INGALLS HOGG

Conceiving the Impossible

"But I say, love your enemies!
Pray for those who persecute you!"
Matthew 5:44

Can you imagine loving or even forgiving the terrorists who flew the planes into the Twin Towers on 9/11? This concept of love and forgiveness at all costs is an extremely difficult one to grasp. This task could be thought of as impossible, but it becomes conceivable if you put all your faith in God. This is proven in Luke 1:37, which states, "For nothing is impossible with God."

All enemies large and small should be forgiven completely. They, too, are people who have made mistakes that have, in turn, deeply hurt people. God has a perfect plan, although we, as human beings, cannot always see or comprehend it.

Keep in mind that Jesus knows precisely what it feels like to be persecuted and betrayed. He never despised those who were his enemies, but as He was dying, He said, "Father, forgive them for they know not what they do."

All people who have wronged you
should be forgiven, loved, and prayed for.

—LINDSAY OBERST

Do Not Be Afraid

"Do not be afraid of the terrors of the night, nor fear the dangers of the day, nor dread the plague that stalks in darkness, nor the disaster that strikes at midday. Though a thousand fall at your side, though ten thousand are dying around you, these evils will not touch you."

Psalm 91:5–7

It's not unusual for a child to be afraid of the dark. The absence of light can cause uncertainty and even panic. But the comfort and assurance of a parent, soothingly saying, "Don't be afraid. I'm here, right beside you," can instantly dispel the fear.

Much violent crime happens at night. With a higher threat of terrorism, the days don't feel very safe. Biological warfare, weapons of mass destruction, school violence, and more impose on our sense of peace.

While we may not be spared from physical threats, we can feel safe spiritually. Even surrounded by chaos and panic, peace can be found. It is such a comfort to trust a Father who whispers in the dark, "Do not be afraid. I'm here, right beside you."

God helps you through times of fear and uncertainty.

—ELAINE YOUNG MCGUIRE

An Unshakable High Tower

"The name of the LORD is a strong fortress;
the godly run to him and are safe."
Proverbs 18:10

My friend Janey served as the White House Web master for several years. On September 11, 2001, Janey was with her coworkers, watching the World Trade Center collapse on television and discussing changes she needed to make to the official Web site, when a Secret Service member yelled, "Everyone out of the building *now*!"

Confused but obedient, Janey took off her high heels and sprinted outside with her colleagues. Later, she found out that a fourth plane had most likely targeted the White House. Janey was shaken but safe when I talked to her the next day.

Where can we run when danger threatens? Since September 11, I've realized that I can't keep myself or my family members protected each minute of the day—but I'm thankful that I can turn to God and let Him comfort my frightened heart. God is an eternal safe place for those who trust in Him.

In prayer, you can run to the Lord, who is your strong tower.

—DENA DYER

Seed for the Harvest

"The generous prosper and are satisfied;
those who refresh others will themselves be refreshed."
Proverbs 11:25

One fall morning after I'd scattered a sprinkling of bird seed along the top of our patio wall, I smiled at the scene unfolding before me. One little sparrow picked up a sunflower seed and fed it to another little sparrow, beak to beak. How absolutely precious, I thought to myself.

I wonder how brightly God must smile when we pause long enough to help another weary traveler along life's road. And how does that sharing begin? It begins by carrying seeds of truth and love from heart to heart.

Love is a seed you can plant daily.

—LINDA KNIGHT

While Waiting for the School Bus

"Understand, therefore, that the LORD your God is indeed God. He is the faithful God who keeps his covenant for a thousand generations and constantly loves those who love him and obey his commands."

Deuteronomy 7:9

I first understood the depth of my mother's faithfulness while waiting for the school bus.

I remember listening for the sound of uneven grinding that marked the bus's approach. I remember the riotous chatter of children drifting from its windows, making my heart race with trepidation.

Most of all, I remember that before stepping onto the bus, I always snuck one last look behind me. I knew that I'd see my mother, lingering in the doorway, watching, praying, and waiting for my return. Her unwavering support buoyed my spirit and filled me with confidence. I could face the day because I felt the words her presence spoke: "I'm here for you. I'll always be here for you."

Her example helps highlight an even greater truth. Though a mother's faithful love lasts a lifetime, God keeps his covenant of love to a thousand generations. His faithfulness buoys the spirit beyond comparison.

Like a mother's faithful love,
God's faithful love is beyond comparison.

—LORI Z. SCOTT

295

My Life as a "Launch Pad"

> "My relatives stay far away,
> and my friends have turned against me."
> Job 19:13

Having unexpectedly lost his job, my friend now found himself at a crossroads; he could either go back to the safer vocation that he had recently left or he could continue to pursue the road on which he had just embarked.

The answer became obvious almost the moment I started praying. God had directed my friend into this new and uncertain path, and He wanted him not to go back, but to continue to move forward and trust Him. But I did not like this answer! I had heard it too many times before regarding too many other close friends, and it usually meant I'd have to "launch" them to who-knows-where.

But lately, through unexpected regular contact with some of the other friends whom I had previously "launched," God has shown me that, not only is the emotional connection between my "launched" friends and me still intact, but the new lives and ministries into which God had used me to launch them are flourishing.

With God for Mission Control, life as a launch pad isn't so bad!

Friends move into and out of your life,
but God remains steadfast.

—HEIDI L. JANZ

Work and Pray

"You will enjoy the fruit of your labor.
How happy you will be! How rich your life!"
Psalm 128:2

A retired secretary on a low income took on typing. Within weeks, word spread about her skill. Customers raved about her work. Soon, she had more work than she could handle.

What was her secret? She thought about and prayed for each client. She never returned an assignment unless she prayed over it. She prayed for people she hardly knew. I wonder how many people God sent her way.

Whatever your trade or job, make room for prayer—it is the greatest form of love. Pray for people you don't know. Remember those touched by your work, and ask God to help you give your very best to them. Give your work to God, and discover your own secret to success.

Spread the Good News at work and at pray!

—S. (SHAE) COOKE

Angels Are People, Too

"Don't forget to show hospitality to strangers,
for some who have done this have
entertained angels without realizing it!"
Hebrews 13:2

I was in a new state and working a new job, knew practically no one locally, and I didn't have a car. My transportation was an old ten-speed bike. Going shopping was an adventure, and juggling bags on the way home, a challenge.

One cold, windy fall day, a tire blew. Though still several blocks away, the store was closer than my apartment, so I started walking the bike there. A man on a bike appeared beside me. He was Hispanic and didn't speak English.

From his gestures, I realized he wanted to fix my tire. He motioned me to stand back and then went to work applying a patch and using a hand pump to fill the tire.

When he finished I said, "Gracias!" and offered him money. He refused, hopped on his bike, and was gone.

Was he an angel? On that cold, windy fall day, he was mine!

Look for opportunities to be someone's angel today.

—SRC

What Name Is on Your Sneakers?

"For shoes, put on the peace that comes from
the Good News, so that you will be fully prepared."
Ephesians 6:15

An eighteen-year-old just out of high school allows his name to be put on a pair of athletic shoes in a multimillion-dollar contract. Why is his name worth so much? Because his name is LeBron James and he was the 2003 NBA first-round draft choice.

Wearing shoes with LeBron's name on them will not make you run faster or jump higher. They just make you feel cool.

We Christians wear shoes that not only make us feel cool, but have a mission of their own: bringing the Good News of God's peace to a troubled world.

Make sure you put on your Christian jogging shoes this morning and go through your day spreading peace.

*Wherever you walk, go with the
intention of bringing peace to others.*

—MERRY E. VARGO

Embracing Troubles

"Don't sin by letting anger gain control over you.
Think about it overnight and remain silent."
Psalm 4:4

Life hurts, people make us mad, conflicts and anger ensue as we struggle to avoid pain. But the path around a dilemma is frequently not avoidance or pain reduction. God delivers the gift of a trial to us and the correct response could be— are you ready for this?—to embrace it. To tough it out joy-fully, sharing the pain with no one but Him as you wait for His deliverance, even if it never comes on your terms.

Mining the depths of hurt and anger with tools given through the Holy Spirit can yield the most precious jewels. These are the gems of experience, maturity, and wisdom with which He adorns our lives as He quietly heals the hurts.

When they come, if all we do is struggle against trou-bles, we may miss the opportunity to grow and be strength-ened in grace and mercy. In fact, we just may miss Him.

God walks with you through troubles and joys.

—SRC

God Knows Us Personally

"But now, O Israel, the LORD who created you says:
'Do not be afraid, for I have ransomed you.
I have called you by name; you are mine.'"
Isaiah 43:1

Since the ultrasound was unable to reveal the gender of our first child, we jokingly referred to our mystery bundle as "Pat." We were overjoyed when we gave birth to our perfect baby girl, on Labor Day, no less. As we held her tenderly, we spoke intimate words of love and affirmation to our Kylie Rae. She was no longer a Pat. She was our little girl.

Jesus Christ's name is above every name in heaven and on earth. Yet, He sees us, not as faceless, nameless creatures, but as His dearly loved children . . . His delight. We are created in His image, connected by His blood, called by name.

Because God knows you intimately,
you can walk in assurance and security.

—BROOK CHALFANT

Under God's Wings

"May the LORD, the God of Israel, under whose wings
you have come to take refuge, reward you fully."
Ruth 2:12

Have you ever woken up in a strange bed, far away from home? You might have just moved or started a new job or a new school. You may feel lonely and isolated.

Ruth knew what it was to leave her homeland. Her husband died and her mother-in-law, Naomi, wanted to return to Israel. Ruth went with Naomi and left behind Moab, the place where she grew up and where her family still lived.

In Israel Boaz spoke to Ruth. He asked God to bless her for her faithfulness to her mother-in-law and her self-sacrifice. He reminded her that as a bird gathers its chicks under her wings to protect them, Ruth was under the protection of God's wings.

When you leave behind those you love and familiar situations, remember that you can take refuge under the wings of God. Nothing will provide better shelter and comfort.

God is your refuge wherever you are.

—Maryann Breukelman

My Mother's Bible

"For the word of God is full of living power. It is sharper than the sharpest knife, cutting deep into our innermost thoughts and desires. It exposes us for what we really are."
Hebrews 4:12

After her car wreck, our mother remained in a coma. Neurologists warned she would be a "vegetable" if she lived. Eventually, she did open her eyes but remained unresponsive.

One night, I sat by her hospital bed quoting familiar Bible promises. I was quoting Romans 8:28: "We know that all things work together for good . . ." when suddenly, Mother interrupted to finish the verse: ". . . to them who love God and are called according to His purpose."

They were the first rational words she had spoken in three months! Over the coming weeks, we discovered all the verses she had memorized were still there in the scrambled corridors of her brain. Slowly but surely, she returned to us through the healing ministry of the Word. She lived another sixteen years, learning all over again to walk, to feed herself, and to read. The first book she asked for was her Bible.

The Word of God is powerful beyond human comprehension.

—KATHRYN THOMPSON PRESLEY

The Uncharted Path

"Then John's two disciples turned and
followed Jesus. Jesus looked around and saw them
following. 'What do you want?' he asked them."
John 1:37–38

I awoke one morning and realized that life had taken a new turn. While I was looking the other way, my sixty-fifth birthday had arrived. I no longer felt wise and middle-aged, I felt outdated and old. What did I want now? I had more questions than answers. Will I be incapacitated? Not needed? How will I die? I was on a strange and unmarked path.

I suspect that the disciples, when asked what they wanted, didn't know the answer to that question, either, but they wanted more. They wanted to be near Jesus, so they had to know where He was staying. They chose to follow him down an unfamiliar path.

On the uncharted path of old age, I don't know where I'm going or what lies ahead. But, like the disciples, I want to be near Jesus. If He walks the path with me, it is enough.

Stay near Jesus. His presence is sufficient.

—NANCY BAKER

Desiring His Purpose

"He fulfills the desires of those who fear him;
he hears their cries for help and rescues them."
Psalm 145:19

I was out of college, married for a few years, and a daddy to a little boy. The best jobs I could find where we lived in Ohio had nothing to do with my degree. I worked construction, janitorial, and sales but really wanted a job in publishing.

I checked the classifieds in the magazine *Christianity Today*. A Christian trade magazine in Illinois needed an editor. I had never heard of the magazine, but the job description intrigued me. I prayed, sent my resume, and they called me for an interview.

The magazine was well known in its market. I had no experience and little hope of getting the job. Still, the interview process went well. They sent me home with an assignment to write a feature for the magazine. A couple of weeks after mailing the completed article, they called me again. I was hired and began fulfilling God's call for my life.

God will enable you to fulfill His purpose for your life.

—SRC

Surface Scan

"My servant grew up in the LORD's presence like a tender green shoot, sprouting from a root in dry and sterile ground. There was nothing beautiful or majestic about his appearance, nothing to attract us to him."

Isaiah 53:2

At a garage sale, I rummaged through an assortment of gaudy jewelry, trinkets, and ornaments.

"Let's go," I said to my sister. "It's all useless junk!"

She poked around the basket, then grabbed something. "Look what I found!" she said. "An antique thimble!" In her hand was a black blob. I rolled my eyes skyward and headed for the car.

Her idea of a treasure and mine were galaxies apart.

A few weeks later, Sarah dropped by for coffee and showed me the "blob."

"It's exquisite!" I couldn't believe it was the same object. I examined the delicate engraving etched into the shimmering silver, and commended her for her find.

Simeon and Anna also recognized a treasure while worshiping at the temple in Jerusalem. Stirred by the Holy Spirit, they identified an ordinary-looking baby as the Messiah—Savior of the world. The Holy Spirit can stir our hearts to see the hidden value in people, too.

Look below the surface of those around you.

—S. (SHAE) COOKE

The Student Who Taught the Teacher

". . . and asked Jesus, 'Do you hear what these children are saying?'

'Yes,' Jesus replied. 'Haven't you ever read the Scriptures? For they say, 'You have taught children and infants to give you praise.'"

Matthew 21:16

My friend Joni had always dreamed of being a teacher and loved the idea of working with the disabled. Soon after receiving her teaching credentials, she landed a job at a school for children with Down syndrome.

One September morning she noticed seven-year-old Joseph was watching her closely. "Can I help you with something, Joseph?" she offered. Joseph looked at her with a serious expression and asked, "Do you know Jesus?"

Caught off guard, Joni smiled and answered lightly, "Oh yeah. He's a great guy, isn't he?"

Joseph cocked his head and frowned. Then he said with authority, "No, Jesus isn't a great *guy*. Jesus is the *Lord*!"

Joseph made his point!

Later, as Joni expressed the valuable lesson she learned, I found myself learning from her the beauty of humility. She was able to accept correction from this little guy!

God uses even the simplest of
vessels to remind you of valuable truths.

—CAROLYN COTÉ

Peace in a Chaotic World

"I have told you all this so that you may have peace in me. Here on earth you will have many trials and sorrows. But take heart, because I have overcome the world."

John 16:33

The war on terrorism hit close to home when Tina, one of my best friends, called to tell me that her brother had been killed.

As he sat in the cafeteria of a veteran's hospital, the news broke out that America was bombing Afghanistan. An older veteran went crazy, pulled out a gun, and shot Tina's brother.

In the aftermath, my mind and heart have been trying to process all that's happened. To be honest, some days—like today—I have more questions than answers.

But as I poured out my grief to God, one of the first verses He brought to my mind was John 16:33. As I meditated on it, I realized that Jesus says "in me" you will have peace. We cannot have peace by trusting the government to keep us secure, or by opening the mail with gloves to protect us from harmful chemicals. We'll find peace in spending time with Jesus.

In Jesus you can experience the
peace that "passes understanding" always.

—DENA DYER

The Power of ALL Has Conditions

"The righteous face many troubles,
but the LORD rescues them from each and every one."
Psalm 34:19

David begins this Psalm with a bold promise to the Lord; that he will praise Him and boast of Him at ALL times. What has caused him to make such a commitment? He tells us why.

"I prayed to the Lord, and He answered me, freeing me from ALL my (debilitating) fears. . . . I cried out to the Lord in my suffering, and He heard me. He sets me free from ALL my (debilitating) fears. . . . The Lord hears His people when they call to Him for help. He rescues them from ALL their troubles" (Psalm 34: 4,6,17).

In my periods of unemployment and financial stress there were times when I felt alone and rejected. I experienced debilitating fear at times. This psalm was powerful in my life. Call on Him and He will hear and deliver you. That is the condition for the promise to be fulfilled.

*You can be delivered from
debilitating fears if you accept the conditions.*

—KENNETH M. HANSEN

The Lines of Communication

"Seek the LORD while you can find him.
Call on him now while he is near."
Isaiah 55:6

"I really need my phone," Sally explained. She was told that it would be on by the weekend.

On the weekend she plugged in her phone but there was no dial tone. A week passed and Sally visited the phone office. "I came to check when my phone will be turned on," she explained. The clerk checked the records. "The phone was hooked up a week ago," she said.

When Sally arrived home she discovered the jack was dead, and all week long she had been connected to the wrong power source.

If we haven't heard God's voice for awhile, perhaps it's because we've been plugging into the wrong jack (such as too much TV or other distractions) and our lines of communication are dead. However, God is still there, waiting to hear and answer our prayers, but first we have to plug in to the right source.

*Turn off the TV, hyperactivity,
and other noise, and connect with God.*

—ELAINE INGALLS HOGG

A Pitcher Full

"And may you have the power to understand, as all God's people should, how wide, how long, how high, and how deep his love really is. May you experience the love of Christ, though it is so great you will never fully understand it. Then you will be filled with the fullness of life and power that comes from God."

Ephesians 3:18–19

As much as students dread the start of school, teachers also feel anxiety. I question if I will be able to be all that my students need. Even those students with the best home life are in need, yet many of my students are so broken, so desperately in need of love, and so unwilling to admit it or receive it.

The only way I can begin to meet their needs is to fill up my pitcher with living water each morning by meeting with Jesus first thing. If my pitcher is nearly empty, I have little to share, will probably be stingy with what little I do have, and will probably spend most of my time searching to fill my pitcher in other ways instead of looking to fill others. If my pitcher is overflowing, I am fully equipped, empowered, and perfectly willing to share.

You need to meet with Him daily
in order to minister to others effectively.

—MARLENE MECKENSTOCK

OCTOBER

TIME TO WALK THE DOG
—THOMAS SMITH

"A fool gives full vent to anger,
but a wise person quietly holds it back."

PROVERBS 29:11

*M*Y FATHER AND I WERE CHILLED OUT comfortably on our downstairs couch, riveted to the TV. The latest *Star Trek* episode was nearing its climax. As the show cut for a final commercial break, my father turned to me and asked if I had removed the air conditioner from my bedroom window.

Every fall I had to remove the air-conditioning unit from the window in the bedroom I shared with my brother and put it away in our storage closet.

"I'll take it out after the show is over," I replied to my dad. Unfortunately, this did not bring the closure I had expected. My father, angered that I had left this task to the final days of fall (still within the required timeline, in my mind), insisted the job be done immediately. Meaning now.

I plodded upstairs, seething with a rage mixed with adolescent hormones and self-pity. I reached the bedroom, threw back the drapes, jerked open the window. Bad move.

To my horror, the air conditioner tumbled backward out the window, end over end, and landed squarely on the roof of my father's two-day-old Buick. The whole incident took no more than a few seconds, and yet my mind saw it all unfold in horrific, agonizing slow motion. I looked down. My dad's Buick looked like it had been sledgehammered.

I went downstairs, stood by his chair, and, over the final strains of the *Star Trek* theme, said, "Dad, I just dropped the air conditioner through the roof of your car." Nothing.

Still engrossed in the TV and without looking up, he finally said, "Son, stop fooling around and put the air conditioner away."

I stepped between my dad and the TV and persisted, saying, "I'm serious, Dad. I just dropped the air conditioner through your car roof." This time, he looked up and turned off the TV.

My ashen face and sweating brow seemed to lend new credence to my words. He knew I was serious. My father got up and walked outside. I waited.

"Son," he said when he came back in, "I am going to take the dog for a walk." With that he left for what turned out to be one of the longest romps in the park our pooch ever enjoyed. The rest we'll just leave to your imagination, but know that I survived the episode, and so did my dad.

I am now a lay counselor to teens, and the father of three girls. I can see clearly the wisdom behind my dad's actions on that day. Knee-jerk reactions to bad news hardly ever lead to the kind of positive results that the rational wisdom of a measured, thoughtful response does.

God's Mammogram

"We are pressed on every side by troubles,
but we are not crushed and broken.
We are perplexed, but we don't give up and quit."
2 Corinthians 4:8

I'm standing in a dimly lit room, naked from the waist up except for a thin paper covering not made for human beings with arms. It's my annual mammogram.

The technician positions my body to hang from the cold, metal contraption; my feet are barely touching the floor. As she leaves the room she says, "Don't move. Don't breathe."

I know if I try to get away, if I move, if I even breathe, I will have to start all over again. Agony prolonged.

Spiritual lessons can be like that. Sometimes we try to get away, or move, or breathe, but if we stand firm, still, and quiet, the Holy Spirit will work in us.

We submit to physical tests for our good. We submit to spiritual tests for our good. Unlike the mammogram technician, our God stays with us. He never leaves us alone during the test.

*You can stand firm in times of
testing with the help of the Holy Spirit.*

—SHANNON RULÉ

An Opportunity

"Oh, the joys of those who are kind to the poor.
The LORD rescues them in times of trouble."
Psalm 41:1

I was griping to a friend at church about our school lunch program. When students forgot their lunch money, they weren't allowed to have IOUs. They simply went without lunch. I complained that I was often making up the difference by giving them the money. It was either that or try to teach hungry students.

Mary simply exclaimed, "What a ministry opportunity you have!"

I was taken aback. I wasn't looking at it as an opportunity at all.

When I expect others to meet the needs I see, I stop being God's hands and feet. I deny Him the opportunity to show love and grace through me. With just a few words from my friend, God took my complaint and showed me His ministry to my students.

God honors those who are generous in sharing His love.

—MARY J. BAUER

What Makes Jesus Happy?

"But when Jesus saw what was happening, he was very displeased with his disciples. He said to them, 'Let the children come to me. Don't stop them! For the Kingdom of God belongs to such as these.'"

Mark 10:14

Five-year-old Keifer walked the aisle of the small chapel; he slowly lit the candles. He stretched high on tiptoe to reach the tall tapers. Then he joined the other children waiting for the children's sermon.

"Keifer, I think it makes Jesus happy to see you light the candles," I said. He smiled shyly and lowered his eyes. The children crowded closer. Their faces were innocent, eager, and expectant, awaiting today's story.

I put on my happy-face hat. Giggles broke out. "Children make Jesus happy," I said. "He says that if we want to enter His kingdom we all have to be like little children." Their faces were radiant.

Lord, help me to be as innocent, eager, and expectant as the little children. Help me to be humble and willing to serve like little Keifer.

The qualities of childlike innocence
and humility make Jesus happy.

—SHANNON RULÉ

Obedience Is Always God's Will

"And then he told them, 'Go into all the world and
preach the Good News to everyone, everywhere.'"
Mark 16:15

Our church singles group decided to take a one-week mis-
sions trip to Mexico. I made a commitment to be included.
Then I lost my job! Despite being jobless, I knew, somehow,
I would still make the trip.

I had already paid part of the money I needed prior to the
job loss. Then, my landlords gave me some money and waived
a month's rent. And finally, our singles group pastor let me
know someone in the congregation had paid all the rest.

It was one of two trips I made to Mexico, and one of the
greatest blessings I ever received.

When the idea was first brought up, I'd asked a friend,
"Do you think it's God's will for me to go?" Her reply was
stunning: "How could it *not* be God's will?"

When it comes to sharing the Gospel, God's will isn't a
question, it's a matter of doing.

God's will is that you act on all of
His commands at every opportunity.

—SRC

A Tiny Spark

"So also, the tongue is a small thing,
but what enormous damage it can do.
A tiny spark can set a great forest on fire."
James 3:5

During Fire Prevention Week, my daughter's class took a field trip to the fire station. Firefighter Ken showed the children several seemingly innocent toys. But, with one quick flick of a button, tiny flames appeared.

Here, the fireman gave a stern warning about the danger of playing with matches or lighters, no matter how cool they seemed. "Used correctly, a lighter is a helpful tool. But be careful. It only takes one careless spark to start a big fire," he said.

A careless spark of gossip, the flash of harsh words, or an ember of angry verbal lashings can wreak an immense amount of injury on others. It can create fires in our relationships that can destroy all we've built.

However, used correctly, the tongue can help prevent those fires. Encouraging words aptly spoken and prayer are good examples of tongue fire safety.

Practice good "fire prevention"
techniques by guarding your tongue.

—LORI Z. SCOTT

His Team

"But the LORD said to Samuel, 'Don't judge by his appearance or height, for I have rejected him. The LORD doesn't make decisions the way you do! People judge by outward appearance, but the LORD looks at a person's thoughts and intentions.'"

1 Samuel 16:7

It was exciting when the University of Georgia Bulldogs donated old football uniforms to a local junior high team. But it presented the coach with a challenge. He had to match the available equipment with the sizes of the starters.

Most of the uniforms had been given out when one last boy appeared at the door. He was a small kid, and the coach felt terrible telling him nothing was left that would fit him. The boy smiled and said, "That's okay, Coach. I just want to play with the team."

I often worry about how I look, what I will wear, and what people will say. I know, deep down, that these things don't matter. I realize God is looking straight at my heart. I hope one day to say, "That's okay, Lord, I just want to play on Your team."

Outward appearance doesn't matter.
What is in the heart is what counts.

—ELAINE YOUNG MCGUIRE

The Cells at Work

"We are all parts of his one body, and each of us has different work to do. And since we are all one body in Christ, we belong to each other, and each of us needs all the others."

Romans 12:5

The cells of our body are intriguing structures. Within the nucleus of each is the complete DNA code for our entire body.

Soon after we become a fertilized egg, our multiplying cells migrate to various locations and begin to utilize specific DNA instructions in order to function. In the end, some will become lung cells, some skin cells, others kidney or liver cells and so on. When all is arranged and functioning, each cell has utilized 2 percent of the genes available within our DNA code. Cells that function outside these instructions cause disease.

Such is the exquisite beauty of Christ's body—the church. Each individual has a very unique spiritual DNA—giftings of talents, skills, experiences, and wisdom—which contributes to the proper functioning of the Body of Christ. The health of Christ's Body depends on our obedience to His plan for our life.

God has a specific call for each of His children.

—CAROLYN COTÉ

Letting Go of Guilt

"Wash me clean from my guilt. Purify me
from my sin. For I recognize my shameful
deeds—they haunt me day and night."
Psalm 51:2–3

David, we are told, was a man after God's own heart. Still he had trouble seeing the depth of his sin of adultery and murder, and the damage he had caused to his relationship with God, until Nathan confronted him.

David's first request of God was for "mercy," appealing to God's compassion. His second request was for God to "blot out the stain of my sin."

David's third request was the one we all deal with the longest and which the Enemy uses most against us. "Wash me clean from ALL my guilt." David was haunted "day and night," riddled with guilt.

Until we are rid of sin's guilt we cannot have the "joy of salvation." We have a harder time forgiving ourselves than God does. And hell's imps love to pile on the guilt.

We need the Comforter and Counselor, the Cleaner of hearts. Is your conscience clean? Do you sleep well at night? The Lord can restore your joy!

*Guilt is one area from which you can't lift yourself
by your own efforts. You need the blood of Jesus.*

—KENNETH M. HANSEN

God's Unfailing Love

"Show us your unfailing love,
O LORD, and grant us your salvation."
Psalm 85:7

It seems God's response comes right after we've reached the end of ourselves and things can't get much worse. I had reached that moment the day I found an eviction notice on our doorstep.

"Lord!" I anguished. "We need $1,000 in two days or we're homeless! You said you would never leave us or forsake us—are you going to take care of us?" At this point, I could pray no longer and sobbed, "Lord, just show us you love us!"

That evening, while my family was getting ready for bed, a friend from our home Bible study group knocked at our door. "My wife and I were praying tonight and feel the Lord wants us to give you this," he said as he handed us a check for $1,000!

Before leaving he added, "Oh, and the Lord told me something else. He said, 'Tell them I love them.'"

God demonstrates His love when you need it most.

—CHERYL KNIGHT

Check for Messages

"Yet faith comes from listening to this message
of good news—the Good News about Christ."
Romans 10:17

When I heard the news of the terrorist attacks on September 11, I panicked. My husband was in Washington at the time and I hadn't heard from him.

Worry tortured me. Was he okay? What if he wasn't?

Hours later, it occurred to me to check the answering machine for phone messages. I nearly collapsed in relief when I heard his voice. My husband had called immediately after the Pentagon was hit. He left a recorded message letting me know he was okay. His assuring words were right under my nose the whole time. I should've checked the machine first and saved myself a day of tears and anxiety.

My actions during this tragic event mirror the way we often approach everyday crises. We anguish over the what-ifs and surrender to fear instead of looking to God's Word for answers. The Bible clearly presents assurances with messages recorded for our benefit.

God's Word is true, and His promises faithful.

—LORI Z. SCOTT

Good Versus Evil

"Don't let evil get the best of you,
but conquer evil by doing good."
Romans 12:21

"Two wrongs don't make a right," my best friend scolded.

We were in second grade walking home from school and she had hit me with her backpack. So, being the typical eight-year-old, I took my backpack and struck her back.

No way was I going to let her get away with hitting me.

When someone hurts us, it's sometimes easier for us to retaliate than it is to shrug it off or return with a good deed. As Jesus tells us, we are to "turn the other cheek" when someone does us wrong. If only it were that simple. With Christ, it is.

If we have the joy of the Lord in our lives, not only will it be easy for us to turn the other cheek, but we will want to do something good for the person who hit us. We might just be the only example of Christ that person will see.

"Retaliate" with love, patience, and kindness.

—STORMY NIEVES

Worthy in His Sight

"And I have put my words in your mouth and hidden you safely within my hand. I set all the stars in space and established the earth. I am the one who says to Israel, 'You are mine!'"

Isaiah 51:16

Someone called me "loyal" today, and, I have to admit, I like that. I like to be thought of as someone who can be counted on for the long haul. Many of the things others call us aren't nearly as nice.

What does God call His children? In Matthew 5:13 He calls us "the salt of the earth." He calls us "valuable" in Matthew 6:26, and in 1 Peter 2:9 we are "a chosen people."

It sounds as if our Heavenly Father holds us in very high esteem. It also sounds like our worth comes from Him and not from man. It is from God alone and not from our works, our position, our wealth, or our personalities. There is nothing we can do to be worthy in His sight. He has done it all.

God holds all in high regard.

—LINDA ROBERTS

A Son's Compassion

"The LORD is good to everyone.
He showers compassion on all his creation."
Psalm 145:9

The woman sat there unconcerned that she had spit up a chocolate milk shake all over herself. Aging had reverted her mental capacity to that of a child. She couldn't understand why the milk shake was taken away from her. She reached out angrily, wanting it back.

The one who took it was her son, who now was busily cleaning her up. He was talking to her in a quiet, gentle voice, reassuring her that her milk shake would be returned to her soon. He was oblivious to the people around him in the restaurant. He had only loving and compassionate eyes for his mother, who now needed his care as he had once needed hers.

God has shown us the ultimate example of His love and grace. Because of that love, we are able to reach out to those around us and share that gift of compassion. God has given us all that gift.

God shares His compassion through you,
so that you may be witnesses of His love.

—JAY D. ROHMAN

The Worry Exchange

"Don't worry about anything; instead, pray about everything. Tell God what you need, and thank him for all he has done. If you do this, you will experience God's peace, which is far more wonderful than the human mind can understand. His peace will guard your hearts and minds as you live in Christ Jesus."

Philippians 4:6–7

I tossed the wet clothes in the dryer. I hope it starts, I thought as I slammed the door. We'd bought the worn dryer a few months before and we couldn't afford to buy a new one. I pressed the button and it rumbled reassuringly. As I picked up the empty laundry basket and headed for the basement stairs I realized that I worried about the dryer working every time I did a load of laundry.

I paused with my foot on the first step. "Lord," I prayed, "I'm so tired of worrying about that dryer. You provided it for us. If it breaks, I trust You to provide a repair or another one." Relieved, I went upstairs.

We never had any trouble with that dryer. In fact, we gave it to the man who delivered our brand-new dryer six years later.

Exchange your worries for God's peace.

—SARA ROSETT

Feeling Faint

"He gives power to those who are tired and worn out;
he offers strength to the weak."
Isaiah 40:29

"I'm going to faint. I'm going now. . . ." my daughter wisely informed me. We were in the elevator, leaving the doctor's office. At Samantha's twelve-year well check, she'd been given a tetanus shot. Shots terrify her.

My child was right. She passed out in the elevator. Due to her warning, I was holding her. Together, we crumpled down to the floor. She fainted but she wasn't hurt since I was supporting her.

This has caused me to think of my relationship with the Lord. There are times I may be overwhelmed, but the Creator of the Universe offers me strength. If I wisely let Him in on the details of my life, He will be there to support me when I feel faint and weary. He will hold me in His strong arms just as I held my daughter in mine.

In your weakness, God is strong.

—LORI WILDENBERG

Soaring Moments

"He fills my life with good things.
My youth is renewed like the eagle's!"
Psalm 103:5

A seagull-like bird, a shearwater, leaves its nest as a fledgling and does not set foot on land again until it reaches maturity three or four years later.

In its yearly migration, a hummingbird flies from the Yucatan Peninsula in Mexico at night, straight across the Gulf of Mexico, more than 600 miles over water, to South Texas.

The same God who fashioned these tiny feathered dynamos promises to renew our strength and give us energy. Even when we are middle aged, we will have playbacks of earlier days, bursts of good things, good energy—only this time, we will be equipped with wisdom.

When I was a child, I used to wonder what older folks meant when they said, "I just don't have the energy!" That was because I was a youth and an eagle. My flights are shorter now, and not as high, but God still grants me soaring moments—if I lift my wings and trust.

God will renew you all through your life.

—JAN SEALE

It's My Pleasure

"So you should not be like cowering, fearful slaves. You should behave instead like God's very own children, adopted into his family—calling him 'Father, dear Father.'"

Romans 8:15

When Michael and his brother were young, their mother remarried. A family of three quickly doubled in number! The new father in their life took great pleasure in adopting the boys and giving them his last name. That adoption changed Michael's life forever.

Chosen. Adopted. To be loved, cherished, encouraged, protected. Put apart from the past and entering a new future, belonging to a new family.

Michael is an adult now and the man he calls "Pop" is as surely his father as if he had been a part of the original birth process. The bond between them is strong and certain.

Six years ago Michael reclaimed his adoption from another Father who loves him no less intensely than this earthly man. Chosen by God, adopted into His family, to be loved and protected, encouraged and cherished. A new birth and a new life. God's unchanging plan. And God smiled.

God's goal has always been to
bring you into relationship with Him.

—ANNA SEDEN

An Eye for Quality

"Then the angel of the LORD came and sat beneath the oak tree at Ophrah, which belonged to Joash of the clan of Abiezer. Gideon son of Joash had been threshing wheat at the bottom of a winepress to hide the grain from the Midianites. The angel of the LORD appeared to him and said, 'Mighty hero, the LORD is with you!'"

Judges 6:11–12

I love snooping in pawn shops. On one occasion I found a sad-looking guitar plastered with ugly stickers and sporting a single rusty string. I'm a guitar player with an eye for quality, and I recognized this as a hidden gem for a mere thirty dollars. It took me a month of weekends to clean up my bargain, repair the broken parts, and restring my new toy.

Now this guitar absolutely sings when I play it. It's the envy of my musician buddies who all own much more expensive instruments!

I love the story of Gideon—the youngest and least-significant son of a large family, yet God saw much value within this man.

I may not always feel or act like a "mighty man of God," but I am humbled by the fact that when God looks at me through Christ's eyes, He sees much value, too!

God looks beyond your shortcomings,
your flaws, and your failures.

—THOMAS SMITH

333

Invisible God

"It was by faith that Moses left the land of Egypt.
He was not afraid of the king. Moses kept right on going
because he kept his eyes on the one who is invisible."
Hebrews 11:27

I used to write secret messages to my friends with invisible ink. The lemon juice ink vanished as the paper soaked up its essence. The process was somewhat frustrating because I often forgot what I had already written since I couldn't see it. However, I continued to write because I knew the unseen letters existed, no matter how garbled my note. Eventually, exposure to a heat source, like a lightbulb, brought the hidden words to life.

There are times when God seems like invisible ink. We forget to keep our eyes on Him because we cannot see Him. Sometimes it isn't until we're under a heat source, like stress or fatigue, that his words of wisdom and comfort become clear.

Like Moses, we can keep right on going because we know God exists and that He has our best interests at heart.

God makes His invisible presence known to you.

—LORI Z. SCOTT

Following God's Plans

"'For I know the plans I have for you,'
says the LORD. 'They are plans for good and
not for disaster, to give you a future and a hope.'"
Jeremiah 29:11

Did you know God is a matchmaker?

We both worked for a Christian organization. We felt drawn to pray together for the people who came for help. We began daily devotions together before and after work. One evening, God gave us Jeremiah 29:11 as our very own. We were excited to know that God really wanted us to lean on Him and that He had great plans for us—together!

We were obedient and saw God's plan unfold. We married and left our jobs and the security of "stable employment." Following God's guidance, we started our own businesses.

One year later, we are totally dependent on His provision and He has truly given us "a future and a hope." We are able to share food, prayer, hugs, and more with others in need. And our needs are met daily.

God has plans for you. If you allow, He will direct your days into blessings!

*Releasing your entire way of life into
God's hands enables Him to bless you daily.*

—JACK AND PAM GIBBONS

Wordless Journeys

"Teach them to your children. Talk about them when you
are at home and when you are away on a journey, when
you are lying down and when you are getting up again."

Deuteronomy 11:19

"I want to collect something. Everybody gets to collect something except me." Her little voice sounded indignant as we walked along past the freshly fallen autumn leaves. "My sisters have books and dolls and I have nothing." She bent and picked up a bright red maple leaf. "I think I'll collect leaves and put them in a book. I can't read but I can look at them and remember our walk today. I won't even need words."

"Honey, everyone needs words. One day, you'll learn how to read." How would I convince my five-year-old otherwise? We walked in silence for some time. I was taking in the scenery and she was collecting her leaves. I drew in a deep breath and said, "I love you. What picture would you paint that could replace those three little words?" She answered, "I would paint a picture of God. You say that God is love and He loves me."

She was right. Sometimes we don't need words because we can experience God's love in our hearts.

You can both teach and learn from children.

—MICHELE STARKEY

The Chance to Grow

"We can rejoice, too, when we run into problems and trials, for we know that they are good for us—they help us learn to endure. And endurance develops strength of character in us, and character strengthens our confident expectation of salvation."

Romans 5:3–4

I always won the 100- and 200-meter races at school. But anything longer and I was more likely to come in last. Not because I couldn't run, because I would never really try. I'd run 300 meters, feel the first hint of tiredness, and stop running. I'd just wander off the track and sit down.

The day the coach asked for cross-country runners, I suddenly felt compelled to enter. "It's three miles," he warned me.

"I can do it," I said.

I started the run and when I felt the first hint of tiredness, I kept going. I finished the race, coming in second. I hadn't won but I felt better than ever. That's when I finally got it. I'd endured. And I was a stronger person for it.

I think life has to challenge us sometimes, just so we get the chance to go the full distance.

*Every challenge life throws at
you is a chance to endure and grow.*

—SHELLEY WAKE

Stand Up, Stand Up for Jesus

"Oh, the joys of those who do not follow the advice of the wicked, or stand around with sinners, or join in with scoffers. But they delight in doing everything the LORD wants; day and night they think about His law."

Psalm 1:1–2

My son Barrett was six years old when he had his first experience with shoplifting. He and a classmate went to a store for candy one day after school. His friend stole a toy, and on the way home, gave it to Barrett.

The excursion took much longer than it should have. When he finally got home, I asked what had happened. His story brought tears to my eyes. Barrett had gone back to the store, returned the toy, and apologized. He told me he knew God saw what happened and it was wrong.

Ten years later I'm still marveling as I watch my son growing into a godly young man who loves the Lord with all his heart. Truly, a life of righteousness brings joy and beauty to everyone it touches.

Training children in godly ways reaps eternal rewards.

—RACHEL WALLACE-OBERLE

Green-Eyed Monster

"Do your part to live in peace
with everyone, as much as possible."
Romans 12:18

Two people (or two countries) find it hard to live peacefully together when one wants something the other has. Think of wars that started as fights over land, or siblings who argue about possessions. We don't usually make the effort to be nice to someone when we're jealous of them. But maybe we should.

I met Marilyn when we competed against each other for a part in a play. I won the part and Marilyn was cast in a smaller role. I figured she wouldn't want to talk to me anymore. Instead, she marched right up to me at the first rehearsal and offered congratulations. She was smiling, genuinely happy for me. She ignored any jealousy she might have felt and reached out to me. And we both won, becoming friends.

Just think how many friends we could make if, instead of envying people, we reached out to them instead!

Reaching out to others instead of
envying them is a first step toward peace.

—KIM SHEARD

A Moving Experience

"But when you ask him, be sure that you really expect him to answer, for a doubtful mind is as unsettled as a wave of the sea that is driven and tossed by the wind."

James 1:6

What is God's will? Does He want us to move?

"Go out there and see if God speaks to you," my pastor advised. Reluctantly, I did. We had already relocated twice. I had stopped praying even though another move was in the works.

A friend told me she was praying for me to find a new home. "Quit praying that prayer!" I commanded. "My mission's to see if I can hear God's voice." I couldn't picture my family in any of the locations the real estate agent and I had visited. Our final destination was a newly developed neighborhood. I stopped in my tracks. The home I had in my mind's eye was right in front of me. "Move" was the answer to the prayer I had been praying all along.

Change is unsettling. But it allows us to see God's hand and to be dependent upon Him. He has our best interest at heart.

Trust in the Lord. Listen to His voice.

—LORI WILDENBERG

The Couple Dressed in Black

"Don't be concerned about the outward
beauty that depends on fancy hairstyles,
expensive jewelry, or beautiful clothes."
1 Peter 3:3

"That couple over there, are they in the wrong funeral parlor?" people began to whisper to one another, and they nodded over their shoulders at the young people in the black leather jackets behind them.

"They have their own rock band," another explained.

Eventually the crowd thinned. The son of the deceased woman crossed the room and moved in their direction, not knowing what to say but sensing he should say something by way of greeting. He offered his hand and said, "Thanks for coming."

"Oh, you're welcome. We wanted to come. You see, she always visited my mother when she was sick and she always brought us our own batch of shortbread and cookies. No one had ever done that for us before. Imagine it, a sweet little old lady baking us cookies. We will never forget her."

The widow, my mother-in-law, had not judged others by appearance. Instead she spent her senior years showing God's love by baking cookies for others.

Look for the good God sees in others.

—ELAINE INGALLS HOGG

The Complete Christian Warrior

"Use every piece of God's armor to resist
the enemy in time of evil, so that after
the battle you will still be standing firm."
Ephesians 6:13

You've finally done it! You've got it all on: the belt of truth, the armor of righteousness, the shoes of peace, the shield of faith, and the sword of the Spirit.

How do you look? Medieval pictures of the Christian warrior show a knight in full battle dress. You'd probably look more like a member of the local SWAT team in a painting.

God wants everyone to be saved. He knows our strengths and our weaknesses. He doesn't throw us out to battle the Evil One in an unfair fight. He has given us all the equipment we need.

The battle is already raging. Put on your armor, Christian warrior, and step into the fray!

God's armor helps you withstand
the assaults of the Evil One.

—MERRY E. VARGO

Statue of Liberty

"God alone made it possible for you to be in Christ Jesus. For our benefit God made Christ to be wisdom itself. He is the one who made us acceptable to God. He made us pure and holy, and he gave himself to purchase our freedom."

1 Corinthians 1:30

"On October 28, 1886, the people of New York had a parade to welcome her," I read out loud to my daughter, Meghan, from the fact book about the Statue of Liberty she had purchased. Then I added, "The Statue of Liberty is a symbol of freedom, but the Cross was the first and best symbol of freedom."

"What's a symbol?" Meghan asked.

"A symbol is a picture helping you remember something, like pictures outside bathroom doors," I said. "So the cross . . . well, do you know why Jesus died for us?"

"To save us from our sins."

"That's why, for people who believe in Jesus, the cross is a symbol of freedom."

"So Jesus is a Statue of Liberty?" Meghan inquired.

"Close enough," I laughed. How blessed we are today with forgiveness and freedom from sin. Let's have a parade!

Celebrate the freedom purchased for you on the cross.

—LORI Z. SCOTT

The Big Picture

"The heavens tell of the glory of God.
The skies display his marvelous craftsmanship."
Psalm 19:1

English astronomer Edmond Halley, born October 29, 1656, saw a huge comet in 1682 and proved that it was the same comet seen over England in 1531 and 1607. He predicted it would return in seventy-six years—and it did.

The strange brilliance of comets has always touched us with awe. They travel at speeds up to 140,000 mph. The same force that moves this star provides a tiny seed with the ability to develop into a beautiful flower. From the tiniest molecule to the largest galaxy, God's awesome creation is filled with beauty, order, and design. Truly, the wonders of the heavens are marvelous—and though we may not understand why things, like comets, are the way they are, we know they serve a plan in ways known to Him.

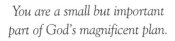

*You are a small but important
part of God's magnificent plan.*

—S. (SHAE) COOKE

Visitations

"One of the things I always pray for is the opportunity, God willing, to come at last to see you. I'm eager to encourage you in your faith, but I also want to be encouraged by yours. In this way, each of us will be a blessing to the other."

Romans 1:10, 12

We need each other.

Every encounter with a friend is an opportunity to be blessed and be a blessing. Being visited by friends is a validation. The very act of them coming to see you speaks of their love and care for you. When they come seeking comfort, it's an opportunity to reflect love and care back to them.

From time to time, a friend who lived out of town would ask to spend the night. He sometimes had very early meetings following a late night of work. But it made no difference how late he arrived, we always spent two to three hours talking. One of us was always in need of a little encouragement.

Each visit yielded new spiritual strength and refreshed faith. Yet, all that was taking place was two friends talking about ordinary life stuff. Those late hours of sharing are priceless treasures in my bank of memories.

Every encounter is an opportunity
to be encouraged and to offer encouragement.

—SRC

Carving Pumpkins

"The LORD is good. When trouble comes, he is a strong
refuge. And he knows everyone who trusts in him."
Nahum 1:7

Ellie labored over the pattern, putting the finishing touches
on her cat pumpkin carving. She set the pumpkin on the
floor and walked away, forgetting to keep an eye on her
puppy, distracted by something else. The carving lost its
head to a puppy attack.

She looked to me to wipe the tears and fix the mess.
Onto a small leftover pumpkin, I traced the pattern of the
cat's head and carved a new head. Toothpicks were used to
suture the new head to the original carving.

I also get busy and distracted, forgetting to take heed of
things that are greater priorities for my time and thoughts.
Fortunately, my Father in heaven is there to pick up the
pieces and carve out new beginnings after I mess up, and I
start anew.

God can forgive your mistakes and help you start fresh.

—AMY CARR

NOVEMBER

THANKFUL FOR HIS CARE
—ELAINE YOUNG MCGUIRE

"The LORD keeps watch over you as
you come and go, both now and forever."

PSALM 121:8

$\mathcal{A}$ SIMPLE BUT BEAUTIFUL CHRISTMAS-SEASON wedding had been planned, for December 13, 1941, between a young woman, my mother, and her PFC (private first class) boyfriend, my dad. Mom would wear a lovely blue velvet dress made by her mother, and would descend the winding front stairway of their white antebellum home, near Nashville, Tennessee. There would be a wedding cake and flowers and candles and many family members and friends there to celebrate the union that would be performed by the family's local preacher. There would be photographs of the wedding to linger over later as the special day was recalled.

But the declaration of war, on December 8, 1941, the day after Pearl Harbor, changed everything. Daddy was stationed at Fort Oglethorpe, Georgia, just over the border from Chattanooga. Soon, his call came. All leave was canceled.

Mom dissolved into frantic prayers and tears, with the unspoken fear that she might never see her soldier again. He could be killed before there could be a wedding. Rumors ran rampant, with all uniformed personnel believing they would be shipped out immediately. The young couple, still reeling from the news, was more focused on the state of their own affairs than on the state of the world.

Mom sobbed all that day and into the late evening hours before another call came. Under the circumstances, maybe, just maybe, he could get a few hours' leave, if he informed the base of his whereabouts and if he could return quickly when called. "Can you come here?" he asked. *Could* she? She quickly packed the blue velvet dress and headed into the darkness for the four-hour drive to her brother's home in Chattanooga.

She spent the rest of that night, and the next day, in tears, but finally, in the late afternoon, the good news came. Leave was granted. My parents raced to the courthouse just as it was closing for the day. A kindly judge let them in and granted a marriage license even though Mom was six months under the legal age of consent and a parent wasn't present to sign the required documents.

That night they were married by a stranger, my mother looking radiant, if a bit red-eyed, in her blue velvet dress, with no flowers or candles adorning the simple living room, and with no photographer to record the affair. The nine guests who were present listened to my parents pledge to one another the vows that would last through decades, and then they all shared my aunt's Christmas fruitcake.

My uncle drove them to a tiny motel on Signal Mountain, where they spent their wedding night. The next morning, having to check out early, they went to the elegant Reed House for breakfast and then to see the movie *Sergeant York*. That afternoon, it was time for Daddy to kiss his bride of twenty hours goodbye and to return to base, while she returned home alone. And the war went on and on and on. But eventually, Daddy came home, and a few years later, I came along. Some forty years after that rushed December wedding, Daddy passed away.

I've never spent too much time worrying about wars, even with a son serving on the front lines of Desert Storm, even with the current War on Terror filling the news. Worrying does no good, because I can't physically do a thing to change or stop it. I can only pray. I remember that the Bible says there will always be wars and rumors of wars. I know that God, alone, is in control, because Scripture says, "He raises up nations, and he destroys them. He makes nations expand, and he abandons them" (Job 12:23, New Living Translation).

I know that failing to have a picture-perfect wedding day pales in comparison to losing a child, because I've experienced the loss of a son. On each December 7, I remember and mourn the losses of the families of two nations on that fateful day in 1941. Even though I don't entirely understand, I believe that God allowed all those events for His plans and purposes and for the ultimate good.

As each December 9 arrives, I remember and experience great comfort in the sure knowledge that God not only cares about the affairs of nations, but He knows and loves us individually as well. I read, in Matthew 10:29–31 that, "Not even a sparrow . . . can fall to the ground without your Father knowing it. . . . So don't be afraid; you are more valuable to him than a whole flock of sparrows." I know, without a doubt, He cared for two "sparrows," young lovebirds, during those days of December long ago. With joy and assurance I know He cares for me, too, and for that I am truly thankful.

Excuses

"But Moses again pleaded,
'LORD, please! Send someone else.'"
Exodus 4:13

Moses tried every excuse he could think of to avoid going to Egypt when God told him to. He said he wasn't famous enough, that the people wouldn't believe him, and that he couldn't speak well enough. But God addressed his excuses and gave him detailed instructions, the ability to perform miracles, and the company of his brother on his mission. That mission succeeded.

What excuses do you use when God asks you to do something, like tell a friend about your faith or pray in public? Do you claim that you're not smart enough to explain it well or think that people will laugh at you?

Next time, counter those excuses by remembering that God helped Moses to do what He asked of him. He will give you the help you need, too.

*No matter what your excuses,
God will assist you in doing what He asks.*

—KIM SHEARD

Good News Brings Good Health

"A cheerful look brings joy to the heart;
good news makes for good health."
Proverbs 15:30

Among the items I keep on my desk, one is special. It is a piece of my skull. I had an accident several years ago that fractured my skull and caused blood clots on my brain. A neurosurgeon had to open my head to stop the bleeding. He replaced the bone he removed, stitched me up, and sent me home.

Over the next three years that piece of my skull began to disintegrate and a noticeable indention formed. I had to go back to surgery to have that piece replaced by an acrylic prosthesis. Just before going to surgery, I asked the doctor to keep the piece he removed for me.

That thin piece of bone—about the size of a half-dollar—now sits in a plastic specimen jar on my desk. It is a great reminder of my gratitude for being alive. The accident could have killed me but I feel that God brought me through that ordeal. I am alive and well and living the Good News.

The Good News of God's Word will bring you health.

—DON M. AYCOCK

God's Generous Grace

"For the grace of God has been revealed,
bringing salvation to all people."
Titus 2:11

"Don't make me come back there!"

When we heard these words from the front seat of our car, my sister and I froze. Suddenly, we were the perfect little lady and gentleman, sitting up straight, our hands folded in our laps, and our faces looking as angelic as possible.

Only moments before we had been thoroughly engaged in mutual torment. This usually culminated with me putting my back to the door and, using my long legs, pushing my sister onto "her side" by pushing her against her door. She would then loudly complain, "Dad! Make him stop squishing me!" And that would be the last straw.

Fortunately, being relatively smart children, we never pushed things to the point of finding out what would happen if Dad actually did "come back there." By stopping our shenanigans instantly we received his grace, time after time.

Our Heavenly Father extends even greater grace toward us and our sinfulness.

God's grace is always available to those who seek Him.

—SRC

The Problem Poplar Tree

"'My thoughts are completely different
from yours,' says the LORD. 'And my ways
are far beyond anything you could imagine.'"
Isaiah 55:8

One bright November day I watched through our picture window as our troublesome poplar tree was cut down and arranged into neat stacks of firewood. The stump was then burned until all that remained was a black hole. We hoped that the cracked pavement and clogged plumbing would become distant memories.

That winter, the tree became a symbol of my own problems. I prayed, "You see the havoc that problem is causing in my life, Lord. Just get out your chain saw and get rid of it. It would be such an easy task for you!" I was young in my faith and in the ways of trees.

Spring soon arrived as expected but with something very unexpected—hundreds of baby poplar trees growing where the one had been. The Lord spoke to my heart: "It's the roots that give life to the tree, my daughter. I remove the tree's roots first. My ways are not your ways."

God's ways are not your ways.

—CAROLYN COTÉ

Alone, but Filled with Hope

"Yet I am confident that I will see the LORD's
goodness while I am here in the land of the living."
Psalm 27:13

In Psalm 27, David begins by affirming his relationship to
the Lord: "He is my light . . . my salvation . . . my hiding
place." He is alone, without family, and with enemies
seeking his life.

When I was terminated from a position after years of
faithful service, there was a deep sense of despair and loneliness. Like David I whispered, "Do not hide yourself from me.
Do not reject your servant in anger. Don't leave me now . . .
don't abandon me." It was in a time like this, which you may
be experiencing, that David believed that he would "see the
Lord's goodness while I am here in the land of the living."

A hope in heaven's later judgment was not enough for
him. He would have given up on life had he not believed
that God would bless him sooner rather than later. Believe
His deliverance is on the way.

*Your hope needs to be not just in heaven
but in seeing God's goodness in this life.*

—KENNETH M. HANSEN

Her Father's Eyes

"So God created people in his own image; God patterned them after himself; male and female he created them."
Genesis 1:27

I assigned myself the gigantic task of sorting through my life-time collection of pictures, in order to pare down the collection to a reasonable size. The volumes were neatly stacked along one shelf in a large closet, and when this space was overgrown, I'd started to fill boxes. I put the "keepers" in one pile, but if I didn't recognize the people in the pictures, I threw them out.

One picture in particular puzzled me. It was the picture of a lovely baby about six months old. Studying what the baby was wearing was of no help. I started thinking of my friends who had babies in that particular year. In the end, the baby's eyes gave me the clue that allowed me to identify the child. The baby girl had her father's eyes!

This sorting process caused me to ponder about the characteristics others see when they are looking at us. It left me wondering if our neighbors and friends see a resemblance to our Creator when they look at us. Do we look like our Heavenly Father? Does our countenance reflect the image of His holiness?

Do you have your Father's eyes?

—ELAINE INGALLS HOGG

Why Should I Say Thanks?

"And you will always give thanks for everything to God
the Father in the name of our LORD Jesus Christ."
Ephesians 5:20

I crept out of bed, careful not to disturb my sleeping husband. Tonight I had some heavy praying to do. Our daughter was struggling with an eating disorder. Two close friends had a sixteen-year-old daughter, pregnant and unmarried. Another pair of friends had a son in prison.

Kneeling in the living room, I began, "Lord, please help." But in my spirit I sensed the need to thank God, not petition Him.

"For what?" I wondered. Then I bowed my head and prayed, "Thank You that You are greater than any eating disorder." I continued to thank God through the rest of my prayer time.

Now when burdens press heavy, before I petition, I give thanks. In so doing, I change my focus from the problem to my sufficient Provider.

Expressing thanks to God for difficult circumstances lifts your eyes above the situation to your faithful, all-powerful God.

—JEWELL JOHNSON

The Things We Try

"O LORD, I will honor and praise your name, for you are my God. You do such wonderful things! You planned them long ago, and now you have accomplished them."

Isaiah 25:1

My husband was always very careful in our family planning and was not yet prepared for children. "I don't know why you're so concerned," I chided. "You heard the doctor. I'm clinically infertile. I can't get pregnant!"

I had just been to one of the area's leading infertility specialists. He confirmed our worst fears. "It will be difficult, if not impossible, for you to get pregnant," he said, "but there are things you can try." Invasive, expensive, and heart-breaking things. We had seen three couples who were very close to us go through this. It was devastating. We weren't ready to go through it ourselves.

Shortly thereafter, my husband got laid off from work and we put our plans for a family on hold. The timing wasn't good. Apparently, God disagreed and surprised us with a pregnancy anyway. How much better though was His plan than ours! Today, we have our miracle baby son, a true reflection of God's perfect glory.

God's timing for His blessings is always perfect.

—STEPHANIE KANAK

Mt. Rainier

"God is our refuge and strength,
always ready to help in times of trouble."
Psalm 46:1

Five years ago, my family was transferred from California to Kent, Washington, a suburb of Seattle. On an overcast November day as we brought in the last piece of furniture from the moving van, the rain started. It was either overcast or rainy for three months solid.

One day, the clouds parted briefly just as I looked out an upstairs window. I gasped out loud when I saw the most awesome view I had ever seen—snow-capped Mt. Rainier. I was amazed that for three months I had not realized it was even there.

Each time Mt. Rainier makes an appearance, it seems more beautiful and more immense than before and I am reminded of God. When my days are cloudy, directionless, or filled with stress, God is ever present and powerful—even when I don't see Him.

God is always there, even when you don't feel His presence.

—CHERYL KNIGHT

God's Security System

"In every battle you will need faith as your shield
to stop the fiery arrows aimed at you by Satan."
Ephesians 6:16

We have burglar-alarm systems and smoke alarms. We rust-proof our cars, childproof our homes, and waterproof our shoes. We wear insect repellent to protect ourselves from mosquitoes, and sunscreen to shield us from solar rays.

Those things are all fine to protect the body, but what are we going to use to protect our soul?

Because God loves us so much, He has given us the ultimate security system—the shield of faith. It keeps evil from getting to us—even the biggest temptations!

You wouldn't forget your deodorant when you get dressed. Don't forget your shield of faith, either. Think of it as your "anti-evil stick"!

Your faith will protect you in
your contests with the powers of evil.

—MERRY E. VARGO

Seize the Day

*"I have fought a good fight, I have finished the race,
and I have remained faithful."*
2 Timothy 4:7

My husband's duty in military service took us all over the country. We moved nine times in seven years. Each assignment had challenges and rewards. In every case we knew our time was temporary. We had to make the most of each opportunity.

For the last twenty-four years we have lived in one place, but we still get "orders." Our Heavenly Father stations us for a season in different service areas—at work, at church, in the community—then moves one or both of us to our next assignment. To be chosen for service is an honor; to fulfill it is a blessing.

Now we may not know our departure date, but we do know all duty is temporary. We will be relieved. On that day, we want to be able to report with Paul that our mission has been accomplished.

Your duty to God never ends.

—MARCIA SWEARINGEN

The Scent of Humility

"So he got up from the table, took off his robe, wrapped a towel around his waist, and poured water into a basin. Then he began to wash the disciples' feet and to wipe them with the towel he had around him."

John 13:4–5

I couldn't smell the stew for some other odor that pervaded the room. I had volunteered with my church to work at a winter shelter for homeless men.

We prepared dinner, as well as sack meals for the next day. Then we drove an hour, in the rain, in rush-hour traffic, to the mission in the heart of Atlanta.

The men waited patiently until we checked them in. I was amazed at how "normal" they seemed. Their prayers were simple, but eloquent, and their conversation lively.

We put away tables and brought out cots. I was feeling pretty good about my night of service, despite my discomfort with the offensive odor.

Then I saw them, three doctors, tenderly washing festering sores—the source of the odor—on the men's feet before they began to treat them. That night I saw the Great Physician and knew that the smell filling the room was the sweet scent of humility.

Be humble as Christ was humble.

—ELAINE YOUNG MCGUIRE

Superficial Wounds . . . Deep Scars

"Gentle words bring life and health;
a deceitful tongue crushes the spirit."
Proverbs 15:4

"Mom!" yelled my six-year-old son. "The paper cut me, get a bandage—quick . . . it stings!" I surveyed the finger but all I saw was a tiny cut. His pain seemed out of proportion to the injury.

"Owwwwwwies, make the hurt stop, Mommy!" I washed his hand under cold water, gave it the mandatory mommy kiss, and dried his tears.

Shallow paper cuts on fingers often hurt worse than deeper ones because the hand has numerous nerve endings close to the skin's surface. Small, thoughtless remarks are just like paper cuts. Although they may seem superficial, they can cause much pain, especially to children and loved ones who trust us to be kind. Words are powerful. They can either cut like a sharp razor or act as a salve to a wounded spirit.

We have to put our brains and hearts in gear before putting our tongues in action. The wrong words produce deep scars—kind ones heal and encourage.

Kind words heal and encourage.

—S. (SHAE) COOKE

Treasures in the Rain

"What is faith? It is the confident assurance
that what we hope for is going to happen.
It is the evidence of things we cannot yet see."
Hebrews 11:1

A friend of mine who has battled cancer is asked from time to time what the experience was like. She loves the Lord devotedly, and answers that although it was extremely difficult, it was beautiful.

It's a response that puzzles some, but I know what she means. She laid all her broken pieces at His feet and beneath His tender touch a new vessel emerged. He shaped the old into the new, and although the pieces may be arranged a little differently than before, He fashioned something lovely out of anguish and agony.

I see joy and peace shining in my friend's face. She is uncertain of her health, but she is sure of the love of her Heavenly Father. Often this precious place can only be reached through suffering.

Suffering can teach you to fully trust in God's faithfulness.

—RACHEL WALLACE-OBERLE

Every Pattern and Color

"If you look for me in earnest,
you will find me when you seek me."
Jeremiah 29:13

My grandmother had a pincushion made of twelve stars intricately joined to each other to form a type of pointed ball. Each point of the stars was covered in a different fabric, sixty different fabrics in all. We spent hours taking turns hiding a pin somewhere in the pincushion, then searching every pattern, color, and fold for the tiny silvery head. So difficult to find, yet when finally located, always surprising that the discovery took so long, for it now seemed so obvious.

God bids us to seek Him with all that we have. If we truly look for Him in our lives, we will eventually begin to see Him in every pattern, every color, and every corner, always guiding, directing, willing to make His presence known to us. When we finally perceive His work and presence in our lives, we ask ourselves, "Why didn't I recognize Him sooner?"

If you look you will see He is always at work in your life.

—MARLENE MECKENSTOCK

Saying Grace

"And let the peace that comes from Christ rule
in your hearts. For as members of one body you are
all called to live in peace. And always be thankful."
Colossians 3:15

I have two close friends who were both in accidents that left
them permanently disabled. They became acquainted with
each other in the hospital where their paths crossed and
they've kept in touch. They jokingly refer to me as their
"common denominator."

I've listened as they discussed the miracle of how they
were drawn to God because of their terrible circumstances.
How humbling to witness such thankfulness; one is confined
to a wheelchair and partially paralyzed, the other has lost all
sense of taste or temperature and eats with great difficulty.

I often leave our meetings in tears. I have so much to be
thankful for, yet often I take the blessings in my life for
granted. Through my friends, I receive a heavenly reminder.

An attitude of gratitude should be your daily demeanor.

—RACHEL WALLACE-OBERLE

Absolute Perfection

"As for God, his way is perfect.
All the LORD's promises prove true.
He is a shield for all who look to him for protection."
Psalm 18:30

When I was a small child I trusted my parents completely. I accepted their decisions and never questioned their judgment. They were always right in my mind because they were my Mommy and Daddy. If they had asked me to walk off a cliff, I would have faithfully done it.

This is the type of absolute trust we must have in God. His way is perfect, and if we believe this, life will become much easier.

As I've grown older, I have questioned my parents and actually started to doubt their capabilities. The Lord wants us to never distrust Him, but to remain childlike in our faith. Upon asking Him, He will protect us through anything and lead us in the perfect direction He has planned specifically for us.

Everything that the Lord does is perfect.
He protects those who believe in Him.

—LINDSAY OBERST

A Journal, a Sword, a Flag, and an Old Man: Iwo Jima Remembered

"But if you are willing to listen, I say,
love your enemies. Do good to those who hate you."
Luke 6:27

"I see them coming," were the chilling words scrawled in the journal of a Japanese soldier. He penned them, from his lice-infested cave on Iwo Jima, minutes before his last battle.

The old Marine's voice quivered as he read the translated words to my students. He told of being deployed to the volcanic island just after the fierce fighting ended. His eyes misted as he described the pitiable conditions he found there and of his discovery of the body and possessions of his dead enemy.

Carefully, nearly reverently, he lifted a polished sword. Then he ever so slowly unfolded and showed them a tiny square of silk, a blazing red sun set against a field of white—the Japanese flag.

He remembered and cared about his dead enemies.

The lesson was gently reminiscent of the way Christ taught His followers. My students and I learned that day that one way to love an enemy is to treat his memory with respect.

There are many ways to love your enemies.

—ELAINE YOUNG MCGUIRE

369

Thank You, Veterans of Vietnam

"He fell face down on the ground at Jesus' feet, thanking him for what he had done. This man was a Samaritan. Jesus asked, 'Didn't I heal ten men? Where are the other nine?'"

Luke 17:16–17

God loves thanksgiving, yet when our Vietnam veterans returned, I tied no yellow ribbons, waved no flag, and never said thank you until God reminded me years later.

It happened while chaperoning my seventh graders. At the Vietnam War Memorial, I gave them a brief history of the war and then explained how to locate names on the wall.

A short time later, I noticed a student and his father locked in a tearful embrace. I hadn't realized when I so casually discussed the conflict that one on the bus had lived it and knew some of the men behind the names.

We boarded the bus. I felt a bit uncomfortable. I looked into his face and said sincerely, "Thank you." The students stood and cheered. His words were barely audible above his sobs: "In all these years, this is the first time anyone ever said 'thank you' to me."

It is never too late to say, "Thank you."

—ELAINE YOUNG MCGUIRE

The Ultimate Ultrasound

"And Solomon, my son, get to know the God of your ancestors. Worship and serve him with your whole heart and with a willing mind. For the LORD sees every heart and understands and knows every plan and thought. If you seek him, you will find him."

1 Chronicles 28:9

When I was fourteen weeks pregnant, I began to bleed heavily. Fear gripped me; fear that I might lose the treasured little life within me.

"Please, God, not my baby," I prayed, tears streaming down my cheeks.

The ultrasound technician was silent as she examined the monitor. Finally she spoke, "Everything looks fine. Would you like to see your baby?" She swung the monitor around and there on the screen a tiny little person blissfully kicked his feet and waved his arms.

How I loved that ultrasound! To be able to shine a light of understanding on what was happening inside me was such a relief.

God is like the ultimate ultrasound—He can shine His love on our lives, our fears, and our troubles, giving us the reassurance that everything will be okay if we let Him be in control!

God offers you comfort in times of trouble.

—MICHELLE PETERS

371

Cashing in Delight Dividends

"Take delight in the LORD,
and he will give you your heart's desires."
Psalm 37:4

I have an eighty-five-year-old friend who sends inspirational e-mails to all of her friends. Joan learned how to use a computer when she turned eighty-four. When I asked her why she wanted to learn the newfangled technology, she replied, "It's just another tool to spread joy. I'm cashing in some delight dividends and sharing the wealth!"

Sharing delight with the disheartened will fuel our own delight furnace. Joan's furnace is burning brightly!

Jesus was the master of paying out delight dividends. He delivered delight everywhere He went and continues to do so on a daily basis to all who take His lead and follow Him.

We would all like to be content most of the time. However, finding joy in a fragile world is not an easy task. Savoring God's blessings and rejoicing daily in all that the Lord provides allows us to cash in on delight dividends—and to spend them wisely on all nearby.

Share God's delight in you with others.

—MICHELE STARKEY

Psalms and Hymns

"Let the words of Christ, in all their richness, live in your hearts and make you wise. Use his words to teach and counsel each other. Sing psalms and hymns and spiritual songs to God with thankful hearts."

Colossians 3:16

Driving my husband's car one day, I was dismayed to find the radio not working. In my own car I have all the buttons preset so that I can hear singing, news, or classical music as fits my mood. With no radio I began to hum a tune and soon found myself singing a hymn: "O worship the King, all glorious above, / and gratefully sing his wonderful love." I hadn't sung that hymn in years!

The words brought back memories of God's blessing, His leading in our home, and His comfort in times of trouble.

As I continued to sing I was reminded of God's glory and greatness: "whose robe is the light, whose canopy space."

My solitary, silent car ride turned into a praise service that day. I am so thankful for songwriters who express worship so effectively, and thankful that I have this means of praising God wherever I am. Now sometimes I choose to leave the radio off and praise God instead!

Sing your thanks to God.

—SHERRY L. POFF

Thankful Acceptance

"Since everything God created is good,
we should not reject any of it. We may
receive it gladly, with thankful hearts."
1 Timothy 4:4

It is difficult to accept all that God has created and to be thankful for it also. Like spiders, which I *don't* like!

Everything the Lord does is good. Even death and destruction (kind of like life's spiders) are necessary to help us grow closer to God and to allow us to connect with others in related situations. We should not reject unexplainable experiences, but instead be glad for a challenge. When people fail to recognize all there is to be grateful for, they become infuriated with God. However, He obviously knows far more than we do and wants us to fully trust Him.

We should truly consider all that we have. Everything is perfect in its own way. It is easy to overlook or reject some of God's blessings, but if we take the time to consider them, we will feel a lot better about ourselves.

God never makes a mistake.
Be thankful for all that He has given you.

—LINDSAY OBERST

Too Grateful to Be Anything Else

"No matter what happens, always be thankful, for
this is God's will for you who belong to Christ Jesus."
1 Thessalonians 5:18

Some pastor friends and I went to visit a retired professor.
He had risen to the very top of his profession. He taught at a
prestigious university, received numerous awards and all
sorts of recognition, and spoke at nearly every major university and seminary in the nation. His list of published books is
impressive.

My friends and I did not quite know what to expect
since none of us had met him before. We found a warm,
friendly man who treated us like old friends. He even had
cake and coffee ready when we arrived.

After a day of stimulating conversation and deep dis-
cussions, we were drawing our time to a close. I said, "Fred,
you have traveled all over the country, received numerous
awards, achieved more than most of us can imagine, yet you
have remained humble. How is that?" He laughed and said,
"That's easy. My interior world is so filled with gratitude for
what I have. How could I be anything else?"

Let God fill you up from the inside out.

—DON M. AYCOCK

Toss Your Bread into the Ocean

"Give generously, for your gifts will return
to you later. Divide your gifts among many,
for you do not know what risks might lie ahead."
Ecclesiastes 11:1

Picture yourself standing on the beach with a loaf of bread in your hand. You break off one piece, then another, throwing the chunks of bread into the waves until the loaf is gone.

"Cast your bread upon the waters," was a bit of advice King Solomon gave in Ecclesiastes (King James Version). Did he mean for us to actually throw bread into the ocean? No. Writers of the Bible often used word pictures to help us understand truth.

"Be generous!" Solomon is saying. As water is an unlikely place to throw bread, do kind deeds to unlikely people, not thinking of receiving anything back.

What happens when we "cast our bread on the waters"? Kind words and deeds act like boomerangs. Cast them out to a needy person and you'll find that when you're in need, someone will cast bread your way.

*By generously sharing your money, possessions,
and time, you open the door to God's blessings.*

—JEWELL JOHNSON

Thanksgiving by the Giver

"And I have been a constant example of how you can help the poor by working hard. You should remember the words of the LORD Jesus: 'It is more blessed to give than to receive.'"

Acts 20:35

My grandfather developed disgust for his son's habit of borrowing just about every piece of the old man's clothing.

"The only words I ever hear from you are 'Thanks for the clothes, Dad,'" he chided one day. "When will you ever return the favor?"

My uncle just smiled a big smile. His dad continued, "You enjoy being on the receiving end all your life?"

"It would be my pleasure to have you borrow from me," his son replied. "I just thought that you enjoyed being a father who had clothes his son would want to share."

We imitate our Heavenly Father when we give without demanding that the giver reciprocate. Often, our gift is the answer to someone's prayer.

Be thankful for the privilege to give and to receive.

—DORA ISAAC WEITHERS

Give Thanks

"Let us come before him with thanksgiving.
Let us sing him psalms of praise."
Psalm 95:2

A friend battled cancer for six years before her doctor pronounced her cured. Sharing this blessed news, she said, "Every day is Thanksgiving Day to me."

What a wonderful motto for each of us. While our blessings may not appear as dramatic as being cured of cancer, they are diverse and plentiful. We must not let a single day pass without thanking God for His love, His protection, and all miracles, great and small. The breath of life and all good gifts received come from Him.

Today we honor a proclamation issued by President George Washington in 1789 establishing this special day of gratitude. The 200 years that followed brought incredible changes, and the coming 200 will bring innumerable more, but God never changes. He was, is, and will ever be. Believers can proclaim every day is Thanksgiving Day as we acknowledge our blessings of healing, mercy, and grace.

Make today a day of thanksgiving.

—PAT CAPPS MEHAFFEY

A Messy Stable

"An empty stable stays clean, but no
income comes from an empty stable."
Proverbs 14:4

Walking into my kitchen after being away for the afternoon,
I was dismayed to see the sink full of dirty dishes where just
that morning all had been clean.

Passing on to the laundry room, I noticed that someone
had been clearing all the dirty clothes out of their bedroom.
Laundry baskets overflowed.

At such times I am tempted to complain about the
never-ending nature of housework or to think of how difficult it is to have so many people to care for. Then I am
ashamed.

I have the blessing of a family to share my life. Piles of
laundry and dirty dishes are indications that we have clothes
to wear and plenty of food to eat. The busyness that fills my
days comes from the many ways God has blessed me.

How thankful I am for "a messy stable."

The blessings of life are often messy!

—SHERRY L. POFF

Letter of Vision

"Clearly, you are a letter from Christ prepared by us. It is written not with pen and ink, but with the Spirit of the living God. It is carved not on stone, but on human hearts."

2 Corinthians 3:3

I finally located a pastor I had as a teen living only sixty miles from me, though we had both moved from state to state in the course of our lives. At the time, he was convalescing in a nursing home, soon to be released to return home. After sending a note of thanks for his faithfulness over the years, he wrote back, requesting that I fill him in on the nearly thirty years since he last saw me.

I had never attempted a writing assignment quite like this before, condensing nearly three decades into a couple of typewritten pages. Soon, I had my life before me in print, and as I proofread the letter, God's faithfulness to me over the years leapt to life as never before.

I was awestruck, humbled, and blessed by the enormous scope of God's hand of mercy, grace, and protection that had followed me through my life.

Counting your blessings reveals the depths of God's care.

—MARLENE MECKENSTOCK

Speak Carefully

"Let your conversation be gracious and effective
so that you will have the right answer for everyone."
Colossians 4:6

During his early teen years, my son became more indifferent than usual. I had no idea how extensive this change would be, and I felt scared. One day, I said to him, "You cannot be bad, no matter how you try, because my prayers have gone up ahead of you."

Those words expressed faith instead of fear and affirmed my expectation that he would grow up godly. In obedience to my grandmother's counsel to "Say it short, but often," I repeated them as he grew into a young man.

Reminiscing with him on a visit from college, I asked him, "Do you remember me telling you, 'You cannot be bad'?"

"Mom, I hear those words even when I am far from home," he assured me.

"Thank God," I prayed silently, "that I had spoken words worth remembering." May our words speak hope and love to all, but especially to the children.

What you say impacts those who hear.

—DORA ISAAC WEITHERS

DECEMBER

WHERE IS BABY JESUS?
—DEBBIE HASKINS

"The Savior—yes, the Messiah, the LORD—has been born tonight in Bethlehem, the city of David! And this is how you will recognize him: You will find a baby lying in a manger, wrapped snugly in strips of cloth!"

LUKE 2:11–12

"**M**OMMY, BABY JESUS WILL FREEZE WITH-out any covers," said four-year-old Jonathan. His two-year-old brother, Brian, nodded in agreement.

"I think you're right. It's pretty cold out here," I said, and we headed into the house for a small blanket. We swaddled the plastic illuminated Christ child and placed him tenderly into his simulated wood manger near Mary and Joseph. My sons patted the baby and smiled with satisfaction. It was a moment to remember; a perfect finish to our family's outdoor decorating. At that time, I had no inkling of the powerful reminder I would receive through that little replica of the newborn King.

After the lights were lit, we stood back to take in the wonderful sight. Brian clapped and all joined in. Before going inside, the boys visited the manger again to make sure their special baby was all right. They checked on him daily. Usually they'd smooth the blanket, but on occasion, they'd just stand and gaze at the tiny representation of our newborn Savior. I should have taken the time to ask what they were thinking.

Soon I was buried in our typical Christmas activities: shopping, wrapping, candy making, parties, concerts, and numerous other festive things. With a large family, this was often more stressful than fun. The kids made requests for gifts and I'd drive myself crazy working to make everyone's dreams become reality. In an attempt to keep the Christmas spirit, we tried to read aloud an uplifting story of the season together each evening, but sometimes I was so exhausted my heart wasn't in it. Christmas was wearing me out.

One evening, as we arrived home, I heard Jonathan ask, "Where is Baby Jesus?" Looking into his face, I told him, "He grew up to be a wonderful teacher and leader. He blessed and healed people, and then because He loves us all and is the Son of God, He died for everyone's sins and went back to His Father in heaven." Jonathan fidgeted but listened to my explanation. I was surprised when he shook his head.

"No, Mommy, I mean *our* Baby Jesus in the yard. He's gone!" he explained while leading me to the Nativity set. It was true. There knelt Mary and Joseph, gazing down with loving serenity at a limp baby blanket. The Christ child was missing. The whole family searched the yard that night and the next day, but the baby was nowhere to be found.

The view of that lonely manger was more than I could bear, so I fashioned a bundle from old towels and wrapped it in the blanket, making it look as much like an infant as possible. I placed my substitute in the manger. It would do for the rest of the season, but it was not the same. The boys showed no interest in checking on a wad of rags.

As I went about my daily tasks, I obsessed over how the theft might have been prevented. Perhaps the baby and manger could have been secured to wires attached to stakes in the ground. Steps could have been taken that would have made it difficult for someone to steal Baby Jesus. I determined that when we replaced him, I would make certain he did not fall easy prey to another thief. Next time, I would take extra care to protect the baby in the manger.

Then, a gentle voice spoke to my spirit, posing a serious question: "What steps are you taking to protect the presence of the real Jesus Christ in your life and in your family?" Tears filled my eyes. While I'd been consumed with material and worldly holiday things, had the thief of all thieves come and, in a manner of speaking, taken the Christ child out of the manger of my heart? I realized that he'd been trying, but now I was warned and could take action to thwart his intentions.

That moment of spiritual clarity changed Christmas for me. It gave me the strength to say no to activities that didn't enhance the true spirit of the occasion, and our family began to enjoy more fully the peace of God's presence.

A few years later, we located a replacement for our missing baby and again had a complete Nativity set. I don't stake the manger down or wire the infant into it because the thief I'm most concerned about doesn't steal yard decorations. Instead, when I place the Baby Jesus near Mary and Joseph, I take a moment to reflect on how I'm doing in my relationship with the Lord and set spiritual goals for the holiday. It helps me keep worldly distractions in perspective. I ask myself the same question Jonathan asked me: "Where is Baby Jesus?" As long as I seek His Spirit, Christmas will be what it was meant to be: a celebration of the wondrous gift of redemption granted us by our Savior, Jesus Christ.

Sitting to Stand

"But if you are unwilling to serve the LORD, then choose today whom you will serve. Would you prefer the gods your ancestors served beyond the Euphrates? Or will it be the gods of the Amorites in whose land you now live? But as for me and my family, we will serve the LORD."

Joshua 24:15

Rosa Parks's name is synonymous with courage in the face of prejudice. The stand she took by remaining seated on the bus on December 1, 1955, was just the beginning. The American civil rights movement she was a part of led to significant changes in treating each other as equals.

As believers, we have constant opportunities to show courage in the face of prejudice. Knowing that our neighbors, coworkers, or acquaintances think dedicated Christians are ridiculous, we often avoid saying anything in order to keep peace.

Rosa Parks reminds us, however, that there is a place where we must take a stand. When someone disparages a Christian's position, we can quietly say, "Actually, I agree with her." When gossip starts, we can unobtrusively leave the group. We can continually show love to those who are anti-Christian. Whether sitting or standing, we have opportunities to "take a stand" for Christ.

Stand up for Jesus in all you do.

—LANITA BRADLEY BOYD

Different Gifts, One Goal

"There are different kinds of service in the church,
but it is the same LORD we are serving."
1 Corinthians 12:5

Each Sunday a member of my church's congregation leads readings and prepared prayers. One Sunday, Mike improvised his prayer rather than reading the prepared one. He closed his eyes, bowed his head, and prayed from the heart.

I felt annoyed! Didn't he know where to find the prayer before the service? Was he unprepared? Then I realized I was jealous. I could never ad-lib the way Mike had. Yet I know it doesn't really matter that I prepare and practice for my turn instead. The congregation doesn't care, and neither does God.

Mike has a special gift that allows him to pray and speak extemporaneously, but I have been given a gift as well, that of an organized mind. Mike and I use our different gifts for the same goal—assisting the pastor in leading a successful worship service—and that's what matters.

God has given you gifts to use in serving Him.

—KIM SHEARD

Beauty of the Heart

"Charm is deceptive, and beauty does not last; but
a woman who fears the LORD will be greatly praised."
Proverbs 31:30

"Oh, she's so ugly," I overheard an office associate say, as Maria, a volunteer, passed by.

I wondered how anyone could be unaware of Maria's beauty. Maria, who had become my friend, never seemed ugly to me. She touched everyone she met, including me, with her tenderness and warmth, with her time, caring, and bubbly personality. She often gave unexpected hugs, cards of encouragement, and motherly love notes—even to strangers. She had an effervescent personality and the most beautiful smile I had ever seen.

People see the scars, the protruding teeth, the droopy eye, and the thin frame. God sees the whole person. Although our bodies die and wither, the beauty of our soul continues to shine and grow regardless of our outward appearance.

Maria died recently. I am sure she received God's wholehearted and unconditional approval as she entered into His presence.

Inward beauty is a gift from God.

—S. (SHAE) COOKE

These Boots

"And you yourself must be an example to them by doing good deeds of every kind. Let everything you do reflect the integrity and seriousness of your teaching."

Titus 2:7

It wasn't the doll that my husband and I had so carefully chosen to give our daughter for Christmas that captured her heart, it was a pair of brown boots. I can still see the smile that lit up the face of my two-year-old as she pulled her boots on over the feet of her cozy warm sleepers. She wanted them buckled and once they were fastened she turned toward me and beamed proudly, "Just like Grampy's!"

Later in the day I watched from the window as she took her grandfather by the hand and went out to the backyard. Together they made footprints in the snow. Simple brown boots that buckled and looked like her grandfather's were her best gift that Christmas.

Watching her I was reminded that our children are watching us. They not only copy what we are wearing, but they copy our attitudes. If they follow our example, will their footsteps be directed toward God?

Children are watching you,
and learn from your attitude and example.

—ELAINE INGALLS HOGG

Transformations

"You should be known for the beauty that
comes from within, the unfading beauty of a
gentle and quiet spirit, which is so precious to God."
1 Peter 3:4

Last year, my sister gave me an unusual Christmas gift. The package contained hundreds of squares and triangles of fabric, an assortment of threads, a pair of scissors, needles, and a measuring tape.

On its own, it didn't seem like very much of a present, but when I sewed the pieces together using the tools supplied, they were transformed into a beautiful, vibrant, and useful quilt.

Jesus can transform us. He sees the beautiful in us, even when we're in a million pieces.

Jesus can make all life beautiful.

—S. (Shae) Cooke

God Is Faithful

"Then I will praise you with music on the harp,
because you are faithful to your promises, O God.
I will sing for you with a lyre, O Holy One of Israel."
Psalm 71:22

I was alone, divorced, and separated from my young son. Night after night, in my tiny apartment, I cried and prayed myself to sleep. Much of my prayer was entreating God to watch over my son.

One night, as I lay in bed quietly sobbing and praying, I felt the physical embrace of the Lord's arms. Then, I heard His voice: "Your son is in my hands." Still, I cried and prayed. Again, I felt His arms and heard His voice: "Your son is in my hands." It happened a third time before I fell asleep.

Years later, I attended his high school graduation. I had not seen him since he was small. We spoke and hugged and had our picture taken together after the ceremony. On the ride home, my niece, who had accompanied me, asked, "How'd he turn out so well given his circumstances?"

I replied, "God kept his promise."

All of God's promises are trustworthy.

—SRC

Please Pay Attention to Me

"O God, listen to my prayer. Pay attention to my plea.
For strangers are attacking me; violent men are
trying to kill me. They care nothing for God."
Psalm 54:2–3

There are times when we feel no one is paying attention to our entreaties because we believe they can't understand what we are going through. We experience this emotional isolation at work, school, church, or even at home.

As a freelance project manager for many years, I have felt the cold response by many to requests for work. Not exactly holding up a "will work for food" sign, but making numerous networking calls to set up brief meetings. When 95 percent of the calls bear no immediate fruit, I discovered the real definition of being a "self-starter."

How often I have cried out to God to show me His will, to turn on the high beams so I could see further down the road, or to get me some real work. I have prayed Psalm 54 often. Like David, we need to praise Him, and He will rescue us from our troubles in His way, in His time.

You may not feel Him, but He
hears every cry of your humble heart.

—KENNETH M. HANSEN

The Faithfulness of God Extends from Us to Our Children

"'I will continue this everlasting covenant between us, generation after generation. It will continue between me and your offspring forever. And I will always be your God and the God of your descendants after you.'"

Genesis 17:7

As my young son and I share devotional times in the mornings, I cannot help but wonder what kind of man God will fashion him to be.

We parents know that the world offers an increasing number of empty promises and temptations, but what of our children? As they grow into young men and women, will they be able to stand firm against this tide of iniquity?

God's promise to us who have given our lives to Him is that He will not forget our children. Even as we have been included in Christ's new covenant, so that everlasting covenant will extend to our sons and daughters. As God has been our God, so He will be for our children if we cling to Him and trust Him in His promise.

For those in Christ, there is no fear of the future, either for us or for our children.

Your children's futures are secure in the Lord.

—DAN EDELEN

They Came to Worship Him

"... but the angel reassured them. 'Don't be afraid!' he
said. 'I bring you good news of great joy for everyone!'"
Luke 2:10

As our pastor read the Christmas story, my mind began to
picture the scene. What was it like to be a shepherd on that
night so long ago? To be sitting at the fire after gathering the
sheep into the fold for safety, warming your chapped hands,
and watching the sparks drift lazily upward into the night
sky? What was it like to hear the angels' song announcing
the birth of the Promised One, the King of Kings?

Thankfully the shepherds found the Christ Child, but
today there are people all around us who, because they have
never heard the message, do not recognize that the King of
Kings has been born to bring hope, to bring forgiveness of
sin, to bring salvation. As we celebrate this Christmas
season, let's look for ways to share the true message of
Christmas so that those who are waiting to hear may, like
the shepherds, bow at the manger and worship Jesus Christ,
the King.

Live the meaning of Christmas so others can see Him.

—ELAINE INGALLS HOGG

Stillness of Winter

"And now, dear brothers and sisters, let me say one more thing as I close this letter. Fix your thoughts on what is true and honorable and right. Think about things that are pure and lovely and admirable. Think about things that are excellent and worthy of praise."

Philippians 4:8

Surely there is no better time to sit and contemplate God and His world than early in the morning while the house is quiet and there is a snowstorm going on outside. What a reminder of His power and glory! Snow turns the December landscape of browns and grays into a winter wonderland just as the forgiveness of Jesus purifies our hearts.

Snow erases the noise that distracts us from the beauty of nature's sounds. Step outside after a snowfall and listen. The silence is like no other. You can almost hear Him whisper, "Be still and know that I am God."

Snow serves to slow us down. We can't (or shouldn't) drive as fast. We certainly can't walk as fast. In a world that is obsessed with motion and going places, again we are reminded, "Be still."

Spend quiet time in reflection and prayer with your Lord.

—TERESA BELL KINDRED

Giving Him Our Best

"And the LORD said to Moses, 'If you offer a whole burnt offering to the LORD, whether to fulfill a vow or as a freewill offering, it will be accepted only if it is a male animal with no physical defects. It may be either a bull, a ram, or a male goat.'"

Leviticus 22:17–19

From the time of the wandering Israelites of Leviticus until now, God has always wanted our best. Sometimes we offer lip service and intentions, rather than action.

I worked alongside teens in a huge warehouse that sends holiday gift boxes to underprivileged children around the world. My students' eyes were opened, visualizing a place where a pencil or a pair of socks would excite a child.

As they inspected each shoebox they were astounded, however, at finding items some considered "gifts." Unwashed used clothing, used cosmetics, broken toys, and one box filled with shredded construction paper. Shocking secondhand goods donated in the name of the Lord.

Then I wondered, "Do I sometimes offer God my leftover time, talent, and energy?" He whispered, "Yes." I want to follow His example and give my best. Thankfully, it is never too late to begin!

Just as God gave you His best,
you should give your best in His name.

—ELAINE YOUNG MCGUIRE

Showers of Blessing

"And God will generously provide all you
need. Then you will always have everything you
need and plenty left over to share with others."
2 Corinthians 9:8

Years ago, we were pastoring a small church with barely
enough provisions to meet our needs. Near Christmas, a
large church "adopted" us as their Christmas project.

A short while later, a friend visited who was quite ill. I
had prayed for an opening to witness to her, but she was
antagonistic toward the Gospel. While talking, a pickup
truck drove up full of boxes. It was our adopted church
delivering their gifts.

As boxes were brought into our tiny parsonage, my
friend asked why they were doing this. I explained
Christians love each other, even those whom they have
never met. She was overwhelmed by the generosity show-
ered on us. Sometime later I learned she had passed away
but had accepted the Lord before her death. I thanked the
Lord that through the love and generosity of others, her
heart was softened toward the Gospel.

*In the midst of need, God's bounty
and love is poured forth as a witness.*

—BEVERLY HILL MCKINNEY

Purified like Snow

"'Come now, let us argue this out,' says the LORD. 'No matter how deep the stain of your sins, I can remove it. I can make you as clean as freshly fallen snow. Even if you are stained as red as crimson, I can make you as white as wool.'"

Isaiah 1:18

To me winter seems desperately distressing without snow. The bare, lifeless trees scarcely cling to life and all sight of the formerly fresh green is long departed. The chill reaches your bones as the wind howls around you. Kept indoors, and away from the refreshing air, all appears lost.

Until one morning, you find snow gracefully floating down. It possesses a cleansing and heartwarming essence to it. The cool, fluffy crystals provide a reason to be outside and shower beauty as they tumble down. The unspoiled whiteness covers the muddiness, making it new.

In this same way, the Lord can cleanse you from your sins. He does not care how much you have sinned, but He accepts you just the same. He does not look upon your sinfulness, but sees only the beauty you hold deep inside, like the leafless trees that have the capacity to grow beautiful things.

God can purify you and make you white as snow.

—LINDSAY OBERST

"Almost" Carries No Weight

"But since you are like lukewarm water,
I will spit you out of my mouth!"
Revelation 3:16

In our house, it is a ritual to watch *A Christmas Carol* each December. There's a line the first Spirit says to Scrooge that always awakens my heart: "'Almost' carries no weight— especially in matters of the heart."

Scrooge "almost" ran after Belle. Yet, he chose not to do so, thereby clinching his life of misery and loneliness.

How many times have we seen the same in others' hearts? They "almost" get the blessings that are in store for them by living a godly life. They "almost" accept Jesus as their personal Savior. They "almost" serve Him gladly.

But they choose not to do so and suffer the consequences.

"Almost" means nothing. Being sold out fully to God means everything.

Commit your life wholly to Him.

—RHONDA LANE PHILLIPS

Take Time to Rest in the Lord

"Her sister, Mary, sat at the Lord's feet, listening to what he taught. But Martha was worrying over the big dinner she was preparing. She came to Jesus and said, 'LORD, doesn't it seem unfair to you that my sister just sits here while I do all the work? Tell her to come and help me.'

"But the LORD said to her, 'My dear Martha, you are so upset over all these details! There is really only one thing worth being concerned about. Mary has discovered it—and I won't take it away from her.'"

Luke 10:39–42

We live in a hectic world. We work long hours and come home and have to take care of children and our homes. We often forget what we need to be concerned about.

Mary knew. While her sister Martha was running around preparing the meal, she sat at Jesus' feet and listened to his words. Jesus doesn't praise Martha for all the work she was doing for Him. He praised Mary for her quiet hands and listening ears. She knew that it was more important to be still and rest and listen to Jesus. He had the food of life to nourish her.

All year round we must not become so busy with our own lives and what we think is important that we forget to listen to Jesus.

Sit at the feet of Jesus and listen to His words today.

—MARYANN BREUKELMAN

Hope

"Mary responded, 'Oh, how I praise the LORD.'"
Luke 1:46

One Christmas when I was a child, there was no promise of gifts. My father had been out of work all fall. Still I hoped.

That Christmas Eve was a beautiful clear night, and for a long time I stood at the window and watched the stars in the sky. After some time, I noticed an extra-large one and I told my mother, "Mom, Christmas will come. I saw the star!"

After supper our whole family gathered in the living room while Dad played carols on his violin and my mother read the Christmas story. We didn't receive many gifts that year. At first I was a bit disappointed, but the close family times, the singing, and the love my parents shared were the most important gifts they could give. They were sharing their spiritual values, teaching my brothers and me that our hope is in the Lord.

Experience the true meaning of
Christmas through the giving of yourself.

—ELAINE INGALLS HOGG

God Is Standing By

"He will not let you stumble and fall; the one
who watches over you will not sleep. Indeed, he
who watches over Israel never tires and never sleeps."
Psalm 121:3–4

I was nine, old enough to go to sleep by myself. My dad, however, understood how panicked I would get when all the lights were out and the house grew quiet. Then my sister, who usually shared my room, went away for a week.

To keep me from being scared on my first night "alone," my dad sat quietly beside my bed. Once or twice I opened my eyes just a little to satisfy myself that he was still there. Finally I was able to relax enough to go to sleep. The knowledge that my dad was available if I needed him gave me peace.

Years later I still experience moments of near panic when the world seems a dark and lonely place. Knowing that my Heavenly Father stands nearby waiting for my call, just like my earthly dad did, remains an immeasurable comfort.

Your Heavenly Father watches over you night and day.

—SHERRY L. POFF

What Flavor?

"Because God's children are human beings—made of flesh and blood—Jesus also became flesh and blood by being born in human form. For only as a human being could he die, and only by dying could he break the power of the Devil, who had the power of death."

Hebrews 2:14

To help celebrate Christmas, my daughter's preschool teacher gave a box of cake mix to each student. Parents were encouraged to help their child bake and frost a birthday treat for Jesus.

The idea seemed delightful, but I had a long laugh when I saw what kind of cake mix the teacher sent home. Devil's food!

During Christ's life, the devil tried many times to derail God's plan. Jealous King Herod sought Jesus' death, Pharisees and religious leaders challenged Him, and the devil himself tempted Him. Perhaps he believed that God in human flesh was easy prey, or "devil's food."

Not so. God's plan for salvation, which began with the birth of a child in a lowly manger and culminated in Christ's death and resurrection, held firm.

This year I'm making an angel food cake to celebrate Christmas.

Jesus has broken the power of Satan over your life.

—LORI Z. SCOTT

The Altar Dog

"Your righteousness is like the mighty mountains,
your justice like the ocean depths. You care for
people and animals alike, O LORD."
Psalm 36:6

Magna was a faithful worshipper in our area for many years. She accompanied the priest down the aisle on Sunday and lay curled at the foot of the communion table during the service. When the postlude began, she arose and processed out with the others.

The large mixed-breed brown dog attended weddings, often adorned with a flowered collar. At Christmas, when the angels in the pageant went to the manger, Magna joined them to view the Christ child.

Father Snipes felt that Magna helped him connect with his parishioners more effectively. People relaxed when they saw the calm, beautiful dog. They became more loving. "A dog is a symbol of fidelity," he observed. "Magna was great-hearted."

God wants us to synthesize the ordinary and the holy in our lives. A dog at church? "God made all sorts of . . . animals. . . . And God saw that it was good" (Genesis 1:25).

God can use a modest animal for His glory.

—JAN SEALE

Needing Support in Solitude

"For forty days and forty nights he
ate nothing and became very hungry."
Matthew 4:2

Taking a new job, I had to move 2,500 miles from Canada to Salt Lake City. My wife and I decided that uprooting our family should happen after I was settled into the new position. Those few months were incredibly lonely for me. I eventually found a local church where the fellowship picked up my spirits and helped keep me spiritually aligned.

Satan loves to prey when we are alone. Early in His ministry, Jesus spent more than a month in desert solitude, no doubt considering the awesome events that lay before Him. In Jesus' weakened solitude, Satan mounted an aggressive attack, yet God's Son stood firm.

In my alone moments, Satan finds me in a weakened state, too. I am much more susceptible to temptations when I am not surrounded by Christian fellowship. On our own we are weak, but strength comes through fellowship in the Body of Christ.

In your alone moments, you need to hold firm to your faith.

—THOMAS SMITH

In Appreciation

"For God so loved the world that he gave
his only Son, so that everyone who believes
in him will not perish but have eternal life."
John 3:16

First observed in 1769 as "Old Colony Day," the anniversary of the Plymouth Rock landing of 1620 was celebrated with a feast, music, and speeches. Today the holiday is still observed in Plymouth with a parade, though not many Americans celebrate this important day. The holiday is observed quietly, with respect and admiration.

In many ways, the founding fathers of America sacrificed for us as well. And like our relationship with God, our appreciation of our forefathers' accomplishments is not always evident in our daily life.

Our forefathers risked all to ensure our future freedom, including the freedom to worship as we choose. They loved mankind, and had the courage to come to the shores of America so that our faith could be observed openly.

Those who sacrifice for you, love you.

—ROBIN BAYNE

Wake-Up Call

"So stay awake and be prepared, because you
do not know the day or hour of my return."
Matthew 25:13

"Rise and shine, it's 6:00 A.M.! He is risen! Maybe you should get up, too!" That's what I hear when I wake up in the morning. My alarm is set to the Christian radio station, and the announcer gives me the same wake-up call every day.

Jesus gave us a wake-up call, too. Many of us travel through life sleepy-eyed and tired, with our eyes half closed and our attention halfhearted. Jesus told us to "stay awake and be prepared."

Are you awake? Do you rise and shine each and every day? Are you giving the world the attention it deserves and making a difference in the lives of others? If you're not, maybe it's time for you to wake up. The buzzer is going off! Get up and get going. Remember, He arose to give you the power to arise to all occasions.

Be fully awake through the life Jesus gives you.

—MICHELE STARKEY

409

The Gift That Keeps on Giving

"But when the right time came, God sent his Son, born of a woman, subject to the law. God sent him to buy freedom for us who were slaves to the law, so that he could adopt us as his very own children."

Galatians 4:4–5

Right after Christmas our twenty-two-year-old daughter was to report for eight weeks of boot camp. It was hard to let her go, but I knew she would be an asset to the Navy and the experience would be good for her. Together we savored a few moments by the holiday tree.

"Mom, I love my life and wouldn't change a thing. I can't wait to see what's next," she said.

"I feel exactly the same. I wouldn't change one thing. I'd do it all over."

"So you're not sad about the first adoption that fell through?"

"No! I know we were meant to adopt you!" I assured her.

The next day, as I remembered the warmth of that exchange, God added an extra blessing. I suddenly realized it was the twenty-second anniversary of the day her adoption had become final!

Daily God opens His storehouse of blessings, but His greatest gift has always been the Child.

—MARCIA SWEARINGEN

Love Is the Recipe of Life

"Live in such a way that God's love can bless
you as you wait for the eternal life that our LORD
Jesus Christ in his mercy is going to give you."
Jude 1:21

In my first year of teaching, the mother of one of my students taught me something I have never forgotten.

"We're having a hard Christmas, but I wanted to thank you and let you know this gift is from Johnny and me. Please don't tell him what I did. He might be embarrassed, but I wanted to remember you."

She handed me a package wrapped in old newspapers and tied with worn-out string.

On arriving home after school, I unwrapped this strange gift covered in faded newspaper. Imagine my surprise to find a little prune cake baked inside a coffee can. I made hot tea and my husband and I devoured that delicious little cake. Savoring every crumb, I told Emmitt what she had said.

The mother's sacrificial present spoke volumes to my heart. She gave from the little she had. The mother's gift reminded me of another sacrifice: God's great gift of love to the world.

Jesus is a gift of love and that love lasts forever!

Love is a prime ingredient in the recipe of life.

—JOAN CLAYTON

Unopened Gifts

"God has given gifts to each of you from his
great variety of spiritual gifts. Manage them well
so that God's generosity can flow through you."
1 Peter 4:10

When I was a young girl we had big Christmas celebrations. My mother would invite many family members and friends. Gifts were bought for all who would attend. Occasionally someone was unable to attend and his or her gift was left unopened under the tree.

Just as those gifts sat unopened under our tree, some people never bother to unwrap or use their gifts and talents. They just sit there—never possessed, used, or enjoyed.

The Lord blesses each of us with unique gifts and talents that should be used to honor Him. Recognizing our gifts helps us to use them properly. It may be your voice, your hands, or your ability to listen.

Take a look at your life, and examine what gifts you have left unopened.

*Opening your gifts that are meant
for others will bring blessings.*

—ANNETTE BUDZBAN

Music Blessing

"They and their families were all trained in
making music before the LORD, and each of them
—288 in all—was an accomplished musician."
1 Chronicles 25:7

For as long as I can remember, my mother holds open house on Boxing Day, the day after Christmas. (Boxing Day is the day you box up presents for your postman, garbage collector, and the like.) Everyone brings their leftovers and everyone brings their musical instruments. The afternoon is spent entertaining whoever comes in. It's like a marathon of the family von Trapp.

We have three generations playing in the band, as well as in-laws, outlaws, neighbors, and friends. People come from miles around to enjoy the down-home feel and flavor of our Christmas Concert open house. It has become a tradition enjoyed by many.

The TV stays silent and no video games are played. The material gifts of Christmas are abandoned as we reflect on God's greatest gift.

We are truly blessed as we use our God-given talent to bless the hearts and lives of others.

Make your home a place of blessing.

—NANCY F. REVIE

Give with Good Cheer

"You must each make up your own mind as to how much you should give. Don't give reluctantly or in response to pressure. For God loves the person who gives cheerfully."
2 Corinthians 9:7

Boxing Day was first observed in Queen Victoria's England, in the mid-1800s, with servants and tradesmen receiving gifts and money. Children received small gifts from their parents, and the poor would go door-to-door hoping for treats to fill their boxes. The custom is still practiced today in England and Canada, but the concept of charitable giving is upheld in countries all over the world.

Jesus encouraged us to take care of the poor, to share our worldly possessions with those of us less fortunate. Throughout the holiday season, individuals and businesses donate what they can to ease the burdens of others. Make it a habit to think of the poor all year round. Share your material wealth and your spiritual wealth—the knowledge of God's love. Un-box His word and share the joy.

When you decide to give to those in need,
do it with a smile and much love.

—ROBIN BAYNE

Give or Take

"Give what you have to anyone who asks you for it; and when things are taken away from you, don't try to get them back. Do for others as you would like them to do for you."

Luke 6:30–31

Travis and Rachel walked out of the department store empty-handed. "Shopping makes me so depressed," said Rachel.

"I wish we had more money," said Travis. "Not heaps, just enough to actually enjoy shopping."

They kept on walking. "You know what's stupid," said Travis, "The people who own these department stores could probably just give us the money we want and it would be like pocket change to them. But can you imagine how happy it'd make us?"

"Oh, well," Travis sighed. "I guess we'll just go for lunch instead."

"How much for lunch?" asked Rachel.

"About twenty bucks I guess." Travis looked on in surprise as Rachel took out her purse, darted across the road, approached a homeless man, handed him twenty dollars, and darted back.

"What was that about?" asked Travis.

"That was my 'pocket change.' Think how much it must mean to that man."

Give to someone who has even less than you.

—SHELLEY WAKE

Hospitality Pays

"Whenever we have the opportunity,
we should do good to everyone,
especially to our Christian brothers and sisters."
Galatians 6:10

From my first meeting with the school board, Mr. Fallows showed a fatherly interest. "We're your family away from home, if you ever need help," he declared.

He brought me fresh produce from his farm. When my fiancé visited, Mr. Fallows provided him a place to stay for free. His kindness was beyond what I would have asked.

Near the end of my assignment, Mr. Fallows and I were talking. He shared, "I had a friend with the same last name as yours. He was very generous when I visited his hometown. I wished to return the favor, but he died soon after."

I questioned him until I was certain, then I told him, "Your friend was my father. I was just a baby when he died."

Mr. Fallows was ecstatic that he had been so kind to me. He had reaped the satisfaction of returning a favor, and the greater satisfaction of obeying God's practical command.

*The practice of hospitality is obedience
to one of God's practical commands.*

—DORA ISAAC WEITHERS

Hold on to the Hope

"My guilt overwhelms me—
it is a burden too heavy to bear."
Psalm 38:4

While driving, my friend Jennifer accidentally killed another motorist. Following the accident, Jennifer's guilt was an invasive dark cloud.

David of the Old Testament also suffered agonizing guilt. In Psalm 38:4, David says, "My guilt has overwhelmed me. . . ." David was ill, his friends had left him, and enemies were closing in. I can imagine his dark cloud of utter desolation.

The author of Hebrews tells of supernatural cleansing (Hebrews 10:22). Imagine God's purifying water, washing away our horrible burden of guilt, leaving us without ugly blotches or blemishes. God has offered life-saving cleansing to anyone who asks.

He has promised. He is faithful.

David found himself lifted "out of the slimy pit" (Psalm 40:2, NIV) after God heard his cry.

Jennifer believed God's promise. And although life's consequences must be reckoned with, she knows God is faithful. She's holding on to the hope.

Guilt can overwhelm you beyond bearing.
God offers to cleanse you, washing the burden away.

—LAURIE WHITMAN

Exchange This World for the Next

"And this world is fading away,
along with everything it craves. But if you
do the will of God, you will live forever."
1 John 2:17

In *The Great Divorce*, C. S. Lewis imagines the world to come as far more substantial than what we have known in our mortal existence. The very grass itself bends only beneath the feet of those wholly devoted to the Lord. Such "bright people" as Lewis calls them are more real and "weighty" than they ever were in their earthly lives, reflecting their obedience to the Lord they served.

Many of us find ourselves instead living for the moment and not for eternity, investing in the insubstantial rather than doing the will of God. Ultimately, the world we inherit will, in part, be a reflection of how devoted we are to the Lord in the here and now. Mercifully, God grants the grace to make the choice to live for His perfect Kingdom, enabling us to do His will by the Holy Spirit if we only ask Him.

You possess a future more real than the world you now live in.

—DAN EDELEN

CONTRIBUTORS

Don M. Aycock is the pastor of Liberty Baptist Church in Palatka, Florida; he is the author of nineteen books, father of grown twins, and husband to Carla.

Nancy Baker resides in College Station, Texas, with her husband and two cats, and has been published in anthologies and national magazines.

Richard S. Barnett has retired from petroleum exploration and teaching geology at Houston Community College. He attends Wimberley Presbyterian Church in Wimberley, Texas.

Mary J. Bauer is an elementary school teacher in Mountlake Terrace Washington. She has been married a year and has a nine-year-old stepdaughter.

Robin Bayne lives in Maryland with her husband of thirteen years. She enjoys reading inspirational stories and hopes to share some with her readers.

Lanita Bradley Boyd is a former teacher from Fort Thomas, Kentucky. Her writing often draws on her rural childhood, teaching experiences, and family events.

Stephen D. Boyd is a preacher, writer, university professor, husband, father, grandfather, runner, reader, fisherman, traveler, mentor, and friend.

Maryann Breukelman lives in rural Ontario, Canada, where she is currently working on a novel.

Elaine Britt is grateful to God for the call to write and speak. She has one book, *Messages*, and articles in Christian magazines.

Annettee Budzban is a wife, mother, and grandmother. She is an author and weekly newspaper religion columnist (e-mail: *ahrtwrites2u@aol.com*).

Monica Cane, freelance author from California, uses her gift of writing to bring a breath of inspiration to readers everywhere.

DenaRae Carlock has been married for twelve years and lives in the beautiful Pacific Northwest, where she is the mom of four boys in a blended family.

Amy Carr is married and has four children; Casey (18), Jesse (14), Eli (11), and Ellie (7). She also operates a licensed home child-care business.

Contributors

Brook Chalfant is a freelance writer from Dayton, Ohio. She and her family are currently studying and ministering at Hillsong International Leadership College in Sydney, NSW Australia.

Mary Roberts Clark is a freelance writer living with her husband, children, and mother in Richmond, Virginia.

Charlene Clayton is a wife, mother, nurse, and writer. Her passion is discovering and sharing how God's Word relates to everday life.

Joan Clayton is a retired educator. She has written seven books and more than 450 published articles. She is the religion columnist for her local newspaper.

S. (Shae) Cooke, a writer, mother, and former foster child, shares her heart and God's message of Hope internationally in print, and online. Contact her at *shaesy@shaw.ca*.

Melva Cooper is a grandmother from Jonesboro, Arkansas. She encourages many, both in print and on the Internet, with stories from her heart. Read more of her stories at *www.MelvaCooper.com*.

Carolyn Coté has taught as a certified childbirth educator for more than ten years. She currently practices as a professional doula (childbirth assistant).

Virginia Dawkins and her husband attend Church of the Way, in Meridian, Mississippi. She writes a column for a local newspaper.

Wendy Ann Dunham is a wife, mom, registered therapist for differently abled children, and child of God. Writing is one of her many pastimes.

Dena Dyer is a wife and mom who makes her home in Granbury, Texas. She enjoys reading, watching old movies, creative scrapbooking, and decorating.

Dan Edelen shares the beauty of God's world with his wife and son on their farm in Ohio. They attend Vineyard Community Church in Springdale.

Pat Friedrich is Dean of Students in a Louisiana alternative high school. She enjoys spending time with daughter Sarah and writing.

Charlene Friesen is armed and ready with a loaded pen. Spiritual lessons, life's happenings, and family shenanigans afford great writing opportunities.

Victoria Gaines is an Atlanta nurse whose writing bug grew from simple journaling and heart-to-heart correspondence.

Jack and Pam Gibbons, owners and operators of Gibby's Orbits (mini–donut shop and Fair Food diner) in Springfield, Illinois.

Marilynn Griffith lives in Florida with her husband and seven children. Visit her Web site at *www.marilynngriffith.com*.

Kenneth M. Hansen and his wife Wanda live in Milwaukee, while kids Dana, Bryce, and Amanda return seasonally to the nest. He consults to faith-based organizations.

Charles E. Harrel has served as a pastor for thirty years. He enjoys teaching, inspirational writing, and camping trips with his family.

Debbie Haskins lives in Denton, Texas. She has seven children and four grandchildren. She loves to travel, read, and laugh with her family.

Michael Herman, Sr., a former sales manager, retired due to Parkinson's. He enjoys writing devotional essays and poems, glorifying God in his personal relationship with Christ.

Elaine Ingalls Hogg is a palliative care volunteer and started writing stories to help children deal with their grief. She has written several inspirational stories.

Heidi L. Janz, Ph.D., is a university instructor and playwright in Edmonton, Alberta, Canada.

Karla R. Jensen has written for radio, television, and magazines for more than fifteen years. She has published church dramas, an audiobook, and short stories.

Esther B. Jimenez is a parishioner of St. Peter, the Apostle, Itasca, Illinois. She paints, plays guitar, writes inspirational and religious poems, and makes inspirational cards.

CONTRIBUTORS

Jewell Johnson writes from Arizona where she enjoys walking, quilting, and reading. She and her husband, LeRoy, have six children and seven grandchildren.

Kim Jonn is an artist and social worker. She is cofounder of "Gospel on the Go," a Bible outreach for nursing home patients.

Marsha Jordan founded the HUGS and HOPE Club for Sick Children (*www.hugsandhope.com*). She lives in Wisconsin with her husband and their toy poodle King Louie.

Stephanie Kanak, a freelance writer, enjoys life with her husband and son in a small community just outside of Philadelphia, Pennsylvania.

Teresa Bell Kindred is a wife, mother of five, author of several Precious Moments books, freelance writer, magazine columnist, and public speaker.

Cheryl Knight is a teacher and foster-parent liaison. She lives in Kent, Washington, with her husband, two teens, and a daughter in college.

Linda Knight lives in Woodslee, Ontario, Canada. She currently writes for *Woman's World* magazine, Faithville Gospelcast Kid's TV, SPS Studios, Abbey Press, and more.

Deborah R. McCorry-Nunez lives in Scottsdale, Arizona with husband Elizandro and three boys. She taught for ten years and attends Glass and Garden Community Church.

Elaine Young McGuire and husband, Jim, from Lilburn, Georgia, enjoy making short-term mission trips. A retired teacher, she loves writing on her screened porch.

Beverly Hill McKinney was a minister's wife for seventeen years. She is a freelance writer/poet residing in Southern California.

Marlene Meckenstock is a wife, teacher, and business owner. She has served on staff development and leadership teams, and has conducted workshops.

Pat Capps Mehaffey, an ex-banker, retired to a lake cabin where she enjoys birds, grandchildren, and writing.

Jane Morin has been writing for more than twenty-five years. She resides with her husband in the Rocky Mountain region of Colorado. Jane is a speaker and songwriter.

Jessie Ann Moser writes from Wescosville, Pennsylvania, where she lives with her husband and daughter.

Stormy Nieves is a volunteer schoolteacher at her church. She and her husband Juan live in Oklahoma with their two dogs.

Leslie Nivens is a retired nurse, widowed, and living alone; she still finds joy in serving the Lord by serving others.

Lindsay Oberst is a seventeen-year-old junior in high school. She is a member of the yearbook committee and enjoys writing.

Michelle Peters is a social worker and mom. Residing in Winnipeg, Manitoba, Canada, she is active in her church and enjoys sewing and swimming.

Rhonda Lane Phillips is a reading specialist and writes for children.

Michelle Louise Pierre, a published author and speech therapist, currently lives in Hayward, California. She is a Christian writer of short stories, commentaries, and poems.

Sherry L. Poff is a wife, mother, and teacher living in Ooltewah, Tennessee.

Stacy Decker Poole is a homeschooling mother of three young boys in Richmond, Virginia. She enjoys Bible studies, reading children's books, and writing.

Anna M. Popescu is the author of *A Little Bit of Wonderful* as well as articles and devotionals in several magazines.

Cathee A. Poulsen is a native of Florida and seeker of adventures in God. She is married to Bob, mother of four, and grandmother of seven.

Kathryn Thompson Presley is a retired English professor, freelance writer, and Bible teacher. She and husband Roy have two grown children and four grandchildren.

CONTRIBUTORS

Susan Estribou Ramsden is a wife, mother of one daughter, and a new grandmother. She is a retired teacher, who finds joy in writing Christian poetry.

Nancy F. Revie is married to her high school sweetheart, Peter. They have two children, Andrew and Laura, and a cat named Patches.

Sue Rhodes is a fitness professional, married with one son, and serves as a coach for women's Bible studies at Saddleback Church in Southern California.

Linda Roberts is a housewife and mother of three adult children. She works with thirty children and adult Bible study students in her neighborhood.

Jane Robertson is a grandmother to five. She and her husband, Tom, enjoy books, movies, and pets.

Jay D. Rohman is a professional speaker, actor, and freelance writer. He is a recovering alcoholic of more than twenty years.

Sara Rosett lives in Georgia with her husband, two kids, and two dogs.

Shannon Rulé favors inspirational, memoir, and humor writing. She often writes about her "mama," who was apparently everyone's mama.

Doris Schuchard is a homemaker and writer in the areas of education and the family. She lives in Atlanta with her husband and two teenagers.

Elaine L. Schulte is the author of thirty-six novels and many articles. She and husband Frank have two grown sons and live in Fallbrook, California.

Lori Z. Scott lives in Terre Haute, Indiana, with her husband and two kids. She learns more about life from her children than anything else.

Jan Seale lives on the subtropical Texas-Mexico border, where parrots, chameleons, and birds-of-paradise keep her daily in awe of the Creator.

Anna Seden lives in Atlanta, Georgia, where her time and interests are divided between husband Michael, gardening, theater, and work as an advertising coordinator.

Kim Sheard is married, has two dogs, and sings in the Sanctuary Choir of Oakton United Methodist Church in Virginia.

Thomas Smith is an avid musician with a heart for youth. He is married to Gwendy and kept honest by daughters Katie, Carly, and Deanna.

Michele Starkey is a brain aneurysm survivor who enjoys writing. She is living life to the fullest in the Hudson Valley of New York.

Marcia Swearingen is a former newspaper editor and columnist, now freelancing full-time, teaching Young Marrieds at church, and enjoying her husband, grown daughter, and cat.

Lisa Tuttle is a pastor's wife and mother of three who enjoys encouraging and blessing others through her writing.

Merry E. Vargo is a retired high school history teacher living in rural Ohio with her husband, three cats, two dogs, and assorted area wildlife.

Ann Voskamp praises God for farm life (to dwell in the land), family (five blessings with her best friend), and faith (moment by moment).

Shelley Wake is a full-time author, poet, and essayist. Her works have been published in various magazines, e-zines, and anthologies in Australia, the United States, and Great Britain.

Rachel Wallace-Oberle has written for numerous publications. She cohosts and writes for a weekly radio program and loves walking, classical music, and canaries.

Adrian Ward is a freelance writer from Springville, Alabama, where she lives with her husband and their four children.

Dora Isaac Weithers counsels on godly womanhood and parenting. She has two children, Wanda and Wendell, and resides in Houston, Texas.

John C. Westervelt has volunteered with weekday preschool children at Tulsa Asbury UMC since his retirement eight years ago.

Laurie Whitman lives in Michigan with her husband, Jon, and children Luc, Jill, and Ross. She enjoys writing, especially for children.

Lori Wildenberg is a speaker, educator, and the coauthor of *Empowered Parents;* she lives in Colorado with her husband and four children. See *www.LoriWildenberg.com* for more information.

Subject Index

Scripture Index

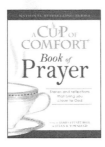